A-to-Z

ALSO BY RICHARD W. KROON

A/V A to Z: An Encyclopedic Dictionary
of Media, Entertainment and Other Audiovisual Terms
(McFarland, 2010)

3D
A-to-Z

An Encyclopedic Dictionary

RICHARD W. KROON

Foreword by RAY ZONE

McFarland & Company, Inc., Publishers
Jefferson, North Carolina, and London

Illustrations are by the author unless otherwise noted.

LIBRARY OF CONGRESS ONLINE CATALOG

Kroon, Richard W., 1964–
3D A-to-Z : an encyclopedic dictionary / Richard W. Kroon ;
foreword by Ray Zone.
p.   cm.
Includes bibliographical references.

ISBN 978-0-7864-6824-9

softcover : acid free paper ∞

1. Image processing—Dictionaries.
2. Three-dimensional imaging—Dictionaries.
3. Three-dimensional display systems—Dictionaries.
4. 3-D films—Dictionaries.   I. Title: Three-D A-to-Z.
TA1637 .K76 2012   621.36'7   2012007048

BRITISH LIBRARY CATALOGUING DATA ARE AVAILABLE

Cover images © 2012 Shutterstock

Manufactured in the United States of America

McFarland & Company, Inc., Publishers
Box 611, Jefferson, North Carolina 28640
www.mcfarlandpub.com

Table of Contents

Acknowledgments

Contributors

Van Beydler
Werner Bloos
Clyde DeSouza
Eric Dubois
Sean Fairburn
Perry Hoberman
David Hoffman
John Krantz
Marc Lambooij

Bernard Mendiburu
Josh Perkins
Del Phillips
John A. Rupkalvis
Mark Schaefer
Clifton Schor
John Schultz
Marty Shindler
Bas Siemons

Svend B. Sorensen
Boris Starosta
Dan Symmes
John Van Leeuwen
Paul van Walree
Vivian Walworth
Andrew Woods
Ray Zone
Dobrányi Zsuzsa

Proofreaders

Janet Corazza
Daniel Coverdale
Harold Geller
Bruce Kroon

Carolyn Kroon
Curt Mayers
Joel Ordesky
Tony Pilla

Mallory Pinkis
Kelly Siegle

Additional Material

Aaron Adair
James Burger
David Eedle
Mike Fleischmann
Ed Hennessy
Warner Johnston

Sharon Klein
Bernie Laramie
Christian Manacmul
Harry Miller
Bill Murray
Nhu-y Nguyen

Holly Pinkis
Mikhail Reider-Gordon
Pamela Troumbly
Wendy Wallace

Foreword: "Z-Space Linguistics" by Ray Zone

"Stereographic photography is not at all difficult for the amateur who has a good stereo camera and viewer. In fact, it's rather simple. Nevertheless, stereoscopy is based upon geometry, optics and human vision. It is not strange that a rather complicated terminology surrounds the subject." — Herbert McKay

Stereoscopic lexicography, like the practice of 3D itself, has had a tenuous history. Precise description of human visual perception, much less the experience of the third dimension, has always been a challenge for scientists and stereographers who have endlessly sought a quantitative language to describe a qualitative phenomenon. In the absence of absolute metrics, the baffling complexity of finding accurate descriptors for the experience of depth through binocular stereopsis has proved a daunting and exacting affair for many inventors, scientists, and artists.

Complicating the difficulties of this task is the fact that for decades a layer of hyperbole has been overlaid atop many technological innovations that were often less than rigorous and composed, for the most part, out of wishful thinking as well as smoke and mirrors. And, frequently, these aspiring architects of the third dimension felt compelled to become neologists as well, to bring their technologies into the world alloyed with a name, something novel, something colorful and descriptive like "Natural Vision," "Tru-Stereo" or "Future Dimension."

Twentieth century stereography had no greater champion than John Norling, who assisted Jacob Leventhal shooting the *Stereoscopiks* 3D films of the 1920s and produced the landmark stop-frame Chrysler 3D film *In Tune with Tomorrow* in 1939 for the New York World's Fair. Norling began his epic paper "The Stereoscopic Art," first published in the *PSA Journal* (November-December 1951), the Journal of the Photographic Society of America, by writing, "That an appreciation and understanding of stereoscopic vision has existed for a long time is evident from Euclid's definition: To see in relief is to receive by means of each eye the simultaneous impression of two dissimilar images of the same subject. On this definition by Euclid (c. 280 BCE) the entire stereo art is based."

This epic paper was reprinted in the *SMPTE Journal* of the Society of Motion Picture and Television Engineers (March 1953), and Norling also contributed several additional important papers on stereography to that publication. When Robert V. Bernier, author of a June 1951 *SMPTE Journal* paper titled "Three Dimensional Motion Picture Applications," began to quibble over stereoscopic terminology with Leslie P. Dudley, author of the book *Stereoptics: An Introduction* (London: MacDonald, 1951) in the Letters section of the *Journal,* John Norling weighed in with correspondence of his own by writing that "these letters confirm my opinion that the Stereoscopic Art needs an authoritative nomenclature."

It became one of the tasks of the SMPTE Stereo Committee of 1952 to draft such a glossary of terms. Besides Norling, also serving on this committee were John T. Rule, Raymond Spottiswoode, Clarence Kennedy, Henry Kogel, Arnold Kotis and William Kelley of the Motion Picture Research Council. As a professor of engineering graphics at Massachusetts Institute of Technology John T. Rule had authored a series of foundational articles published in the *Journal of the Optical Society of America (JOSA)* that formulated a unified theory by which "it may become possible to determine the reasons for observable distortions in the stereoscopic image and to predict the results of any proposed optical system."

Similarly, Raymond Spottiswoode, along with his brother Nigel, Charles Smith and Leslie Dudley, had produced dual-band 35mm 3D movies for the 1951 Festival of Britain, and had authored the book *A Theory of Stereoscopic Transmission and Its Application to the Motion Picture* (University of California Press, 1953) a work of highly exacting mathematics for 3D projection. Clarence Kennedy, a professor of art history at Smith College, was a colleague of Edwin Land and George Wheelwright at the Polaroid Corporation, and he used stereoscopic projection of Kodachrome transparencies as an effective visual aid for instruction at the college. Henry Kogel and Arnold Kotis were officers on the board at SMPTE and William V. Kelley at the Motion Picture Research Council had contributed to the development of the "Stereoscopic Calculator," a circular slide-rule to calculate values for interaxial and

convergence based upon lens focal lengths and distances to subject, a convenient device to be used by cinematographers during production of 3D films. All of these individuals had contributed to articles about 3D for the *Journal of the SMPTE.*

John Norling and John T. Rule had worked together in 1939 on production of *In Tune with Tomorrow.* Stereographers, of necessity, must use descriptors that are exact. But it is likely that Norling and Rule, along with Raymond Spottiswoode, were the most verbally precise stereographers of all. Correspondence between Norling and Rule, and internal memos from the SMPTE Stereo Committee of 1952–53, reveal the great pains these men took to achieve language and mathematics for stereography that were nothing if not descriptive.

A three-page letter on MIT letterhead from John T. Rule to J.A. Norling, dated March 25, 1952, beautifully illustrates the exactitude both men worked to achieve in describing stereoscopic parameters. Rule took particular pains to elucidate and expand the term "hyperstereoscopy." He was attempting to clarify what has been called, variously, the "puppet theater" or "Lilliputian" effect of the hyperstereoscopic image when the interaxial values of the stereo base are greatly increased. "Some clarification is needed here," wrote Rule. At issue, for Rule, was the psychological experience of a visual percept, something nearly impossible to quantify numerically, or even, verbally.

But oddly enough, Norling, with his epic paper on "The Stereoscopic Art" in the *SMPTE Journal,* did just that. "Hyperstereoscopy is the term applied when an interaxial base several times normal is used," wrote Norling, quite simply. The term "normal," in this case would consist of an interaxial about 65mm or 2.5 inches, the average distance between the two human eyes. Hyperstereoscopy, wrote Norling, "has often been employed in mountain photography

MASSACHUSETTS INSTITUTE OF TECHNOLOGY
CAMBRIDGE 39, MASSACHUSETTS

COURSE IX
General Science &
General Engineering

March 25th, 1952

Mr. J. A. Norling,
245 West 55th Street,
New York 17, N. Y.

Dear Jack:

       I have been over your definitions. Some of them I think should be changed. In order they are:

Disparate Images: I don't like your use of the word "image". To avoid confusion we should carefully distinguish between three things:-

1. The stereoscopic image which is the solid image in space seen by the observer. It exists only to the observer.

2. The screen pair or pictures which should not be called images at all.

3. The film pair or pictures which again should not be called images.

An image is an optical phenomenon not a picture.

Focal Distance: I don't like the wording. I think it should read: "The distance from the principal node of the camera lens to the film. Except for extremely close views the stated focal length of the lens is a sufficiently close approximation."

Horizontal Error: I don't understand what you mean by Horizontal Error. A "spacing apart" is always there by choice. It might read: "Any error that causes a different spacing than that desired between homologous points." The error would be there whether it caused eyestrain or not.

Hyperstereoscopy and Hypostereoscopy: are much too loose. I would define a hyperstereoscopic image as one whose three-dimensional image size is smaller than the actual object in space (see toward the end of this letter). Some people tend to define the hypostereoscopic image as one that has exactly the same shape but is smaller than the object, excluding the image in which the depth is exaggerated with respect to the width and height. Some clarification is needed here.

Indicated Interaxial: I don't think this is "established by the distance of the object and the focal length of the lens employed.". I would make the definition read: "The interaxial necessary to obtain some desired effect from the given set of conditions." The desired effect might be either hyperstereoscopic or orthostereoscopic.

Page one of a three-page letter from John T. Rule to John Norling illustrating the exacting verbal felicities the two men worked to achieve for stereography (from the Ray Zone collection).

and serves admirably to reveal details in relief."

Raymond J. Spottiswoode was no less fastidious in his attention to linguistic details for stereography. In a three-page letter dated April 17, 1953, and addressed to the SMPTE Stereo Committee, Spottiswoode reviews consensus of the group. "It seems to me," wrote Spottiswoode, "that the word parallax has come to be accepted as an equivalent of

- 3 -

<u>575</u> - I entirely disagree with the elimination of magnification, since there seems no doubt that divergence is a factor in producing eyestrain, and in our experience a very important factor. It is for the purpose of reducing divergence that we propose a crossing over of aperture centrelines when the screen much exceeds the size for which the film is shot.

<u>576</u> - 1. I agree that dashes could be added.

    6, 7. Agree.

<u>577</u> - Mr. Norling's objections to the nomenclature appear to be substantially the same as John Rule's, and the comments already made under that heading apply here also.

                              /s/ <u>R. J. Spottiswoode</u>

                              Technical Director,
                              Stereo Techniques Limited,
                              36 Soho Square, London W.1.

April 17th 1953.

Page three of a three-page letter from Raymond Spottiswoode to the SMPTE Stereo Committee shows his great attention to details of stereoscopic nomenclature (from the Ray Zone collection).

displacement in stereoscopic analysis but if there is a strong feeling that it should be confined to angular analysis, I would let this go." So exacting is Spottiswoode's attention to detail that, on page three of the letter, he agrees to the addition of dashes to the stereoscopic nomenclature.

The use of a hyphen in the abbreviated term "3-D" or "3D" is occasionally an issue in discussions of stereography, along with the

Stereo Glossary

by Herbert C. McKay

STEREOGRAPHIC PHOTOGRAPHY is not at all difficult for the amateur who has a good stereo camera and viewer. In fact, it's rather simple. Nevertheless, stereoscopy is based upon geometry, optics, and human vision. It is not strange that a rather complicated terminology surrounds the subject. Here, for reference purposes, Herbert C. McKay has prepared a glossary, an explanation of many of the terms encountered in stereo. Some are simple, some are not. Keep this glossary for future reference.

American stereoscope. The common parlor or Holmes version of the Brewster stereoscope. Also Mexican stereoscope.

Anaglyph. A stereogram of two superimposed images in which the images are blocked to their respective eyes, so each eye sees only its own proper image. The original form was the bichrome in which the images are printed in two complementary colors and viewed through correspondingly colored filters. A half century ago the process of using polarized light instead of color was patented, and today is favored over the color type for projection. In motion picture work, alternate frames are dyed in complementary color and the film run at double speed to produce the alternate anaglyph. Both bichrome and polarized types are now in use. Books and magazines, for practical reasons, are usually illustrated in bichrome anaglyphs.

Autostereo plate. An obsolete plate with a parallax grid on the back, used for making direct parallax stereograms. Reversal processing.

Autotransposer. Either a printing frame or machine in which provision is made for transposition by simply pulling 2 levers.

Auxiliaries, stereo visual. Factors in stereo vision which enhance the stereo relief but which are not essential to stereo vision. The two most important are the effects of perspective and overlapping of distant objects by those nearer.

Base. The stereo base is the distance between homologous optical points, usually the optical axes of the camera, but also applied to the separation of viewer lenses and at times to human interpupillary.

Box stereoscope. A stereoscope in the form of an enclosed box as contrasted with the skeleton form of Holmes. Standard in Europe.

Brewster, Sir David. Probably the true inventor of stereoscopic reproduction, although the claims of Wheatstone are also favored by

a rectangular screen image instead of the narrow vertical format of a half frame.

Convergence. The meeting of visual (or other optical) axes when produced from two separate stations to a common object. Absolute convergence is the actual angle between the convergent axes and is identical with the parallactic angle. Relative convergence is the convergence upon one object within a scene compared with that upon another object. Relative convergence is the more important in stereo photography. Convergence is often said to be the primary stereo stimulus, but this has been disproven.

Coronet (Trade name). An inexpensive stereo camera and viewer using 828 or equivalent size film. Comparable to a deluxe box camera.

Diopter. Ophthalmic lenses (and viewer lenses) are designated by power rather than focal length. The power in diopters is equal to 100 divided by the focal length in cm. Thus a 20 cm. lens is 5 diopter, a 10 cm. is 10 diopter, a 5 cm. is 20 diopter and so on.

Diplopia. (Double vision.) Ordinarily an abnormal visual condition, but normal to all stereo vision outside the macular area.

Drawing, stereo. A drawing made in duplicate but with stereo differentiation so that when viewed stereoscopically it will have stereo relief.

Equivalent distance. In stereomicrography, a photograph made at a very short distance is viewed as if it were at some greater arbitrary distance, usually "reading" distance. This apparent distance is the equivalent distance. Also applied to other distortions, deliberate and accidental, of stereo relief.

False stereogram. (See Spreader, Twister, Infusible.) A true stereo pair so mounted that viewing is uncomfortable or impossible.

Flicker projection. Stereo projection in which the two images are projected upon a screen in rapid alternation, and viewed through a shutter which alternately obscures the right and left eyes in synchronism with the projector. High illumination factor, but viewers are slightly awkward to handle. Lateral angle of head does not affect stereo effect as in polarization projection.

Free vision. Any system which permits a true stereoscopic effect to be seen without the use of any kind of viewer.

Fusion. The visual registration of the two images in the eyes. This is distinct from the phenomenon of subjective synthesis to which the term is often applied. Purely a physioneurological factor.

A three-page "Stereo Glossary" was compiled by Herbert C. McKay for a special stereo photography issue of *American Photographer* magazine in March 1950 (from the Ray Zone collection).

question of its first historical usage. To my knowledge, the first published use of this verbal shorthand was within a "Stereo Glossary" compiled by Herbert C. McKay in the March 1950 issue of *American Photography* magazine wherein McKay defines "3-D" as "Popular abbreviation for Three Dimensional." This suggests that first usage of the term may have been in conversation, particularly within the stereo photography clubs that were being formed with great rapidity at this time all over the United States.

The initial oral use of the term may explain why the next subsequent published usage that I have found is parenthetical when Raymond Spottiswoode, N.J. Spottiswoode and Charles Smith in the paper "Basic Principles of the Three-Dimensional Film" in the October 1952 *Journal of the SMPTE* write, "Up to now the production of three-dimensional (3-D) films has been sporadic — scattered all over the world and separated by long intervals of time." Thereafter, throughout 1953, the use of the term "3D," both with and without the hyphen, became commonplace as a universal descriptor for the third dimension.

Herbert McKay was a prolific popularizer of stereoscopic photography. As early as 1935, he had begun to write about stereoscopic photography and motion pictures in the pages of *American Photographer* magazine. His articles appeared regularly and introduced important concepts of stereography such as "Convergence as a Factor in Stereoscopy" in the February 1944 issue or "Hyperstereo" in the August 1947 issue. When the Stereo-Realist camera, invented by Seton Rochwite, was introduced to the popular photography market by the David White Company in 1947, McKay's articles acquired great relevance to the field as stereo photo clubs began to form.

With the March 1950 issue of *American Photographer* magazine, the Stereo-Realist camera was given an "unbiased critique" by Arthur Judge "one of the outstanding authorities on stereoscopy." In 1926, Judge had published the book *Stereoscopic Photography, Its Application to Science, Industry and Education* (American Photographic), which introduced many key concepts and terms and included a brief "Bibliography of Stereoscopic Literature." In the preface, Judge acknowledged "the necessity of maintaining a popular as well as a technical interest in stereoscopy," so "theoretical and analytical sections" were "kept to minimum proportions, and the treatments and accounts given made as simple as possible." A second edition was published in 1935 and in 1950 a third edition was published by Chapman and Hall of London, which "necessitated a thorough revision and the inclusion of a considerable amount of new information" to take into account new developments with polarizing filters, stereoscopic motion picture projection and new 3D cameras such as the Stereo-Realist.

In 1948, McKay collected many of his articles from *American Photographer* magazine and published his book *The Principles of Stereoscopy* (American Photographic). Like Judge before him, McKay attempted to write a pragmatic tome, useful to the layman. Yet he qualified that admission by observing that "the planar [2D] photographer need have no extensive knowledge of the principles of human vision to produce pleasing pictures, but the stereographer can never approach the ultimate possibilities of his art unless he has a more or less complete working knowledge of the principles of stereoscopic vision. For that reason," acknowledged McKay, "it has been necessary to include somewhat more theory in this volume than would be found in the usual photographic reference book." When McKay repackaged his book for a second edition using the revised title *Three-Dimensional Photography: Principles of Stereoscopy* with additional new material in 1953, he included as "Appendix B" the Stereo

Glossary that had been published in *American Photographer* magazine.

The compilation of a Stereo Bibliography is an endeavor very much akin to the creation of a Stereo Glossary. Both represent an attempt to comprehensively gather existing knowledge on a specialized subject. A curious bibliography was sent to Arnold Kotis on June 16, 1953, which he promptly forwarded to Henry Kogel to incorporate into the SMPTE Stereo Bibliography that the Stereo Committee was assembling. The seven-page document had been sent to Kotis by Leslie Knopp in Great Britain and bore the inscrutable title heading "ANONYMOUS." It listed numerous articles in English, French, and German about stereography and included listings for many of McKay's articles about stereoscopic photography that had been published in *American Photographer* magazine.

Leslie Knopp was a technical advisor to the Corporation of Executives and Administrators in the United Kingdom and the general cast of his thought can be surmised from an article that he wrote for the May 28, 1953, issue of *Kinematograph Weekly* titled "Puts You in the Picture." In this article, subtitled "What Is Happening in the United States and Moves for Standardisation Here," Knopp wrote about the changes in motion picture exhibition that were taking place in Great Britain as dual-band 3D movies like *House of Wax, Bwana Devil* and *Man in the Dark* began playing. Not generally enthusiastic about stereoscopic cinema, Knopp wrote that "exhibitors are faced with many additional costs," adding that "the hiring of glasses to the public is both costly and troublesome." Far more hopeful about widescreen, Knopp wrote that "the production of panoramic films is not costly" and that "producers feel that panoramic pictures open up new and hitherto unexplored channels in presentation." Interestingly, Knopp repeatedly makes use of the term "3-D" within his

highly technical article that deals with reels, polarizing filters, projection lenses, and alignment, synchronization of projectors and screen brightness.

Included with the ANONYMOUS stereo bibliography that Knopp sent to Kotis was a seven-page alphabetical list of "Stereoscopic Terms." Someone other than Knopp may have compiled this list because many of the definitions for terms seem imprecise, if not quixotic, and Knopp was exceptionally rigorous in his technical article. For example, consider the nautical twist given to the term "Aft Window," positive parallax that is defined as "a stereoscopic window formed behind the plane of the screen." John Norling and John T. Rule certainly would not have approved the definition for "Hyperstereoscopic image" given as "an image smaller in size but similar in shape to the original object," succinct but hilariously subjective in description.

By October 1, 1953, SMPTE had compiled a thirty-seven page alphabetical "Draft Stereo Bibliography." It included listings for books and articles in German, English, and French from publications that ranged from *Popular Astronomy* and *Hobbies* magazine to *Textile World, Cinema Today, The American Journal of Roentgenology,* and the *Journal of Experimental Psychology.* In this respect I myself would be remiss were I to neglect to mention a fine volume self-published by Sam N. Smith of Calgary, Alberta, Canada, that is titled *The Books, Treatises and Manuals of Stereoscopy: A Chronological Review of Published Work: 1838–2005* (Sam Smith: 2005).

The evolution of the stereographic lexicon can be traced in books on the subject that incorporated Stereo Glossaries. A fine example is *3-D Kinematography and New Screen Techniques* (Hutchison's Scientific and Technical: 1954) an historical overview by Adrian Cornwell-Clyne that includes a three-page bibliography and a seven-page glossary of terms. *Stereo Photography: The Technique*

Stereoscopic Terms

Adjustable Interaxial Camera: A stereoscopic camera provided with means for presetting the lens interaxial for each xxxx scene, i.e. for closeups, medium closeups, medium long shots and long shots.

Aft Window: A stereoscopic window formed behind the plane of the screen.

Anisekonia: A visual defect in which the formation of an image through one eye differs in size or shape from that formed through the other eye.

Angular Alignment: The condition that exists when there is no rotatio between members of the stereoscopic pair. See Rotational Error.

Beam Splitter: An optical attachment composed of mirrors or prisms, which when placed before a camera lens, splits the normal image into two distinct pictures , correctly separated. i.e. a stereoscopic pair

Binocular Vision: Normal vision through two eyes which enables the observer to see depth in a scene by fusing the images in the visual centers of the brain.

Cardboarded Image: An image xixx which with respect to the original object is decreased in depth compared to width and height.

Color Anaglyphs: Stereograms printed or exhibited by employing one color for one member of the stereoscopic pair and a complementary color for the other. The stereograms are viewed through correspondingly colored filters, enabling the spectator visually to combine the two images into a stereoscopic sensation.

Differential Vertical: When either or both pictures are keystoned the vertical displacement of the screen pictures differs across the screen.

Differential Vibration: The effect resulting from differences in steadiness between members of a stereoscopic film while being projected. See Jittering

Dimensional Error: The error in a stereoscopic picture in which one member is of different size than the other. See Anisekonia.

An idiosyncratic list of "Stereoscopic Terms" was sent by Leslie Knopp to Arnold Kotis in May 1953 (from the Ray Zone collection).

of the Third Dimension (Focal, 1957), a practical handbook by K.C.M. Symons, was published with a three-page glossary. Though it contains no stereo glossary, H. Dewhurst's *Introduction to 3-D: Three Dimensional Photography in Motion Pictures* (Macmillan, 1954) contains a bibliography and is itself a veritable stereo glossary with chapter subheads serving as a listing of terms ranging from "relative perspective" and "parallax defined" to "divergent infinity points" and "shutter-occluding."

One of the great terms in stereography, globally descriptive of 3D viewing parameters, is that of "binocular symmetries," first enunciated by Lenny Lipton in his seminal tome *Foundations of the Stereoscopic Cinema: A Study in Depth* (Van Nostrand Reinhold, 1982). Lipton studied causes of eyestrain in stereoscopic displays. "Binocular symmetry differs from conventional symmetry," he wrote, "in that two image fields (the left and right images), and not one field, must be considered — and compared." Lipton's research indicated that "the symmetries of the two fields must be held to within specifiable tolerances or strain will occur. The symmetries are: illumination, aberration (and sharpness), geometry (or linearity), color, image selection, and temporal symmetry and registration."

For literary felicity, wedded to pragmatism, there is the discursive tome *Practical Stereoscopic Photography* (Technical, 1936) by J. Moir Dalzell. The author invokes the great Poet of Stereo in the opening to Chapter Two when he writes, "It was Oliver Wendell Holmes who called a photograph 'a mirror with a memory.' To pictures made with a two-eyed camera, he gave the name of 'sun sculpture.' No one could have said it better." Similarly, this writer is indebted to vision scientist Martin Banks for transference of the term "binocular lustre," a scientifically precise yet marvelously literary expression for the two-eyed experience more commonly known as "retinal rivalry."

Disagreements as to usage of stereographic terms between practitioners can be passionate and elaborately argued. One of the titanic arguments over the precise definition and usage of the term "convergence" took place in 1996 with a series of published articles and correspondence between veteran British stereoscopist Charles Smith and American stereographer Tony Alderson. The debate over the rhetoric began when Alderson published a December 1995 article in *Stereoscopy*, the bi-monthly publication of the International Stereoscopic Union, stating that the term "convergence" should only be used to refer to "toe-in" of the cameras during production and, in any case, its use may cause eyestrain. In response, Smith wrote an article for the *Stereoscopic Society Journal* of Great Britain stating that "convergence control in one form or another is present in all stereoscopy, movie or still."

Subsequent correspondence between Alderson and Smith reveals the great amount of thought that both had invested in the subject. "The only real question here," wrote Alderson, "is: What is the 'correct' usage of the word 'convergence' in the context of stereoscopy?" Alderson opined that "this is the great undeclared war of three-d-dom. As long as I have been involved in the stereo community, I have observed this sectarian squabble arise every time anyone raises the red flag of the 'c' word. The real dispute is concealed by this superficial controversy of 'toe-in or not toe-in' while the issue of definition is never overtly discussed."

Then, after citing McKay, Spottiswoode, Cornwell-Clyne and others, Alderson concurs with Lenny Lipton, who insists upon use of the term "toe-in" to mean camera convergence and in "The Crystal Eyes Handbook" (StereoGraphics, 1991) writes, "Historically, the term 'convergence' has been applied to the process used to achieve the zero parallax condition for stereo imaging. The use of the term creates confusion with regard to the physiological process of convergence in the visual world — a processing requiring rotation of the eyes. Therefore a break with prior usage is called for."

This break with prior usage has yet to happen. The author of the present volume has diplomatically incorporated five separate definitions for the term "convergence" and it appears likely that the "sectarian squabble" that Alderson observed over its usage will continue. Nevertheless, greater precision of usage is now possible because Richard W. Kroon has made the effort to compile this work. It is a task that is Sisyphean in nature because of the continuously evolving nature of digital stereography and language itself.

Every day, new words to describe spatial technologies and experiences are coined, frequently birthed in conversation and then, secondarily, finding their way into print. A recent utterance, for example, heard by this writer from the lips of Hoyt Yeatman, director of *G-Force 3-D* (2009), is the term "three-space" or "3 Space," as the case may be, as an audible percept. By mentioning this, I am undoubtedly adding further exertions to the Herculean task Mr. Kroon has undertaken in compiling this freestanding volume that, in any case, will be remembered as a true and necessary "first" in the history of stereography.

Ray Zone is a film producer, 3D artist, industry historian, and the author of 3-D Filmmakers: Conversations with Creators of Stereoscopic Motion Pictures (2005) *and* Stereoscopic Cinema and the Origins of 3-D Film, 1838–1952 *(2007).*

Introduction

According to some, stereoscopic 3D is a brand-new segment of the media and entertainment industry. In actuality, it is over 180 years old and pre-dates the development of photography. Every 20 to 30 years since the invention of the stereoscope in the 1830s, there has been a resurgence in stereo filmmaking where everything that was once known must be rediscovered again by a whole new generation, with additional twists introduced by technological advancements made during the intervening years. This dictionary documents the current language of the industry and provides historical context for those who are new to this discipline — especially those who have extensive experience producing 2D "flatties," but are still finding their way with 3D "depthies."

This is not the first attempt at a dictionary of stereoscopic terminology, as you will have learned from the Foreword, but it is by far the largest and most ambitious. It covers still and moving image stereography; film and digital image acquisition; production, post-production, distribution, and exhibition; and human visual perception. By necessity, many of the definitions are technical, but we have tried to make them understandable to the non-professional and self-contained within this volume. (You should find that any specialized terms found in one definition will be defined themselves — either directly where they are used or in their own entry elsewhere in the dictionary.) This will make *3D A-to-Z* indispensible to students and hobbyists as well as industry professionals. We like to think of it as a stereoscopic 3D textbook, arranged in alphabetical order.

This book goes beyond the scope of a traditional dictionary, concerned only with the meanings of words, to include encyclopedic entries that provide historical context and introduce the reader to the myriad proper nouns, professional tools, techniques, concepts, and phrases that comprise the stereographic lexicon. The reader will also find editorial notes, cautioning against common usage mistakes and drawing attention to potential points of confusion. Since man does not live by text alone, there are also nearly 300 illustrations — many in color — ranging from historical artifacts to technical diagrams and at least one flying pyramid.

Books such as this are not the work of a single individual. I have done my best to acknowledge everyone who contributed to this dictionary, but so many different people were so generous with their time, expertise, and advice that I am certain to have left someone out. For that, I apologize. I must also apologize to my wife, Melanie, who leads the life of a dictionary widow — lonely at times, but always well informed. This book would not have been possible without her unending support and understanding. This time, the cats did not really help all that much, but there is no telling what they might do to my shoes at night if I do not at least mention them.

If an error has managed to slip through our small army of proofreaders, or if a term has missed the notice of our legion of contributors, please let us know. Send any errors or omissions to updates@hollywords.org so we can address them in the next edition.

Good luck, and remember: If it's not 3D,
it may as well be radio.

THE DICTIONARY

Ø *See* **phi phenomenon.**

µPol *See* **micro-polarizer.**

Abbe's number *See* **dispersion.**

aberration An undesirable visual anomaly caused by an optical element, generally in a camera. *Compare* **artifact; barrel distortion; depth plane curvature; gigantism; lens distortion; Lilliputism; mustache distortion; pincushion distortion.**

above/below; above-below *See* **over/under.**

absolute category rating; ACR A standardized method for measuring the subjective quality of individual video sequences using a five- or nine-point scale, ranging from "bad" to "excellent." Published as part of *ITU-T Recommendation P.910* in September 1999 by the International Telecommunication Union.

Video sequences are presented to reviewers one at a time in a regular pattern. The reviewers rate each video sequence on its own merits during the interval between sequences (generally ≤ 10 seconds). The same video sequence may be presented more than once during a test session to help ensure a more accurate result.

Variations on the ACR method allow for an 11-point scale (adding 0 "A worse quality cannot be imagined." and 10 "No further improvement is possible") a continuous 9-point scale ranging from "bad" to "excellent" without pre-defined choices in-between, and measurements other than simple video quality, including brightness, contrast, jerkiness, and double images.

Also **single stimulus method.** *Compare* **subjective test.**

absolute parallax transition limit The maximum allowable amount of parallax change in an image stream as a function of time. If the presented images exceed this limit, then the viewer will not be able to fuse the images to produce a 3D effect. *Compare* **depth change stress; display parallax transition limit; dZ/dt.**

absolute screen disparity The overall offset of one eye image verses the other. Successful binocular fusion without double vision can be achieved with large absolute screen disparities (well outside Panum's fusion area) so long as the relative screen disparities for the individual objects within the scene remain small (inside Panum's fusion area). *Compare* **relative screen disparity.**

absorptive filter A traditional light filter that allows certain types of light to pass through and absorbs all other types of light, converting the absorbed light energy into heat. Such filters can melt or burn if they absorb too much light. *Compare* **dichroic filter.**

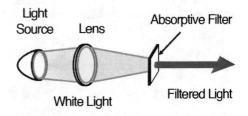

accommodation Changes in the shape of the eye's lens that allow one to focus on objects at different distances, such as when following a close moving object. Similar to adjusting the focus on a camera's lens.

When viewing a stereogram, all objects are the same distance from the viewer (on the surface of the screen), but only appear to be closer or farther away due to parallax (causing binocular disparity and driving eye vergence). Thus, when viewing a stereogram, best image quality is achieved by maintaining constant accommodation. However, breaking the normal accommodation/vergence link can cause the brain to interpret the image as being more flat than image parallax would otherwise indicate.

Compare **convergence.**

accommodation/vergence; accommodation/ convergence; ~ link; ~ relationship The neural association between accommodation (focal adjustments to the eyes) and vergence (turning the eyes in equal but opposite amounts to line up on the same point in space). Useful in the estimation of depth for objects up to 200 meters away (stereo infinity). Matching accommodation and vergence for objects closer than stereo infinity reduces eyestrain, improves depth perception, and decreases the time required to perceive a 3D image.

At an early age one develops the neural crosslinks between accommodation and vergence so that the vergence necessary to align the images of an object in each eye triggers the accommodation necessary to bring the object into focus, and vice versa. The eyes do not need to turn inward from parallel to view distant objects (beyond about 200 meters), since distant left- and right-eye images align when the eyes are pointed straight ahead. However, when viewing closer objects, the eyes must turn inward to align the images. When adjusting the eyes from a far object to near or from a near object to far, the eyes must be turned inward from parallel (convergence) or outward towards parallel (divergence) respectively. As the eyes rotate, accommodation brings the objects into focus. This accommodation/vergence link must be broken when viewing a stereogram. (In most 3D display systems, all objects have the same focal distance and therefore require the same accommodation, regardless of the amount of vergence necessary to align the images.)

In theory, if one has sufficient visual depth of field, the accommodation/vergence link need not be broken and adjusting focus to see an object that vergence says is closer or farther than the screen will not cause the object to lose focus. Depth of field increases with linear distance, so increasing viewing distance should diminish visual conflict over the accommodation/vergence link and reduce eyestrain. This tends to favor theatrical presentation over home viewing for 3D.

Also **vergence/accommodation.**

accommodation/vergence reflex; accommodation/convergence reflex The automatic focal adjustments made as the eyes converge or diverge. This reflexive response must be overcome when viewing a stereogram since the focal distance to the screen is constant even though the amount of vergence changes when viewing different objects at different apparent distances. *Compare* **decorrelation; fundamental disparity.**

accommodation/vergence rivalry; accommodation/convergence rivalry A mismatch between accommodation (actual focal distance) and vergence (based on apparent object distance). Common when viewing stereoscopic images because everything is at the same distance from the viewer (on the surface of the screen) even though different objects appear to be at different distances (thanks to positive or negative parallax).

Accommodation/vergence rivalry has long been assumed to be the primary cause of stereoscopic viewer fatigue. More recent studies indicate that visual depth of field may be sufficient to correct for most accommodation/vergence discrepancies. Instead, conflicts between recorded image vergence and viewer vergence or abrupt changes in vergence may be more important factors in visual fatigue than accommodation/vergence rivalry.

There are two schools of thought regarding the treatment of convergence when toed-in cameras are used to record a stereogram. In the traditional approach, the interaxial distance is held (mostly) constant and the camera convergence is adjusted to set the zero disparity plane. This results in a work that can have significantly different vergence from one shot to the next. Alternatively, the camera vergence is set to match that of the nominal viewer and fixed throughout the work. The interaxial distance is then adjusted to set the zero disparity plane. This use of consistent vergence reduces the time it takes a viewer to adjust to the depth in each new shot and diminishes visual fatigue.

accommodative facility The ease and speed with which one's eyes can change focal distance.

accommodative insufficiency The inability to focus the eyes properly. Often accompanied by convergence insufficiency. *Compare* **amblyopia; diplopia; presbyopia; strabismus.**

achirality A lack of handedness. Achiral objects do not appear in mirror image forms—multiple examples can always be rotated in such a way that they line up exactly. Compounds composed of achiral molecules are not optically active. *Compare* **chirality; polarization handedness.**

ACR *See* **absolute category rating.**

active/active An active stereoscopic display technology coupled with active glasses, as with most consumer 3D televisions. *Compare* **active/passive; passive/passive.**

active display *See* **active glasses-based 3D display.** *Compare* **passive display.**

active eyewear; active glasses Spectacles that can alternatively block the left and right eyes in time with the presentation of left- and right-eye images in a time-sequential stereogram.

The first active eyewear devices were patented by Charles Francis Jenkins in the late 1890s. The first theatrical 3D presentation using active eyewear

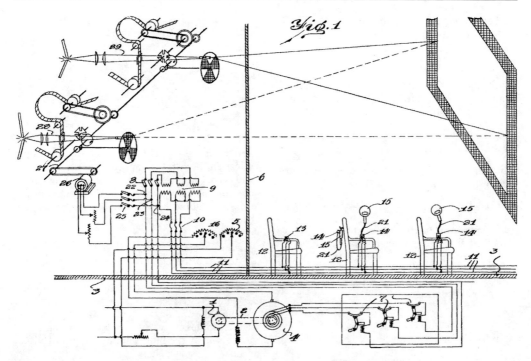

From Laurens Hammond's U.S. patent for a mechanical shutter-based active eyewear system showing the electromechanical linkage between the twin projectors and the viewing device attached to each seat (No. 1,506,524, issued August 26, 1924) (U.S. Patent and Trademark Office).

was in 1922 at the Selwyn Theater in New York City using the Teleview 3D system developed by Laurens Hammond and William F. Cassidy. Viewing devices were attached to each seat with a rotating mechanical shutter synchronized to the projection system. Two separate projectors were used to obtain the double-speed image rate required by active eyewear systems. Contemporary active eyewear uses liquid crystal display (LCD) lenses, called liquid crystal shutters (LCS), that are synchronized electronically to a high-speed display device.

With active eyewear the left eye only sees left-eye images and the right eye only sees right-eye images, so the system can be used with a single image display device so long as it runs at a high enough speed to avoid visible image flicker (generally twice the speed of a standard display device). This applies equally to projectors and televisions. Synchronization is maintained through a timing signal transmitted to the eyewear, typically via an IR or Bluetooth emitter connected to the display device. Active eyewear is more expensive than the passive eyewear used with anaglyphic or polarized systems, but provides superior color fidelity and image resolution compared to anaglyphs and can be presented without the special projector, silver screen, or display filters required by polarized systems.

Also **shutter glasses; wireless shutter eyewear.** *Compare* **eclipse method; hybrid eyewear; passive eyewear.**

active glasses-based 3D display; AGB3D The general class of glasses-based 3D displays (GB3D) that require active eyewear, such as liquid crystal shutters. *Compare* **passive glasses-based 3D display.**

active/passive An active stereoscopic display technology coupled with passive (generally, polarized) glasses, as with RealD theatrical and dual-panel LCD 3D display systems. *Compare* **active/active; passive/passive.**

active retarder *Also* **variable-polarization-angle display.** *See* **dual-panel LCD 3D; ZScreen.**

active stereo A stereoscopic device that requires the viewer to wear active eyewear that switches the right and left lenses on and off in time to the presentation of left- and right-eye images on the display. Auto-stereoscopic devices and technologies based on passive eyewear are excluded. *Compare* **passive stereo; time-sequential.**

acuity Sharpness or clarity of vision; the ability to resolve fine detail. Normal visual acuity is expressed as 20/20 (in the U.S.) or 6/6 (in countries using the Metric system) and corresponds to the ability to resolve details of approximately 1 arc minute (¹⁄₆₀ of a degree). *Compare* **discrimination.**

adaptation The change in sensitivity following prolonged exposure to an unchanging stimulus. *Compare* **aftereffect.**

addressable hologram A holographic image that can be altered as it is being displayed.

adjusting; adjust; depth ~ *See* **convergence animation; depth warping.**

advanced video coding; AVC *See* **MPEG-4 AVC.**

aerial perspective *Also* **atmospheric perspective.** *See* **perspective.** *Compare* **monocular cue.**

aftereffect An alteration in perception that occurs after prolonged exposure to a stimulus. *Compare* **adaptation.**

afterimage *See* **burn-in.**

AGB3D *See* **active glasses-based 3D display.**

AIP *See* **anterior intraparietal cortex.**

Akumira anaglyph The trade name for the first full-color anaglyph optimization process where the colors are mathematically manipulated to improve color reproduction while reducing ghosting, retinal rivalry, and eyestrain. Since being introduced by Brightland Corporation in August 2000, Akumira has been used in a variety of commercial stereoscopic products. The name "Akumira" was coined as a fanciful blend of "accurate mirror." The Brightland Web site is www.brightland.com. *Compare* **optimized anaglyph.** See *Akumira anaglyph* images in color section.

aliasing An undesirable digital artifact that occurs when a high-frequency signal is sampled at too low a rate (generally when the sample frequency is less than twice the frequency of the input signal, also called the *Nyquist frequency*).

When aliasing occurs, the transition from one sample to the next is unacceptably abrupt and noticeable, rather than smooth and unremarkable. This can happen any time an analog signal is converted into discrete samples. Visual aliasing is often referred to as the jaggies because diagonal lines and curves appear jagged rather than smooth, though it can also appear as a twinkling in the picture detail.

In the natural world, an infinite number of gradations are possible. In the digital world, these gradations must be converted into a finite number of values (no matter how much resolution a digital system has, there is still a limit to how

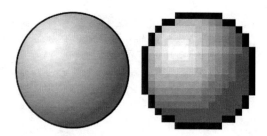

The two images differ only in their digital sample rates. The high-rate image (left) appears smooth and even. The low-rate image (right) shows obvious color aliasing (color bands) throughout the interior and outline aliasing (jaggies) along the edge.

many different values can be represented). So, instead of blending smoothly from one sample to the next, there is a stair step effect where the recorded value jumps slightly between samples. In most cases, these jumps are too small to notice. When the sample rate (or resolution) is too low, these jumps cause a perceptible distortion.

Some of the most common types of visual image aliasing include:

- **Color Aliasing (banding or contouring):** When there are more gradations of color (chrominance or luminance) than the display system can accommodate — most obvious with low-resolution Internet images where there are distinct bands of color in an image. This effect can be exaggerated by an optical illusion that causes dark bands to appear even darker when they are next to a lighter band, and vice versa.
- **Motion (or Temporal) Aliasing:** When fast rotating objects (mostly propellers and wheels) seem to spin in different directions or speeds. Even human vision has a sample rate — if an object is rotating too fast, image sample artifacts will be introduced and the object may seem to spin backwards or forwards at a slower than actual speed.
- **Outline (or Spatial) Aliasing:** The visual jaggies that occur when diagonal or curved lines have visible stair-step increments rather than smooth edges.
- **Raster Aliasing:** If a horizontal line is thinner than a single row of pixels in a video system (or a vertical line is thinner than a single column of pixels), it may be represented as being on different rows (or columns) in different frames, resulting in a visible shimmer effect as it rapidly switches between the two.

Compare **anti-aliasing; posterization.**

alignment error *See* **vertical alignment error.**

amblyopia A developmental disorder of the visual system that causes poor or indistinct vision in an otherwise healthy eye and impairs binocular vision. Rarely affects both eyes and is often confused with strabismus. Develops during early childhood (between birth and two years old); generally treatable if detected early.

Severe amblyopia can limit one's ability to perceive 3D objects in a stereoscopic display. The diminished visual signal may also interfere with depth perception, spatial acuity, and sensitivity to motion while causing a reduced sensitivity to image contrast.

Also **lazy eye.** *Compare* **accommodative insufficiency; convergence insufficiency; diplopia; strabismus.**

AM3D *See* **auto-multiscopic.**

Anachrome The trade name for a variation on the basic anaglyphic process developed by American stereographer Allan Silliphant. Anachrome eyewear provides slight magnification for the red lens to help compensate for the slight image blurring that may be associated with red filters. In addition, the cyan lens admits a certain amount of red light to help combat retinal rivalry and deliver more accurate colors (particularly reds, which are problematic in traditional red/cyan anaglyphs). *Compare* **Prisma-chrome 3D.**

anaglyph; anaglyphic process A frame-compatible stereogram where the left- and right-eye images are color-coded and combined into a single image. When the combined image is viewed through glasses with lenses of the corresponding colors, a 3D image is perceived. Different complementary color combinations have been used over the years, but the most common are red and cyan. Anaglyphs may be projected, displayed on a monitor, or produced in print.

NOTE: There is no international standard for which eye-image is coded with which color. (So long as the glasses match, it does not seem to matter). However, in the U.S., the right lens is often red (capitalizing on alliteration — red/right — as a mnemonic to help keep from confusing the eye filters), while in Europe, the left lens is most often red.

Experiments with complementary color anaglyphic processes may date back to 1717, but the first printed anaglyphs are attributed to Heinrich Wilhelm Dove, working in Germany in 1841. Anaglyphic projection is generally attributed to Joseph Charles d'Almeida, who demonstrated his system in France in 1858, though Wilhelm Rollman may have experimented with anaglyphic projection in Germany as early as 1853. The term itself was coined c. 1862 by Louis Ducos du Hauron, a French citizen living in Algeria, from Greek roots to mean, "again — sculpture."

As with all stereoscopic processes, anaglyphs use two slightly offset images of the same action. The images are filtered through a pair of contrasting colored lenses, usually red and cyan. The audience watches the work through anaglyphoscopes: glasses with corresponding colored lenses. One lens blocks the red image and allows only the cyan filtered image to be seen. The other lens blocks the cyan image and allows only the red image to be seen. In the example of a red ball photographed against a field of green grass to produce a red/green anaglyph, one eye would see a red ball against a black background (that eye's lens having filtered out the color of the green grass) while the other eye would see a black circle on a green field (that eye's lens having filtered out the color of the red ball). The positions of the black circle and the red ball would be slightly offset as perceived by the viewer, simulating the offset images common to human binocular vision. As a result, the viewer perceives the on-screen image as having 3D depth.

The colored filters alter the color composition of the resulting images, so the process works best with black-and-white images. Anaglyphs dominated theatrical 3D for some time. The first U.S. public demonstration was in 1915 at New York's Astor Theater, followed by the first paid presentation in 1922 at New York's Rivoli Theater. In the 1930s, an improved 3D system was developed based on polarized light in place of color-filtered images. Polarized stereograms could be presented in full color and with reduced eyestrain. This process was used during the 3D boom of the 1950s, but generally required special synchronized projectors running two strips of film, one for each eye. Severe eyestrain could still result if the projectors were out of alignment or the film was run through the wrong projector. Despite the popularity of the polarized method, development of the color filter-based anaglyph process has continued, resulting in an improved 3D effect, full-color images, and reduced eyestrain.

Anaglyphs can be recorded on a single strip of film and presented using standard display systems, avoiding the synchronization issues of most polarized processes. Anaglyphs can also be presented on standard color televisions, so long as the viewer has an appropriately matched set of glasses. As a result, until recently, anaglyphs were the only format suitable for home entertainment use. They have also been used in recent theatrical releases including *Spy Kids 3-D: Game Over* (2003) and *The Adventures of Sharkboy and Lavagirl in 3-D* (2005).

Compare **auto-stereoscopic; color bombardment; interocular distance; polarized stereograms.**

anaglyph, black-and-white A black-and-white stereogram encoded as an anaglyph. The resulting anaglyph is a color image, using shades of the two filter colors to encode the left- and right-eye views. Since the original images contain no color, one does not have to trade off depth perception against accurate color rendition. See *anaglyph, black-and-white image* in color section.

anaglyph, full-color An anaglyph produced using full-color stereo images. Results in retinal rivalry if the colors of the anaglyph filters also appear in the original images. Particularly when the stereo images contain red, since most anaglyphic processes use a shade of red in one of the image filters. See *anaglyph, full-color* image in color section.

anaglyph, half-color An anaglyph produced using color stereo images optimized for anaglyphic reproduction by suppressing shades of one of the filter colors from both images. Generally produced by eliminating the reds in the images, since most anaglyphic processes use a shade of red in one of the image filters. This avoids the retinal rivalry associated with full-color anaglyphs, but distorts the colors in the resulting stereogram. *Compare* **optimized anaglyph.** See *anaglyph, half-color* in color section.

anaglyphoscope Special glasses with contrasting colored lenses—generally one red and one cyan — used to view stereograms produced with the anaglyphic process. *Compare* **broadband spectral eyewear.**

analytic photogrammetry The process of using mathematical formulae to calculate physical dimensions from a photograph. May be used to calculate depth data from a stereogram. *Compare* **computational photography; stereophotogrammetry; stereoscopic rendition.**

analytical stereoplotter A device that automates the extraction of elevation contours from a pair of stereo images using a computer. Produces topographic maps from aerial stereograms. *Compare* **analytical stereoplotter.**

analyzer *See* **selection device.**

anamorphic An image magnification by different proportions in the horizontal and vertical directions. Generally, horizontal image compression that uses a special lens to record a widescreen image within the space of a standard image.

> When recording an anamorphic image, the camera lens distorts the image, compressing it in the horizontal direction twice as much as the vertical, making everything look tall and skinny. The display system reverses this distortion by expanding the image in the horizontal direction so that the presented image looks normal.

The principals of the anamorphic lens were first developed by Henri Chrétien during World War I for a tank periscope that gave a 180° field of view. After the war, Chrétien developed the Hypergonar motion picture lens system. It consisted of an anamorphic adapter that could be added to a standard motion picture camera or projector lens. This system was used to produce the first anamorphic film, *Construire un Feu* (*To Build a Fire*, 1928). The process did not catch on until Fox Film Corporation purchased the patents for Chrétien's Hypergonar lens system in 1952 and used them to create CinemaScope, which premiered with *The Robe* (1953). *Compare* **spherical.**

anamorphosis A distorted image that takes on its intended shape when viewed in an unconventional way, such as from an extreme angle (*oblique anamorphosis*) or as a reflection in a distorting mirror (*catoptric anamorphosis*). With perspectival anamorphosis, the 3D perspective of an object is recorded as a stereogram so that the object appears to extend into space when viewed through stereo glasses from the proper angle. *Compare* **Phantaglyph.**

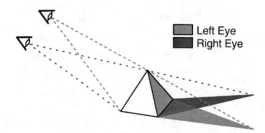

□ Left Eye
■ Right Eye

If the image of the pyramid is recorded as a stereogram using the left and right eye views as noted in the diagram, then when the horizontal stereogram is viewed from the same angle, the pyramid will appear to extend upwards from the surface.

ancillary metadata Data that describe nonaudiovisual attributes of a work, including closed-captions, time code, active format description (AFD) data, cast members, etc.

angle of view A defined portion of the total visual field, represented as a certain number of degrees. When recording an image, the angle of view is defined by the shape of the camera's aperture mask, cutting a rectangular area out of the lens' visual field. When viewing an image on a screen, the angle of view is measured from the viewer to the edges of the screen.

> Most camera apertures and display screens are wider than they are tall, so the angle of view typically describes the angle of the horizontal view as

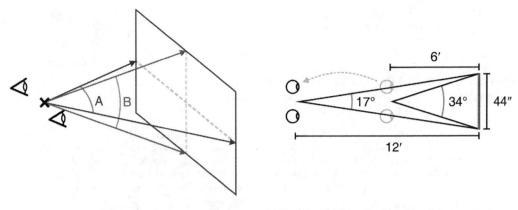

Measuring the angle of view (left) from the center of the viewer's gaze (the mid-point between the eyes) to the edges of the screen horizontally (A) and vertically (B). When viewed from above (right), the relationship between horizontal angle of view and viewing distance becomes apparent. In this case, a screen 44" wide has a 34° angle of view when viewed from 6' and a 17° angle of view when viewed from 12'. If the viewing distance were held constant, then the angle of view would increase with increasing screen width.

measured side to side from the center of the camera lens or the viewer's gaze. This measure fails to account for the image aspect ratio, so some use a diagonal angle of view instead or report both the horizontal and vertical angles of view. However, since the depth information in a stereoscopic work is recorded in the horizontal direction, stereoscopic angles of view are measured horizontally.
Compare **field of view; viewing angle.**

angular resolution The distance separating the smallest points on a display that can be independently resolved, measured as an angle from the center of the viewer's gaze. With the angle held constant, the physical size of the largest practical pixel (2D) or voxel (3D) will grow smaller as the observer moves closer to the display.

angulation *Also* **stereoangle.** *See* **toe-in; vergence.**

aniseikonia; anisoeikonia A visual disorder where perceived size differs significantly between the eyes, leading to double vision (diplopia), dizziness, and eyestrain and interfering with depth perception. Caused by a number of different conditions, including being farsighted in one eye and nearsighted in the other (or attempts to correct this condition with glasses or contacts). *Compare* **diplopia.**

anterior intraparietal cortex; AIP The region of the brain responsive to the visual size, shape, and position of objects one may grasp with the hands. Part of the parietal lobe, located between the fontal and occipital lobes and above the temporal lobe. *Compare* **visual cortex.**

anti-aliasing; antialiasing The reduction of the impact of aliasing in a digital signal. (Aliasing is a bad thing, so anti-aliasing is a good thing.)

The neighboring values of each digital signal element are examined and the signal element is adjusted to better blend with its neighbors and limit the appearance of stair step jumps in value. The process blurs the original signal slightly to give the appearance of a smooth signal rather than a ragged one. Analog signals are naturally anti-aliased since they contain continuously variable values without discrete stair steps.
Compare **aliasing; depth blend; quincunx.** *See* *anti-aliasing* image in color section.

anti-aliasing filter A low-pass filter used to remove any components of an analog signal that are higher than the Nyquist frequency before the signal is subjected to digital conversion. This reduces the incidence of aliasing artifacts in the resulting digital signal. *Compare* **decimation; reconstruction filter.**

anti-imaging filter *See* **reconstruction filter.**

anti-reflective coating *See* **AR coating.**

apparent depth; apparent distance The illusion of depth when viewing a stereogram. Determined by the amount of positive or negative parallax perceived by the viewer (a function of the actual image parallax and the viewer's distance from the screen).

apparent motion The illusion of motion that results from viewing a rapid sequence of still images. *Also* **beta motion; optimal motion.** *See* **phi phenomenon.**

AR coating; anti-reflective coating Material applied to the surface of a lens or other optical element to reduce reflections. This improves the overall efficiency of optical elements and increases image contrast by increasing the percentage of incoming light that passes through the element and eliminating stray light rays that might otherwise have been scattered by the surface of the element.

arc minute; arcminute An angular measure equal to $\frac{1}{60}$ of a degree. One full rotation about a fixed point is 360°. Each degree is divided into 60 minutes (60'). Each minute is divided into 60 seconds (60").

area of primary attention *See* **primary attention.**

artifact; artefact An error in perception or representation introduced into a visual or aural presentation by the equipment used in its capture, creation, processing, delivery, or display. *Compare* **aberration.**

artificial reality A real-time, computer-generated, immersive simulation that combines a visual display system (often a helmet-mounted 3D display) with a means for the user to interact with the simulated world (such as a motion capture device). While virtual reality attempts to create a seemingly real environment, artificial reality is not so constrained and may represent a real or abstract world. The term was coined by American computer scientist Myron W. Krueger in 1973. *Compare* **augmented reality; virtual reality.**

aspect distortion A change in image aspect ratio cause by unequal horizontal or vertical magnification or reduction. For example, the CinemaScope process introduces an aspect distortion by compressing the recorded image two times more horizontally than vertically. This distortion is reversed for presentation by magnifying the image two times more horizontally than vertically.

aspect ratio; AR A comparison of the width to the height of the usable (or visible) image portion of a film or video frame expressed as a numeric value or calculated ratio, such as 16 × 9, 1.33 to 1, or 1.85:1.

Aspect ratios are generally given in terms of the projected or viewed image, rather than in terms of the image recorded by the camera, which may be of a different aspect ratio than the desired projection or broadcast image — typically more square.

Common presentation aspect ratios include:
- 1.25:1— Standard LCD computer monitor; still photographic prints (4 × 5 or 8 × 10 in a landscape orientation)
- 1.33:1— Silent film (aspect ratios varied

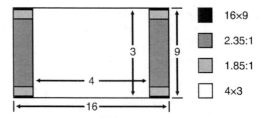

A 16 × 9 widescreen TV image aspect ratio with a standard 4 × 3 television image inset (with pillar bars on either side) along with 1.85:1 and 2.25:1 aspect ratios (with letterbox bars above and below)—1.85:1 is so close to 16 × 9 that such images are generally presented full height with the far left and right edges simply cut off.

greatly during the early Silent Era (c. 1890), but eventually settled on 1.33); standard television or CRT computer monitor (where it is more commonly expressed as 4:3 or 4 × 3)
- 1.37:1— Academy aperture for 35mm (Movietone frame adjusted to provide a more rectangular image while still allowing room for an optical soundtrack)
- 1.43:1— IMAX (often referred to as 15/70 indicating that the frame runs for 15 perforations on 70mm film, as opposed to the standard 4 perforations for a full frame 35mm image)
- 1.60:1— Widescreen computer monitor
- 1.62:1— The Golden Ratio (rounded from 1.6180339887)
- 1.66:1— Continental European standard theatrical aspect ratio (considered widescreen in comparison to Academy aperture)— may be rounded to 1.67
- 1.78:1— Widescreen television (where it is more commonly expressed as 16:9 or 16 × 9)
- 1.85:1— U.S. and UK standard theatrical aspect ratio (considered widescreen in comparison to Academy aperture); normal human vision (unlike motion picture and television aspect ratios, which are based on a rectangular image, human vision is roughly shaped like an ellipse with the aspect ratio measured along its widest and tallest dimensions)
- 2.00:1— VistaVision and Magnafilm
- 2.35:1— Non-anamorphic (spherical) 35mm widescreen; anamorphic 35mm widescreen prior to c. 1970
- 2.39:1— Anamorphic 35mm widescreen since c. 1970 — may still be referred to as 2.35 for historical reasons or may be rounded to 2.40

NOTE: The *:1*— generally pronounced "to one" — is often omitted and aspect ratios are expressed as 1.33, 1.37, 1.85, 2.35, etc. The decimal may also be omitted, resulting in 133 (pronounced "one three three"), 137, 185, etc.

asthenopia; aesthenopia Visual fatigue. Symptoms include blurred vision, double vision. May be caused in stereoscopic systems by retinal rivalry, keystone distortion, depth-plane curvature, crosstalk, and excessive screen disparity. In natural vision often the result of concentrating too long on a visually demanding task and tiring the eyes' ciliary muscles, which control accommodation, and certain binocular vision defects, such as accommodative insufficiency.

Accommodation/vergence rivalry has long been assumed to be the primary cause of stereoscopic viewer fatigue. More recent studies indicate that visual depth of field may be sufficient to correct for most accommodation/vergence discrepancies which may mean that the conflict between recorded image vergence and viewer vergence is a more important factor in visual fatigue.

AS3D; AS-3D *See* **auto-stereoscopic.**

asymmetric coding A method of stereoscopic data compression where one eye image is compressed more or has a lower resolution than the other eye image. *Also* **asymmetric coding.** *Compare* **cross distortion; cross-view prediction.**

asymmetric compression *See* **compression.**

asymmetrical toe-in angle When verging cameras (toed-in rather than parallel) are not oriented symmetrically with respect to their image planes. Each camera will view the subject from a different angle, resulting in image geometries that are not properly aligned.

One may view the respective angles of a properly aligned stereoscopic camera pair based on the amount by which they are turned inward — the angles are equal (of the same magnitude), but opposite (one is measured clockwise while the other is measured counterclockwise). Mathematically speaking, these angles are supplementary, since together they add up to 180° when measured from the same direction.

asynchronous 3D A stereoscopic display system where the left- and right-eye images are presented one at a time. All active eyewear-based 3D systems and some polarized systems are asynchronous. *Compare* **synchronous 3D**

atmospheric attenuation; atmospheric extinction The tendency for air to scatter and absorb light over a distance — the farther light must travel and the greater the optical density of the air it travels through, the greater the effect.

Optical density is most affected by atmospheric pressure (altitude and temperature) and airborne aerosols or particulates (water vapor, dust, smoke,

Atmospheric attenuation (photograph by Melanie B. Kroon).

The left camera pair is configured with symmetrical toe-in angles with respect to the line connecting the cameras' principal points (the point in each camera where the optical axis of the lens intersects the image plane). In the right camera pair, the right camera is toed-in more than the left camera with respect to the line connecting the principal points. In normal human vision, the eyes always toe in symmetrically, so stereograms recorded with the right camera pair will exhibit geometric distortions that interfere with the perception of depth.

Camera
Principal
Points

Symmetrical   Asymmetrical
Toe-In Angle   Toe-In Angle

smog, etc.). In addition, the longer the light must travel from object to observer, the more scattered solar light is integrated into the light path. This results in a characteristic aerial perspective — where distant objects are fainter, less distinct, and bluer — that acts as a monocular depth cue.

atmospheric perspective *Also* **aerial perspective.** *See* **perspective.** *Compare* **monocular cue.**

audience space The perceived area in front of the plane of the screen in display/viewer space. When objects in a stereogram appear to extend off the screen or float in front of the screen, they are said to occupy the audience space. Such objects must lie within the flat-sided pyramid that extends from the center of the viewer's gaze through the edges of the screen (the stereo window). *Also* **personal space; theater space.** *Compare* **display plane; negative parallax; screen space.** See diagram at **display plane.**

audio essence The collection of data that represent an audio stream. Often used within the parlance of Society of Motion Picture and Television Engineers (SMPTE) standards, especially MXF.

audio synchronization When picture and sound play back in proper time; the process of matching picture to sound in proper time.

augmented reality A system that adds enhanced imagery to one's view of the natural world, as with a head-up display (HUD). For example, an augmented reality system may overlay the results of a CT or MRI scan of a patient's internal organs atop a surgeon's field of view during an operation. *Compare* **artificial reality; virtual reality.**

auto cha-cha A sequential stereogram recorded from a moving platform (such as a car or train) so that the interaxial separation is equal to the horizontal distance traveled between exposures. (Vertical travel will introduce unwanted vertical parallax.) *Compare* **sequential stereogram; shifty method.**

auto-multiscopic; automultiscopic; ~ 3D; AM3D Having the ability to present a multiscopic image in which the viewer can perceive depth without wearing glasses. Multiscopic displays have multiple viewing positions or provide more than two views of the same subject, allowing a wider range of viewing options than a standard auto-stereoscopic display.

auto-stereoscopic; autostereoscopic; ~ 3D; AS3D Having the ability to present a stereoscopic image in which the viewer can perceive depth without wearing glasses. Auto-stereoscopic displays often have a fixed presentation direction, so the viewer must be correctly positioned (in the sweet spot) to perceive the effect. Multiple viewing positions generally require more than two eye images, or views, per frame. There are four main types of auto-stereoscopic displays: two-view, multi-view, integral, and volumetric.

The first auto-stereoscopic device was patented in 1903, but the first documented public demonstrations did not take place until the early 1930s.

In 1946, the first color 3D feature film with sync sound was presented using an auto-stereoscopic process. Contemporary auto-stereoscopic displays capable of presenting full motion are generally limited to specialized computer monitors and handheld PDAs.
Also **non-glasses–based 3D display; NG3D.** *See* **multiple pixels per point; single pixel per point.**

avatar A real-time graphical representation of a person in a virtual environment.

AVC; advanced video coding *See* MPEG-4 AVC.

AV/R A camcorder control interface developed by Sony as a replacement for the older LANC system. AV/R uses a 10-pin mini-DIN connector and transmits both bi-directional LANC protocol device control data and uni-directional video out. Adapters are available to connect newer AV/R camcorders to older LANC equipment. *Compare* **LANC; ste-fra LANC.**

axial offset *See* **sensor axial offset.**

background The space behind and subordinate to the principal subject; the area that appears to be farther from the camera than the principal subject or action of a scene; objects that appear behind the subject.

Moving out from the camera one will encounter the foreground, the middle ground (where the subject is), and then the background. What appears to be far away on screen may actually be near and vice versa. It is important to note where objects are according to the audience's perception, rather than simply by their physical relationship to the camera.
Compare **multi-plane camera.**

band-reject filter; band-stop filter A signal frequency filter that discriminates against frequencies in a specific band. The most common band-reject filters are relatively narrow notch filters. The opposite of a *bandpass filter*, with both high- and low-frequency roll-off so that only fre-

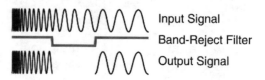

Input Signal
Band-Reject Filter
Output Signal

quencies in-between are allowed to pass. *Also* **notch filter.** *Compare* **comb filter.**

banding; color ~ *Also* **color aliasing.** *See* **aliasing; posterization.**

bandwidth; BW A measure of the data-carrying capacity of a communications channel, or the channel capacity requirements of a digital signal, measured over time.

barrel distortion A lens aberration where straight lines bow outward away from the center of the image and rectangles take on the shape of a barrel due to a decrease in focal length moving outward from the center of the lens. Most common in short focal length (wide angle) lenses. The effect becomes more pronounced as the image aspect ratio increases. The amount of barrel distortion is generally expressed as a percentage of the overall picture height. *Also* **fisheye effect.** *See* **lens distortion.** *Compare* **mustache distortion; pincushion distortion.**

 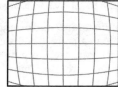

The effect of barrel distortion (right) on an undistorted grid (left).

base/dependent... *See* **B-D...**

baseline The line connecting the optical axes of the two camera views in a stereogram measured between the lenses' entrance pupils or rear focal points. For toed-in cameras, the distance between the optical axes varies depending on where it is measured, so it must always be measured at the baseline. For parallel cameras, the interaxial distance is the same regardless of where it is measured. *Also* **stereo base.**

Bates stereoscope *See* **Holmes stereoscope.**

B-B mode; base/base mode Presentation of a 2D image stream from a 3D master. Instead of presenting different images for each eye (as with a traditional 3D stream), B-B mode presents the same full-resolution base view to both eyes, creating a presentation that may be viewed normally without special glasses.

B-D mode; base/dependent mode Presentation of a stereoscopic image stream from a B-D master consisting of an independent base view (presented to one eye) that can be decoded without

any additional information and a dependent view (presented to the other eye) that requires information from the base view for proper decoding.

B-D view; base/dependent view A stereogram created from a full-resolution, independent base view (encoded as a 2D image) and a lower-resolution, dependent view, requiring additional stereoscopic metadata for correct reconstruction. This results in a recorded stereogram that is significantly smaller than one employing full-resolution images for both eyes. In the MPEG4-MVC standard, the dependence or independence of each view must be clearly identified in the accompanying metadata, since either eye could contain the base (independent) view. *Compare* **2D+delta.**

BDA *See* **Blu-ray Disc Association.**

beam splitter; beamsplitter An optical device that divides incoming light into two parts using prisms or mirrors, such as a 50/50 two-way mirror; a device that is both reflective and transmissive, though not necessarily in equal measures.

> NOTE: More correctly, but rarely, called an *image splitter*, since the volume of light is divided by the beam splitter, not the individual beams of light. A true beam splitter would be a refracting prism, which divides a beam of light into its constituent colors.

Beam splitters are not perfect optical devices. Surface imperfections may distort the reflected image. Even with special surface coatings to improve transmissive properties, different wavelengths of light may not be divided equally, leading, for example, to a characteristic blue color cast to the reflected image and a green color cast to the transmitted image.

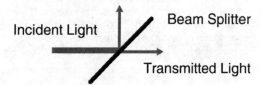

beam-splitter rig *See* **mirror rig.**

beam-splitting polarizer *See* **reflective polarizer.**

beta motion; beta phenomenon *Also* **optimal motion.** *See* **apparent motion; phi phenomenon.**

bezel The fixed frame that surrounds a television screen. *Compare* **surround.**

binocular Having two eyes or coordinating the use of both eyes.

Because humans have two forward-facing eyes separated by the width of the nose, the human vision system can make use of parallax to help determine the distance to a perceived object. Similar in function to the binaural hearing system that enables one to judge the direction of an incoming sound. The effects of binocular vision can be simulated by recording two, slightly offset images and presenting them separately to the left and right eyes.

binocular aliasing *See* **depth aliasing.**

binocular artifact A visual anomaly in a stereogram that interferes with binocular depth cues and disrupts the 3D effect. Generally, a difference between the eye images that is not explained by binocular disparity, but may also include an unexpected area of zero disparity (a flat, 2D image) within an otherwise 3D image. *Compare* **monocular artifact; retinal rivalry.**

binocular convergence *See* **convergence.**

binocular cue; binocular depth cue Depth information that can only be interpreted by calculating the differences between two simultaneous views of the same scene taken from different perspectives, generally those of the two eyes separated by the width of the nose.

When the two images in a stereogram are fused by the brain into a single image, the points in each image that represent the same point in the original view (the conjugate points) are compared. If the conjugate points align, they are assumed to be at the distance where the eyes converge. (The amount of inward turning of the eyes, or vergence, may be used to calculate this distance for objects within about six meters of the observer.) If the conjugate point in the left-eye image is to the left of the conjugate point in the right-eye image (positive parallax), they are assumed to be farther away than the point of convergence. If the conjugate point in the left-eye image is to the right of the conjugate point in the right-eye image (negative parallax), they are assumed to be closer to the observer.
Compare **monocular cue.**

binocular depth perception The ability to perceive 3D space and judge distances based on the differences in the images recorded by the left and right eyes (disparity) and the angle of the eyes (vergence). *Compare* **binocular vision; depth perception; stereopsis.**

binocular disparity; disparity The differences between the images perceived by the left and right eyes due to the physical separation of the eyes.

Those same differences are simulated in stereoscopic systems to create the illusion of 3D depth from otherwise flat images. *See* **retinal disparity.** *Compare* **parallax.** See *binocular disparity* image in color section.

binocular free-viewing; binocular freevision *See* **free-viewing.**

binocular fusion *See* **fusion.**

binocular luster; binocular lustre 1. A difference in the reflective brightness of an object in left- and right-eye images. Such objects, when fused into a single 3D view by the human vision system, appear to have a shiny, or lustrous appearance. This is a natural phenomenon often associated with the surface reflections of metal or polished gemstones and is caused by differences in the amount of light reflected into each eye. The human eye is particularly sensitive to luster, and will immediately notice related errors in computer-generated images and may detect digital image compression artifacts as unnatural luster. 2. Retinal rivalry. *Compare* **binocular rivalry.**

binocular omni-orientation monitor; BOOM 3D virtual reality display device with separate left- and right-eye monitors. The unit is suspended from a counter-weighted boom, allowing the viewer to adjust the position of the device to view the scene from various angles. A predecessor of the head-mounted display developed by the University of Illinois at Chicago's Electronic Visualization Laboratory.

binocular parallax *See* **parallax.**

binocular rivalry When the differences between left- and right-eye images are so large that binocular fusion is not possible, resulting in a confused visual state. The brain may alternate between the eye images, may select portions of each eye image and blend them into a sort of variable mosaic, may interpret the overlaid eye images as static, etc. *Compare* **binocular luster; cue conflict; retinal rivalry.**

binocular stereopsis *See* **stereopsis.**

binocular suppression When the brain ignores some portion of the image from one eye and only registers the overlapping image from the other eye. Occurs in response to diplopia, since the suppression of the one eye image eliminates the double vision that would otherwise have resulted, and allows for clear vision with monocular depth cues but no binocular depth cues in the affected area.

binocular symmetries The common characteristics that may be shared by the left- and right-eye images in a stereogram, including color, focus, geometry, illumination, registration, and temporal symmetry. Thanks to horizontal disparity (parallax), the two images are not identical. Such differences can be interpreted to produce depth information.

binocular viewing device A stereoscopic presentation device where each eye has its own lens. *See* **stereoscope.**

binocular vision Visual perception based on two eyes working together. Binocular vision provides a number of evolutionary advantages, hence its popularity within the animal kingdom. The most important feature of binocular vision for 3D systems is depth perception.

Prey animals tend to give up binocular depth perception in return for a wider angle of view. With eyes on opposite sides of their heads, the right and left visual fields do not overlap enough to produce binocular depth cues. Such animals must rely solely on monocular depth cues instead. Predatory animals, on the other hand, tend to have their eyes on the front of the head so the visual fields overlap, producing binocular depth perception.

Binocular vision and visual perspective were first described by Euclid of Alexandria in *Optics* c. 280 BCE. However, the scientific principle of stereopsis, where depth perception is derived from the differences between the left- and right-eye images (or disparity), was not put to practical use until 1832 when Charles Wheatstone developed the first stereoscope. (Wheatstone's findings were later presented to the Royal Society of London on June 21, 1838.) All stereoscopic display systems rely on binocular vision and stereopsis to produce a 3D effect.

Not everyone has sufficient binocular vision to appreciate the 3D effect in a stereoscopic presentation. Approximately 3 percent of the population in completely incapable of binocular vision, while a further 7 percent has a measurable defect impacting their binocular vision. For the 90 percent of the population with "normal" binocular vision, there is still a wide variation in stereo ability. A key factor in this equation is the distance between an individual's eyes, which is significantly different for children and adults.

In *Handbuch der physiologischen Optik* (*Handbook of Physiological Optics*, 1867), Hermann von Helmholtz described the basic geometry of binocular vision, which can be applied to the illusion of depth created in a stereogram. A simple approximation of perceived depth can be derived from Helmholtz's work.

Assume an interocular distance of E (the space between the viewer's eyes) and a 3D display that is Z distance away. If the screen disparity (the distance between the conjugate points in the left- and

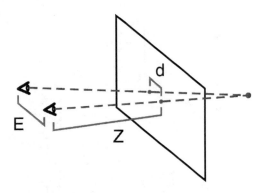

right-eye images of a stereo pair) is d, then when the conjugate points are fused into a single image, the perceived depth (pd) from the viewer to the image can be calculated as below.

This equation is a simplification, and does not work if $d \geq E$ or d is zero, but it does show how these different factors relate. The perceived

$$pd = \cfrac{Z}{\left(\left(\dfrac{E}{d}\right) - 1\right)}$$

depth in an image will increase if the distance to the screen or screen disparity increase or if the interocular distance decreases. Also, the perception of depth in a stereogram will change with the size of one's head, or more specifically, the distance between one's eyes (interocular or interpupillary distance). Images suitable for a child will seem unnaturally flat for an adult, while images optimized for viewing by the average adult will seem exaggerated to the average child.

With the left- and right-eye conjugate points offset to the left and right of each other, the fused image appears to be beyond the screen (positive parallax). As the screen disparity approaches zero, the left- and right-eye images become indistinguishable and the visual result is identical to that of a traditional flat 2D image. When the conjugate points cross each other, with the conjugate point in the left-eye image now to the right of the conjugate point in the right-eye image, the fused images appears to be in front of the screen (negative parallax).

In all of these examples, the image remains fixed on the screen, so the focal distance between the viewer and the screen is constant. Humans are conditioned to expect the focal distance to change as the angle of the eyes changes. (This is the accommodation/vergence link, where accommodation changes the optical characteristics of the eye to focus at a specific distance as cued by the amount of vergence, or inward turning of the eyes.) To view stereograms, one must ignore this conditioning, let the focal distance remain constant (as it would when viewing a flat 2D image) while continuing to adjust the angle of the eyes so

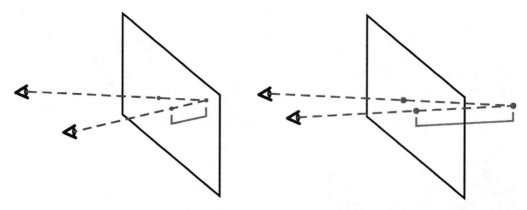

In both images, the distance between the conjugate points on the screen is the same, but the interocular distance is different, resulting in a difference in the apparent depth in the image. The person with the smaller head (right) will perceive greater depth in the image than the person with the larger head (left).

the left- and right-eye images can fuse into a single 3D image. In some cases, this may lead to eyestrain or physical discomfort. *Compare* **monocular vision.**

binocular vision disability A defect in the vision system that prevents proper interpretation of binocular depth information. Approximately 5–10 percent of the population suffers from a binocular vision disability sufficient to interfere with the perception of depth in a stereoscopic presentation. *See* **stereo blind.** *Compare* **accommodative insufficiency; amblyopia; diplopia; convergence insufficiency; strabismus.**

black-and-white anaglyph *See* anaglyph, black-and-white.

black light *See* ultraviolet.

bleeding *See* **crosstalk.** *Compare* **stereo extinction ratio.**

blending; blend; depth ~ *Also* cut-cushioning. *See* convergence animation.

blockiness *See* pixelation.

Blu-ray; ~ disc; BD A 4¾" (12 cm) high-capacity optical disc standard, introduced in June 2006 with support for high-definition (HD) video and the larger storage capacity that HD material requires. Intended to replace the DVD format.
  BD uses a 405-nanometer wavelength blue-violet laser instead of the traditional DVD 650-nanometer red laser. The smaller laser wavelength allows the disc to use smaller pits and tighter tracks. It also uses a thinner cover layer (0.1 mm) than a standard DVD. This moves the data closer to the reading lens. All of these factors combine to fit more data on the same size disc. Blu-ray supports 25 GB in a single-layer configuration or 50 GB in

a double-layer. Four-layer and eight-layer discs can store 100 GB and 200 GB, respectively. This capacity is sufficient for two to four hours of HDTV content on single- and double-layer discs. BD also supports MPEG-2, MPEG-4, AVC, MVC, and VC-1 format video and AACS. BD+, and ROM Mark content encryption/access controls.

Blu-ray Disc Association; BDA The industry consortium that develops and controls the Blu-ray disc format, established in 2002 by Sony in association with Hitachi, LG Electronics, Panasonic (Matsushita), Pioneer, Royal Philips Electronics, Samsung Electronics, Sharp, and Thomson. Formerly known as the Blu-ray Founders. The BDA Web site is www.blu-raydisc.com.

Blu-ray disc player A stand-alone electronic device capable of reading a Blu-ray disc and decoding the recorded data to produce an audiovisual stream that can be played back on a video monitor.

Blu-ray 3D; BD 3D A Blu-ray disc that contains full HD-resolution, MVC-encoded stereoscopic content developed to accommodate the Blu-ray Disc Association (BDA) specifications. Blu-ray 3D discs can be played in a standard Blue-ray player, although the images displayed will be 2D. Anaglyphs or half-resolution stereograms can be delivered via Blu-ray, but would not meet the specifications for Blu-ray 3D. *Compare* **3D DVD.**

blue leak *See* **polarizer blue leak.**

blur gradient The smooth transition between sharp and soft focus associated with distance. Generally, the object the eyes focus on will be in sharp focus while closer and farther objects that lie outside the depth of field are progressively more blurry as their distance from the subject of interest increases.

blur gradient depth cue A monocular depth cue used to estimate the depth in a scene by comparing the relative level of focus of each object to the object upon which the eyes are focused (objects that are closer or farther away will be progressively more blurry).

In most stereoscopic display systems, the entire image is presented on a flat screen so that all objects in the scene are the same distance from the viewer. This eliminates the blur gradient depth cues found in the natural world and may interfere with the illusion of depth in the image unless the depth of focus in the recorded images approximates the natural blur gradient. Even then, as the viewer's gaze shifts from one depth to another in the image, the focal clarity of the other objects in the scene do not change as they would in the natural world. This causes stereograms to appear flatter than they should be.

BMP file; .bmp A device independent, uncompressed digital file format for still images, often associated with the Windows operating system. *Compare* **PNG file.**

BOOM *See* **binocular omni-orientation monitor.**

bounce mirror A high-quality optical mirror, such as used to redirect laser light without changing its optical characteristics or in a projection mirror rig.

Most bounce mirrors are silvered on their front surface, rather than on the back as with a common household mirror. This avoids optical distortions and double images as the light passes through or is reflected off of the glass that supports the mirror, but makes the mirror particularly susceptible to damage and difficult to clean. To maintain optimal performance, such mirrors may have to be resurfaced periodically.

Compare **folded cone method; mirror rig.**

brain shear The brain's inability to accurately

Blur Increases Beyond the Depth of Field

Blur Increases Nearer Than the Depth of Field

Subject in Focus

Pronounced Blur Implies Increased Distance from Subject

Slight Blur Implies Proximity to Subject

Subject in Focus

Top: Blur gradient. *Bottom:* Blur gradient depth cue (photographs by Melanie B. Kroon).

interpret and integrate poorly developed or displayed stereographic input into a cohesive 3D image, forcing the eyes to over compensate, causing eye fatigue, double vision, headache, or nausea. Coined by American film director James Cameron in 2009.

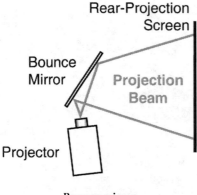

Bounce mirror

breaking the frame; breaking the window *See* **edge violation.** *Compare* **floating window; pinching the presentation.**

breaking the mask Extending out from the screen into the audience space; an object depicted with negative parallax.

brightness 1. A subjective measure of light volume as perceived by the human eye, either produced by a light source (a lamp, the sun, a video screen, etc.) or reflected off a surface (an object in the camera's frame, a projection screen, etc.). Objective measures of brightness are expressed in lumens, for light sources, or nits (candela/m²), for light reflected from a surface or a screen. **2.** The luminance level of a video signal or individual pixel. **3.** A control on some video monitors used to adjust the black level.

broadband light Light composed of frequencies covering a large portion of the visible spectrum.
    If the relative strengths of the component frequencies are equal, this equates to white light. Most projection systems use a broadband light source that is then filtered to produce an image. For example, in a film projector the broadband light source is filtered by the image on the film, while in a single-chip DLP video projector, broadband light passes through a spinning color filter wheel to produce varying amounts of red, green, and blue light that combine to form the image. In either case, a significant portion of the broadband light is absorbed by the filter and converted to heat, resulting in reduced light output and requiring a light source significantly brighter than the desired image.
Compare **narrowband light.**

broadband spectral eyewear Spectacles used to view traditional anaglyphs with a single color filter for each lens; anaglyphoscopes. Red/green and red/cyan are the most common color com-binations, but others are also used, including amber/blue, green/magenta, and magenta/cyan. *Compare* **narrowband spectral eyewear; spectral eyewear.**

browser A visual guide system, including indexes, lists, or animated maps, that provides an overview of and facilitates navigation through the physical, temporal, and conceptual elements of a virtual world.

burn-in Physical damage caused to a CRT or plasma monitor when the same image is displayed for too long and it becomes a permanent feature of the display, generally visible as a ghost image. Such images can be incorrectly interpreted as depth cues, interfering with the 3D effect. *Also* **afterimage.**

camera convergence *See* **convergence.**

camera coordinate system A three-axis (X, Y, and Z) system of Cartesian coordinates (oriented so X, Y, and Z represent width, height, and depth, respectively and grow in a positive direction to the right, up, and away, respectively) oriented to a camera's imaging plane so that the origin is aligned with the principal point (the point where the optical axis of the lens intersects the image plane). *Compare* **world coordinate system.**

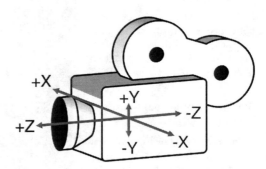

camera field of view *See* **field of view.**

camera inner orientation; camera interior orientation *See* **camera parameters.**

camera parameters; geometric ~ The factors that determine how a camera maps a 3D image (measured in world coordinates) onto a 2D plane (measured in camera coordinates). Often used in computer vision applications or when reconstructing 3D objects from a series of 2D images. *Compare* **extrinsic camera parameters; intrinsic camera parameters.**

camera rig A mechanical framework designed to support two identical cameras in perfect alignment when shooting a stereogram. The two most common configurations are side-by-side rigs and mirror rigs. Computer graphics systems employ a virtual camera rig that emulates the behavior of a physical camera rig in the real world. *Compare* **motion-control rig; mirror rig; parallel rig.**

camera/scene space The area within which an image is recorded, as opposed to the display/viewer space where it is viewed. It is best if the intended display/viewer space is known when a stereogram is recorded, since the display depth budget can influence the camera configuration. *Compare* **display/viewer space.**

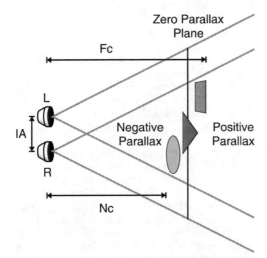

Key characteristics to consider when recording a stereogram include the interaxial (*IA*) distance between the left (*L*) and right (*R*) camera lenses, the lenses' focal length, and the distances from the image plane to the nearest (*Nc*) and farthest (*Fc*) depths recorded by the cameras.

camera separation *See* **interaxial distance.**

camera space *See* **object space.**

capture artifact A visual anomaly caused by the image creation process. *See* **coding artifact; compressed depth artifact; decoding artifact; display artifact; network artifact; production artifact.**

cardboarding; cardboard cutout; cardboard effect The lack of a true 3D effect in a stereogram, giving the appearance that the images is made up of a set of flat cardboard cutouts like a child's pop-up book. Generally caused by inadequate depth resolution in the image due to a mismatch between the focal length of the recording lens (or virtual CGI camera) and the interaxial distance between the cameras. Also a common side effect

of poor-quality 2D to 3D conversion. *Also* **cutout planar effect; depth contouring; diorama effect.**

cataphote *See* **retroreflector.**

cathode ray tube; CRT The basic television vacuum tube, developed in 1897 by Carl Ferdinand Braun of the University of Strasbourg. An electron gun mounted at the back of the tube emits a stream of particles that strikes the fluorescent-coated interior at the front of the tube, producing a glowing picture on the outside of the tube. The exposed face of a CRT makes up a traditional television's screen.

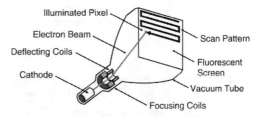

A simplified black-and-white cathode ray tube (CRT). A color CRT would have three cathodes producing separate beams to illuminate red, green, and blue pixels.

catoptric anamorphosis *See* **anamorphosis.**

CAVE CAVE Automatic Virtual Environment; an immersive virtual reality environment where the viewers stand within a box 10' on each side and 9' high. Stereograms are projected onto three walls (rear projection) and the floor (down projection) while the viewer wears wireless active eyewear. The displayed imagery is adjusted to respond to the viewers' movements. Some installations have as many as six active image walls. Developed in 1992 by the University of Illinois at Chicago's Electronic Visualization Laboratory.

>   NOTE: *CAVE* is a recursive acronym, where the C in CAVE stands for CAVE.

CCD; charge coupled device An electronic device consisting of a tightly-packed array of photoelectric detectors. As light photons strike an individual detector (pixel), an electric charge builds up. The amount of cumulated charge corresponds to the brightness of the pixel. Red, green, and blue filters placed over the detectors allow for the recording of a full-color image. All of the values registered by the CCD are converted from their native analog state to an equivalent digital value and then recorded at one moment in time (a global shutter). The device is then re-set to record another image. *Compare* **CMOS.**

CCD width *See* **imaging sensor width.**

center of perspective The point where a compound lens' optical axis intersects the entrance pupil. If the lens (and the attached camera) is rotated about this point, then the relative perspective of near and far objects within the frame will remain constant. If the lens is rotated about any other point, there will be perspective distortions.

The center of perspective is an ideal point to use when measuring the interaxial distance between lenses when recording a stereo image. This point is fixed for prime lenses, but moves depending on the focal length of a varifocal (zoom) lens. It can be identified mathematically or experimentally. *Compare* **entrance pupil; nodal points.**

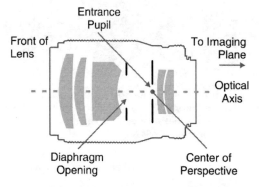

In a compound lens (such as the one depicted above), the entrance pupil is the apparent size and position of the lens diaphragm opening when viewed through the front of the lens. This may differ from the physical position of the diaphragm due to the optical properties of the lens elements. The lens' optical axis passes through the center of the entrance pupil at the center of perspective (illustration by author; based on materials from Paul van Walree).

Certifi3D *See* **Technicolor Certifi3D.**

CFF *See* **critical fusion frequency.**

cha-cha; cha cha; ~ method *See* **shifty method.** *Compare* **auto cha-cha; sequential stereogram.**

channel separation The complete isolation of left- and right-eye images in a stereoscopic image delivery system. Improper channel separation will interfere with depth perception in the resulting image. *Compare* **crosstalk; ghosting; stereo extinction ratio.**

charge coupled device *See* **CCD.**

checkerboard; CK; ~ 3D A time-sequential

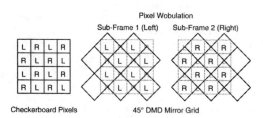

stereoscopic display system where the left- and right-eye images are alternated one pixel at a time to create a combined image with a checkerboard pattern of left- and right-eye image pixels. The checkerboard image is then presented using a digital micro-mirror display (DMD) projection system and matching active eyewear.

With a checkerboard 3D display, a half-resolution DMD grid is rotated 45° to create a diamond pattern. The checkerboard image is treated as if the left- and right-eye pixels represent image subframes, so each frame is presented twice, resulting in a doubling of the image refresh rate. When this is combined with a one pixel horizontal wobulation (optical shift), the left-eye image pixels are positioned above the DMD mirrors and appear in sub-frame 1, followed by the right-eye image pixels in sub-frame 2. Synchronized active glasses combine to create a 3D image display. (With standard wobulation, the image is offset along a 45° angle. With the DMD already rotated 45°, a horizontal pixel offset achieves the same effect.)

As with all half-resolution techniques, this allows both left- and right-eye information to be encoded in a single standard video image frame that can be processed, recorded, and transmitted using standard 2D systems and techniques. Unlike other half-resolution techniques, this method is only supported by DMD video projection systems and certain plasma displays, but is not compatible with CRTs, LEDs, LCDs, or most plasma displays.

chip; film ~ One of the two views in a still image stereogram. *Also* **still stereo view.**

chipset; chip set A packaged set of integrated circuits designed to work together to perform one or more related functions.

chirality Handedness. Chiral objects appear in mirror image forms, such as human hands and the molecules within optically active materials, and can be differentiated by their left- or right-handed nature. *Compare* **achirality; polarization handedness.**

ChromaDepth The trade name for the patented stereoscopic system based on chromatic stereoscopy. Developed originally by Chromatek, Inc. and now owned by American Paper Optics. The ChromaDepth Web site is www.chromatek.com.

Right Hand   Left Hand   Right Mitten   Left Mitten

Hands are chiral; the left hand cannot be rotated into exactly the same orientation as the right hand. If both hands are held out so the palms face up, the thumbs will face opposite directions. If the left hand is rotated so that its thumb points in the same direction as on the right hand, then the palms will face opposite directions. Because of this, a left-hand glove will not fit properly on the right hand. A mitten, however, can be achiral. It can fit either hand equally well. Similarly, feet and shoes are chiral, while socks are achiral.

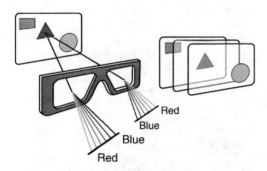

Red
Blue
Blue
Red

Objects with different colors in a two-dimensional image (left) appear to be different distances from the viewer (right) when seen through ChromaDepth glasses. The prismatic effect of the lenses is reversed for left and right eyes, so that colored light bends in opposite directions, creating image parallax differences characteristic of binocular depth perception.

chroma mismatch *See* **color rivalry.**

chroma shift *See* **color shift.**

chromatic dispersion *See* **dispersion.**

chromatic flicker *See* **color flicker.** *Compare* **luminance flicker.**

chromatic stereoscopy A stereoscopic system where the position of each color within the visible spectrum is used to represent depth within an image.

The colors of the visible spectrum range from red on one end to violet on the other. As light passes through an optical device such as a prism, each different wavelength is bent by a different amount. Eyewear configured so that each lens bends light in a different horizontal direction can convert a single flat image into a stereogram. Each color in the perceived left- and right-eye images

will have a different amount of disparity. Generally, red objects are encoded so they appear closer to the viewer than violet objects, with all other colors representing the depths in-between. The effect works best when the image is placed against a dark background. *See* **ChromaDepth.**

chrominance mismatch *See* **color rivalry.**

chrominance ringing *See* **color ringing.**

chromostereopsis A visual phenomenon where objects may appear to be different sizes or at different distances due to the different reception of different wavelengths of light on the retina. As a result, red objects may appear closer than otherwise identical blue objects, with the other wavelengths lying in-between. *See* **chromosteropsis** example in color section.

circle of isolation The area of sharp focus surrounding the subject of a stereogram when set against a completely de-focused background. Coined in 2010 by Indian stereographer Clyde DeSouza after the circle of confusion, the concept describing the area of sufficiently sharp focus that defines a lens' depth of field.

When viewing a stereogram, the brain will attempt to fuse the conjugate points that are in focus in the left- and right-eye images, creating a sense of 3D depth. In the natural world, un-fused points are generally out of focus. If the viewer's attention is drawn to one of these points, the eyes adjust and the new point comes into focus. The amount of focus in a stereogram is generally fixed at the time of recording and attempts by the viewer's brain to fuse out-of-focus elements will lead to visual confusion and eyestrain. The brain may make this attempt automatically if the points are nearly, but not quite, in sharp focus. Viewers may also consciously shift their gaze to discernable, but un-focused, elements within the stereogram.

Attempts to fuse insufficiently focused points may be averted by using an infinite depth of field when recording a stereogram so that nothing is out of focus and the eye can freely travel over the image (a common practice), or by ensuring that the subject is enclosed within an areas of sharp focus (the circle of isolation) with everything else so far out of focus that the brain will not attempt to fuse those points. A proper circle of isolation may be maintained by carefully controlling the image depth of field or by identifying the intended subject and electronically de-focusing the remainder of the image.

circular polarization; CP An electromagnetic wave, such as visible light, where the wave's electric vector travels through space in a helix, or corkscrew, pattern rotating either clockwise (right-hand) or counterclockwise (left-hand) over time.

The left- and right-eye images in a stereogram can be encoded with left- and right-hand circular polarization then presented together as a single image on screen. Eyewear with matching left- and right-hand CP lenses can decode the combined image for stereoscopic viewing.

Circular polarization can be broken down into the sum of two linear polarized waves, where each wave has the same amplitude, is 90° out of phase from its companion, and travels along right angle planes (rotated 90° from each other). When these planar waves combine, they create a 3D wave that follows a helix, or corkscrew, path through space over time. When measured in a specific plane orthogonal (at a right angle) to the light ray, the tip of the wave's electric field vector travels in a clockwise or counterclockwise circle, depending on the handedness of the CP wave.

NOTE: In optics (and therefore most stereoscopic applications), the direction of CP spin is measured from the perspective of the viewer (right-handed for clockwise, left-handed for counterclockwise), while in electrical engineering, it is measured from the perspective of the source.

Compare **linear polarization; polarization.**

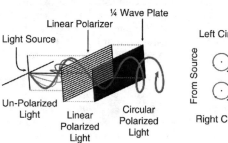

CK *See* **checkerboard.**

clear single binocular vision *See* **Panum's fusion area.**

cloning Creating copies of nearby material to fill in the gaps in the background exposed during a 2D to 3D conversion. Quicker, easier, and less expensive than actually re-creating the missing background elements, but not as accurate. Coined after the *clone* tool in digital paint programs, which performs a similar function in 2D image manipulation. *Compare* **2D to 3D conversion.**

CMOS; complementary metal oxide semiconductor An electronic device consisting of a tightly-packed array of digital memory cells (pixels), each one connected to a photodetector, am-

plifier, and analog-to-digital converter. As light photons strike an individual detector (pixel), an electric charge builds up. The amount of charge corresponds to the brightness of the pixel. Red, green, and blue filters placed over the detectors allow for the recording of a full-color image. CMOS chips do not draw as much power, produce as much heat, or costs as much to produce as comparable CCDs. However, unlike a CCD, the CMOS values are read sequentially (a rolling shutter), which can cause image distortions with fast-moving subjects or when the amount of illumination changes significantly during the exposure. *Compare* **CCD.**

CMOS width *See* **imaging sensor width.**

coding artifact A digital signal anomaly caused by the compression/decompression process. *See* **capture artifact; compressed depth artifact; decoding artifact; display artifact; network artifact; production artifact.**

cognitive dissonance **1.** In psychology, the discomfort that results from holding two contradictory beliefs or goals simultaneously, such as the desire for something that tastes good but that is also bad for you. Coined in 1957 by American social psychologist Leon Festinger. **2.** The mental discomfort that may result from contradictory depth cues in a stereogram and the brain's unconscious attempt to resolve them.

cognitive ergonomics A focus on the link between human cognition (perception, learning, and reasoning) and the design of a machine, user interface, process, etc.—in this case, the design of stereoscopic recording and presentation systems and the production of stereoscopic works.

coincident Occupying the same point in space. Conjugate points in a stereogram are coincident if they overlap exactly (have zero parallax).

color **1.** Any hue distinguished from black, gray, or white; the wavelengths of the electromagnetic spectrum perceived by the human eye to be visible light of various colors (the visible spectrum) ranging from red through orange, yellow, green, blue, and violet and every color in between. Just beneath the range of human vision is infrared. Above human vision is ultraviolet (black light). **2.** One of the parameters of binocular symmetry. In a stereogram, the left-

and right-eye images differ due to horizontal disparity (parallax), but may share a number of other characteristics, including focus, geometry, illumination, registration, and temporal symmetry. *See* **color** diagram in color section.

color aliasing; color banding *Also* **banding; contouring.** *See* **aliasing; posterization.**

color bleed *See* **color shift.**

color bombardment; color-bombardment A phenomenon that causes eyestrain when viewing images where the colors do not align properly. This is a common side effect of viewing anaglyphic pictures, where colored filters are used to separate the left- and right-eye images.

> The brain expects an object to be the same color regardless of which eye is viewing it. When the colors do not match, the brain becomes confused. This process is exaggerated in anaglyphic systems when the two images (for left and right eyes) are not in perfect synchronization. The component color images do not move in perfect synchronization, resulting in color fringing. The brain does not expect this color misalignment and has difficulty interpreting it. Over time, the result of color bombardment can be physically painful to the viewer.

Compare **color rivalry; retinal rivalry.**

color droop *See* **color shift.**

color flicker Repeated variations in the color of conjugate points in a stereogram. This can interfere with the 3D effect or cause entire objects in a stereogram to switch repeatedly from one color to another. May affect one or any combination of the three elements that make up perceived color (hue, saturation, or value) to varying degrees. *Also* **chromatic flicker.** *Compare* **color rivalry; luminance flicker.**

color ringing A digital compression artifact affecting the edges between areas of contrasting color, causing a loss of color fidelity along the borders. *Compare* **depth ringing; Gibbs phenomenon.**

color rivalry; color mismatch When the colors of conjugate points in a stereogram are contrary to what the brain expects given their parallax difference or other available depth cues, leading to contradictory depth information in the fused image.

> Color is often described as being made up of hue (the color's shade), saturation (the purity of the hue), and value (its relative brightness). Color rivalry could be the result of varying levels of mismatch between one or any combination of these

elements. Video signals may also be described as being made up of chrominance (color) and luminance (brightness). Thus, color mismatch may also be described as *chroma mismatch.* *Compare* **cue conflict.**

color saturation *See* **saturation.**

color separation The process of dividing a color into its constituent color components, typically red, green, and blue (RGB) for images produced with light (film and video) or cyan, magenta, yellow, and black (CMYK) for imaged produced with pigments (printed materials). *See* **color separation** images in color section.

color shift A video artifact that results in a horizontal (color bleed) or vertical (color droop) misalignment of the colors in an image, typically seen as an area of solid color (most often red) that extends beyond its intended borders. Often displaying bands of incorrect color on opposite edges of a solid color — one band represents an area where the color is missing and the opposite band represents an area where the color has been incorrectly added.

> Color shifting has two common causes. One results from the misalignment of the three primary colors in a video monitor or projector during presentation. (This does not happen with LCD, plasma, or single-chip DLP displays.) The other is a side effect of the fact that most video signals sub-sample the color (chrominance) component — there is physically more resolution in the luminance (brightness or black-and-white) component. The larger pixel blocks used to represent color may overlap the more precise black-and-white component of the color signal, causing the color to spread out beyond its intended borders.

Also **chroma shift.**

color skew The unequal treatment of different wavelengths of light by an optical device, such as the mirror in a beam splitter camera rig. May be compensated for by white balancing the cameras or color timing the finished work.

color space A mathematical model used to specify, create, and visualize color. A color space provides a means of representing all of the possible colors in a particular gamut, or range of colors, according to defined mathematical rules.

> Different color spaces contain different sets of possible colors (not all colors are represented in all color spaces) and the same color may be represented differently in each color space. For human vision, color is often defined by its attributes of hue, saturation, and brightness. For a printing press, color may be defined in terms of the reflectance and absorbance of cyan, magenta, yel-

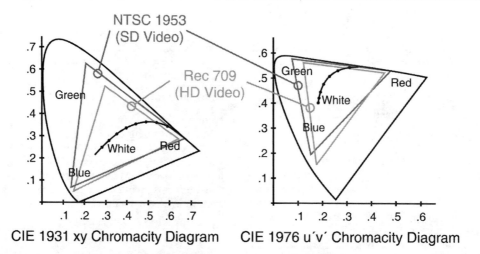

CIE 1931 xy Chromacity Diagram   CIE 1976 u´v´ Chromacity Diagram

Two different representations of the visible color space developed by the CIE (International Commission on Illumination) in 1931 (left) and 1976 (right). Different media reproduce different subsets of all possible colors, as noted by the SD and HD video color space triangles inscribed in the CIE color space diagrams.

low, and black inks on the paper. In computer and video production, color is often defined in terms of the excitations of red, green, and blue phosphors on the face of a screen or the pickup on a camera's imaging sensor. In video, color values may be converted from the RGB color space to a more compact form for transmission, processing, and storage, such as the Y, B–Y, R–Y color space.

Within each of these broader models are more specific color space definitions that specify exact transfer characteristics (linear, log, or gamma), white point, resolution (number of bits per image sample in digital systems), and chromaticity coordinates in relation to standardized CIE values. Some of the models used in video and film production are SMPTE-C, SMPTE-240M, Rec-601–1, Rec-709, and Cineon. To accurately produce color from one color space on a display that supports a different color space, a color space conversion must occur. Conversions may use a CLUT (color lookup table) in which the value from one color space is translated into another.

ColorCode 3-D The trade name for a patented system for encoding full-color stereograms using a special set of amber and blue image filters selected so that one eye receives a nearly full-color image while the other eye receives an essentially monochrome image. Depth is encoded as parallax differences between the conjugate points in each image, as

with a standard stereogram. ColorCode 3-D images look more like 2D images when viewed without glasses and contain more color information than traditional anaglyphs when viewed with special ColorCode glasses. Developed by Sirius 3-D of Kongens Lyngby, Denmark. The Sirius 3-D Web site is www.colorcode3d.com. *See* **ColorCode 3-D** images in color section.

colorimetry mismatch *See* **color rivalry.**

column A vertical array of pixels in a raster image. The 2D grid of pixels that make up a raster image (computer, television, laser printer, etc.) is arranged into a set of vertical columns and horizontal rows. *Compare* **row.** *See* **raster** diagram among the color illustrations.

column-interleaved; ~ 3D A 3D raster image format where left- and right-eye stereoscopic image information is presented in alternating columns within the image. By convention, one starts with the left eye in the leftmost column of the image and moves to the right. May be used with interlaced or progressive scan images. Gen-

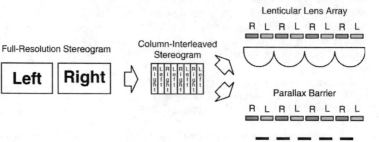

erally viewed on a lenticular or parallax barrier display. *Compare* **time-sequential; row-interleaved.**

comb filter A type of electronic notch filter with a series of deep dips in its frequency response, generally spaced at multiples of the lowest frequency notch. When applied to a signal, it cancels frequencies that have the opposite polarity of the notches. *Compare* **interference filter.**

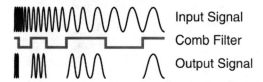

Input Signal

Comb Filter

Output Signal

common objective rig A stereo camera configuration where the two cameras share a single lens. *Compare* **single-lens camera.**

compatible 3D content Audiovisual material created for stereoscopic viewing but structured so that it can also be converted for presentation in 2D. For example, MVC-encoded Blu-ray 3D programs can be viewed in 2D with a standard 2D Blu-ray player. *Compare* **3D-exclusive content.**

complementary color bombardment *See* **color bombardment.**

complementary metal oxide semiconductor *See* **CMOS.**

complex distortion *See* **mustache distortion.**

compressed depth artifact A visual anomaly occurring as a side effect of digitally compressing a stereogram (compression artifacts in the horizontal dimension of one or both eye images that interfere with the 3D effect) or caused by using a digitally compressed disparity map in the creation of a stereogram (resulting in the loss of depth information from the original scene). *See* **capture artifact; coding artifact; decoding artifact; display artifact; network artifact; production artifact.**

compression; data ~; digital ~; signal ~ A process by which digital data are reduced in size to decrease the required storage space, processing time, transmission time, or transmission bandwidth by representing redundant or less important data in such a way that an acceptable approximation of the original can be reconstructed at a later time.

Compression is often used with audio and video to reduce storage and transmission costs. By reducing the size of the data representation, compression allows more content to be transmitted in the same bandwidth or in less time.

All compression algorithms are described as being some combination of lossy or lossless and symmetrical or asymmetrical.

- **Lossy codec:** Sacrifices fidelity for compression performance; the uncompressed file is not identical to the original file.
- **Lossless codec:** Produces uncompressed files that are identical to the original source material, but takes longer to run or consumes more resources than lossy codecs and produces larger output files.
- **Symmetrical codec:** Takes as long to compress as it does to uncompress a particular signal. Often used for live transmissions, such as videoconferencing or television broadcast.
- **Asymmetrical codec:** Takes longer on the compression end, but is faster during decompression. Since a source file is generally compressed once but decompressed and viewed many times, this is an acceptable tradeoff.

Video compression can be performed either within a single frame at a time (intra-frame) or across multiple frames over time (inter-frame). Since raw video contains a great deal of data that must be processed, most of which are not necessary for the reproduction of an acceptable image, most video compression algorithms are lossy and, with the exception of those used for live transmissions, asymmetrical.

There are four primary methods of lossy video compression:

- **Discrete Cosine Transform (DCT).** Samples an image at regular intervals, mathematically transforms the image sample into frequency components, and discards those frequencies that do not affect the image as perceived by human vision. DCT is the basis of a variety of digital image compression standards, including JPEG, MPEG, H.261, and H.263.
- **Vector Quantization (VQ).** Analyzes data as arrays rather than single values. VQ generalizes the data in each array, compressing redundant data while retaining the data stream's original intent.
- **Fractal.** Based on VQ techniques. Fractal compression is performed by locating self-similar sections within an image, then using a fractal algorithm to approximate each section.
- **Discrete Wavelet Transform (DWT).** Mathematically transforms an image into frequency components before discarding those frequencies that do not affect the image as perceived by human vision. This is similar to how DCT operates, but in DWT the process is performed on the entire image at

the same time rather than first dividing it into smaller pieces. The result is a hierarchical representation of an image, where each layer represents a frequency band.

Data compression techniques are designed to be lossless, since the recreated content must exactly match the original for it to be of any use, while audio and video compression techniques are often lossy, since this results in much greater compression ratios at the cost of an acceptable level of distortion.

> NOTE: *Compression* and *encryption* are often confused. Compression is used to make something smaller. Encryption is used to make content unusable for those not authorized to receive the content. There is no attempt to make the encrypted content smaller than the unencrypted content. Of course, the two technologies may be employed together to make content both smaller and more secure at the same time.

computational photography The computerized manipulation and enhancement of digital imagery to achieve visual results that would not be possible using a physical camera. *Compare* **analytic photogrammetry.**

Computer Assisted Virtual Environment *See* **CAVE.**

cone A receptor cell in the retina responsible for color (photopic) vision and the detection of fine details and fast motion. *Compare* **rod.**

cone of 3D The volume within which all objects in a stereogram must reside. Technically, a flat-sided pyramid extending from the center of the viewer's gaze through the sides of the screen. *Also* **stereo window.**

conflict of cues *See* **cue conflict.**

conjugate points The pair of points in the left- and right-eye images that represent the same point in 3D space. When each image is viewed by the corresponding eye, the positional difference between the conjugate points in the two images is interpreted by the brain as being caused by visual parallax (disparity) and is converted into

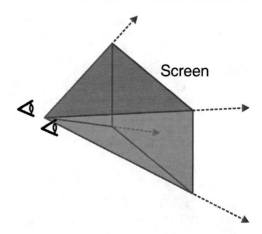

In the diagram, the "cone of 3D" has its apex at the center of the viewer's gaze and then extends outward to intersect the edges of the screen. Technically, it continues to extend into the screen as well, limiting the placement of objects behind the screen (with positive parallax) as well as those in front of the screen (with negative parallax). The one sheet poster for Famous Studios' *Boo Moon* (1954) shows Casper extending well beyond the cone of 3D based on the relative positions of the screen and the audience below.

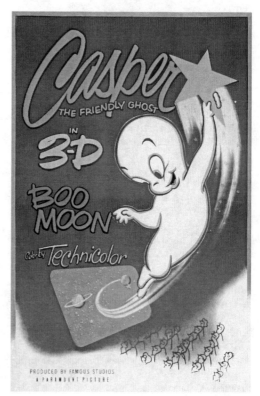

Courtesy Heritage Auctions, www.ha.com.

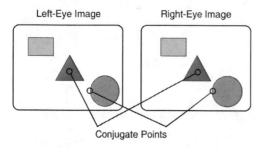

Conjugate Points

depth information. *Also* **corresponding points; homologous points.** *Compare* **disparity; parallax.**

contamination Visual imperfections present in only one half of a stereogram due to foreign bodies in a camera's light path, generally dust or water. Significant contamination can disrupt the 3D effect. *Compare* **visual mismatch.**

contouring; depth ~ *See* **aliasing.**

Control-L *See* **LANC.**

converge in post Adjustments typically made during post-production to 3D images shot with parallel cameras. *Compare* **monocular area; reconverge.**

convergence 1. The coordinated inward turning of the eyes when focusing on a close object, such as when reading; visual convergence. The inability to maintain proper convergence (convergence insufficiency) commonly leads to double vision (diplopia). The amount of convergence necessary to achieve image fusion can be used as a depth cue for objects up to six meters from the observer. **2.** The amount of symmetrical inward turning (toe-in) away from parallel of left and right stereoscopic cameras; angulation; stereoangle. **3.** When the two separate images registered by each eye in binocular stereoscopic vision combine in the perception of the viewer to form a single image with apparent 3D depth; fusion. **4.** When the two separate images in an over/under, split-lens 3D projection system are brought together on the screen, eliminating vertical image disparity. **5.** When parallel lines do not appear parallel in an image, but instead seem to approach each other. *Compare* **divergence; lens convergence; vergence.**

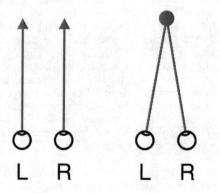

Eyes are set parallel (left) when viewing distant objects and converge inward (right) when viewing close objects. The closer the object, the more the eyes converge.

convergence/accommodation... *See* **accommodation/convergence...**

convergence angle The amount that the optical axes of a pair of lenses are rotated inward from parallel, measured in degrees. May apply to eyes in binocular vision or cameras in a toed-in configuration. An important factor in stereoscopic calculations.

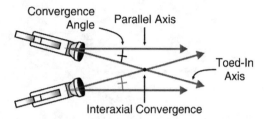

convergence animation Subtle image disparity adjustments made at the tail of the outgoing shot and/or the head of the incoming shot in an edited sequence to help smooth the cut between the two shots. This helps avoid abrupt depth changes between shots, which can be quite jarring for the viewer.

The depth characteristics on either side of a cut can be adjusted in three different ways:
- The outgoing (or hand-off) shot and incoming (or receiving) shot are both adjusted so that the cut comes at a mid-point between the two.
- Only the outgoing shot is adjusted.
- Only the incoming shot is adjusted.

The duration of the adjustment can also vary:
- Adjust: Change the convergence of an entire shot.
- Blend: Change the convergence over the course of X frames during the head or tail of a shot.
- Drift: Change the convergence over the course of an entire shot.

Experiments conducted during the production of *Legend of the Guardians: The Owls of Ga'Hoole* (2010) found that the smoothest transition occurs when only the incoming (or receiving) shot is adjusted, since there is a natural period of visual adjustment at each cut that help hide the convergence animation taking place. Most of the convergence animation sequences in *Legend* were only 8 frames (⅓ second) long—the longest approximately 40 frames (1⅔ seconds). Rather than match the depth characteristics exactly at the cut point, most of the convergence animation sequences eliminated only 50 percent of the depth difference, leaving a slight jump at the cut.

Also **blending; cut-cushioning.** *Compare* **convergence ramp; depth change stress; depth warping; horizontal image translation.**

convergence distance The space from the mid-point between a pair of toed-in stereoscopic cameras (measured from the point used to calculate the interaxial distance) to the point where the optical axes cross. An important factor in stereoscopic calculations.

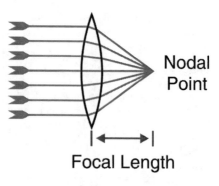

Nodal Point

Focal Length

converging lens

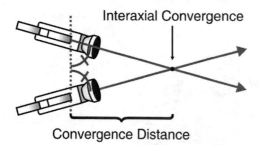

Interaxial Convergence

Convergence Distance

convergence insufficiency The inability to maintain visual convergence for an extended time. May also affect the ability to properly track a near moving object or to switch rapidly between near and far objects. Causes eyestrain, blurred vision, double vision (diplopia), and headaches when one tries to view close objects. *Compare* **accommodative insufficiency; amblyopia; diplopia; strabismus.**

convergence, plane of *See* **plane of convergence.**

convergence ramp Live convergence animation. Adjusting the left/right image disparity while a stereogram is being viewed or recorded, such as during a live 3D broadcast. Brief, infrequent adjustments may go unnoticed, but can lead to eyestrain if overused. *Also* **depth ramp.** *Compare* **depth change stress; horizontal image translation.**

convergence tracking 1. Adjusting camera convergence during a shot, generally to keep the cameras converged on the subject of interest. This keeps the subject at the screen plane (zero parallax), but can lead to some visually odd (and often physically uncomfortable) results. **2.** Adjusting camera convergence for each shot in a stereoscopic work, or between cameras in a multi-camera shoot. This can make shots difficult to edit together without using convergence animation to smooth the transitions. *Also* **pulling convergence; tracking convergence.** *Compare* **accommodation/vergence rivalry.**

convergence viewing *See* **cross-eyed viewing.**

converging lens A lens that causes parallel beams of light to come together at a single point as they pass through the lens. In general, such a lens is thicker at its center than at its edge. *Also* **positive lens.** *Compare* **diverging lens.**

conversion A transformation, such as from linear to circular polarization; from over/under to side-by-side encoding; from 2D to 3D; etc. *Compare* **dimensionalization.**

coordinate transform The process of converting coordinates in object space to corresponding coordinates in image space using mathematical transformations.

Converting stereograms from object space to image space involves three separate steps:
- Converting from three-dimensional X, Y, Z object space to two separate two-dimensional X, Y coordinate pairs representing the left- and right-eye images as recorded by the cameras' imaging sensors.
- Converting from the two-dimensional X, Y coordinates of the left and right image sensors to the X, Y coordinates of the stereoscopic display's image space (or X, Y, Z coordinates of a volumetric display).
- Converting from the X, Y (or X, Y, Z) coordinates in image space to the X, Y, Z coordinates of the 3D image in the viewer's perception.

Additional, intermediate coordinate transforms may be necessary to account for the visual resolutions and aspect ratios of different electronic formats, particularly when down-converting from a higher-resolution image capture to a lower-resolution storage or transmission format.

Color is also transformed from its original state in the object space to the color space of the recording device, to the color space of the display device, to the colors as perceived by the viewer, in addition to any transforms necessitated by intermediate electronic formats.

corner mismatch A stereoscopic image distortion that increases with distance from the image center, making it more obvious in the corners. *Compare* **keystone.**

corresponding points *See* **conjugate points.**

counter-panning Moving the left- and right-eye images of a stereogram (or the position of objects within a stereogram) in opposite directions— either closer to one another (to diminish the apparent depth in the image) or farther apart (to increase the apparent depth).

CP *See* **circular polarization.**

critical fusion frequency; CFF The minimum rate at which a flashing light will be perceived without flicker. The exact rate depends on a number of factors, including ambient light (the less light, the lower the rate), image illumination (the brighter the image, the higher the rate), the orientation of the eye (flicker is more apparent in peripheral vision), and viewer fatigue (the more tired, the lower the rate). In general, the CFF is taken to be somewhere between 50 and 60 flashes per second. To achieve flicker-free viewing of an audiovisual work with a frame rate lower than the CFF, most theatrical projectors are equipped to flash each image two or three times. This results in a flicker frequency of 48 or 72 images per second (96 or 144 for sequential stereograms) from a work with a basic frame rate of only 24 frames per second. *Compare* **persistence of vision; phi phenomenon.**

cross-angled polarization Orthogonal polarization (a system of two linear polarization grids arranged at right angles) where the polarization grids are aligned at orthogonal 45° angles. For theme park applications, the grids are at 45° for the left eye and 135° for the right eye. *Compare* **crossed polarization elements.**

45° and 135° Polarization Angles

**Separate Eye   Superimposed
Images   on Screen**

cross distortion Visual anomalies caused by asymmetrical coding.

crossed axes *See* **cross-eyed viewing.**

crossed linear polarizer *See* **cross-angled polarization.**

crossed parallax *See* **negative parallax.**

crossed polarization elements A pair of identical polarized filters rotated so they block all light, either two linear polarizers set at right angles or a pair of circular polarizers overlapped so they rotate in opposite directions. *Compare* **cross-angled polarization.**

crossed stereoscopic disparity; crossed disparity The horizontal image displacement that is characteristic of objects closer than the horopter; the relationship between conjugate points in an image pair where the left point is to the right of the right point and vice versa. This gives the impression that the point lies in the audience space, closer than the plane of the screen. *Compare* **negative parallax; un-crossed stereoscopic disparity.**

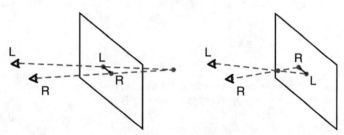

With un-crossed stereoscopic disparity (left), the left-eye image is to the left of the right-eye image, the eyes' views do not cross, and the represented object appears behind the screen. With crossed stereoscopic disparity (right), the left-eye image is to the right of the right-eye image, the eyes' views cross before reaching the screen, and the represented object appears in front of the screen at the point where the views cross.

cross-eye When the eyes are angled inward by an excessive degree, as when trying to focus on an object very near the face. *Compare* **wall-eye.**

cross-eyed viewing; cross-fusing; cross-viewing A stereogram presentation technique where the left-eye image is placed on the right and the right-eye image is placed on the left. The 3D effect becomes apparent when viewers cross their eyes, causing the two images to align in the center. There is no specific limit to how large the individual images may be, but the larger the image, the more convergence required to view it, the more blurry the image may appear to be, and the fewer people who are capable of viewing it. In practice, this is rarely used for images wider than 10". This works equally well with color or black-and-white images and does not require special glasses. However, prolonged eye crossing does cause muscle strain and, if our mothers are to be believed, there is a very good chance that our eyes may freeze that way. *Also* **convergence viewing.** *Compare* **free-viewing; mirror-viewing; parallel-viewing.**

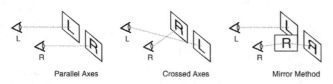

Parallel Axes   Crossed Axes   Mirror Method

In cross-eyed viewing, the optical axes of each eye are crossed, as noted above. When viewing the images below, slowly cross your eyes until the two images overlap in the center. The circle should appear in front of the triangle with the rectangle in the background.

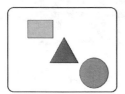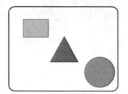

crosstalk; cross-talk; cross talk; XTALK When one channel inadvertently bleeds into another in a multichannel system. In the case of stereoscopic systems, when the left- and right-eye images are not completely separated from one another, resulting in an apparent double exposure. Crosstalk may be introduced at many points in the stereoscopic stream, including encoding, presentation, and reception. Unlike ghosting, which is subjective, crosstalk is an objectively measurable defect. *Also* **bleeding; leakage.** *Compare* **channel separation; ghosting; stereo extinction ratio.**

cross-view freevision *Compare* **cross-eyed viewing.**

cross-view prediction A method of stereoscopic data compression employed with MVC video streams that takes advantage of the fact that the left- and right-eye images are quite similar to each other.

> One (independent) eye is compressed using standard means while the other (dependent) eye is compressed even further by considering the differences from the independent eye. The independent eye can be uncompressed on its own (allowing it to be used for 2D presentation), while the dependent eye does not carry enough data to be uncompressed without also using data from the independent eye.

Compare **asymmetric coding.**

CRT *See* **cathode ray tube.**

CrystalEyes The trade name for a line of liquid crystal shutter (LCS) active eyewear developed by StereoGraphics and now produced by RealD. The RealD Web site is www.reald.com.

cue conflict When two or more depth cues provide contradictory depth information for an image. For example, when monocular depth cues (blur gradient, interposition, relative size, etc.) do not agree with each other or conflict with binocular depth cues, especially image parallax. *Also* **depth cue confusion.** *Compare* **binocular rivalry; color rivalry; retinal rivalry; luminance rivalry; perspective-stereopsis rivalry.**

cut-cushioning; cushion cuts *Also* **blending.** *See* **convergence animation.**

cutout planar effect *See* **cardboarding.**

cybersickness Motion sickness caused by virtual reality systems. If one views immersive scenes of motion while remaining physically stationary for an extended time, one is likely to experience symptoms of motion sickness, including nausea, eyestrain, and dizziness. An estimated 80 percent of virtual reality system users will experience some form of cybersickness after 20 minutes of operation. Coined by Michael McCauley and Thomas Sharkey in 1992. *Also* **simulator sickness.** *Compare* **latency; vection.**

cyberspace The conceptual place where human interaction occurs over computer networks: through e-mail, games, simulations, etc. First appeared in print in 1984 in *Neuromancer* by William Gibson.

d-cinema; dCinema *See* **digital cinema.**

dark adaptation The increase in light sensitivity of the human visual system that occurs over time as illumination levels decrease. *See* **light adaptation.**

dashboard effect Difficulty and time lag associated with adjusting to an abrupt change in visual depth, as when switching from viewing the road ahead to reading the gauges on a car's dashboard. *Compare* **depth jump cut; stereoscopic latency.**

DCDM; digital cinema distribution master The collection of all uncompressed, full-resolution picture, sound, and data elements necessary for theatrical digital projection. The DCDM may then be compressed and encrypted to form the digital cinema package (DCP), prior to delivery to theaters.

DCI; Digital Cinema Initiatives, LLC A joint venture of six motion picture studios (Disney, Fox, Paramount, Sony, Universal, and Warner Bros. Studios— MGM, one of the original founding members, withdrew in 2005), established in 2002 to develop, document, and promote voluntary digital cinema standards. The DCI publishes the *Digital Cinema System Specification* (*DCSS*, issued March 2008), the *DCSS Compliance Test Plan* (May 2009), and a *Stereoscopic Digital Cinema Addendum* (July 2007). The DCI Web site is www.dcimovies.com.

DCIP; Digital Cinema Implementation Partners, LLC A joint venture of three theatrical circuits (AMC Entertainment Inc., Cinemark USA, Inc., and Regal Entertainment Group) with more than 14,000 screens in the U.S. and Canada. Established in 2007 to help plan and implement the conversion to digital cinema in North America. The DCIP Web site is www.dcipllc.com.

DCP; digital cinema package The collection of all picture, sound, and data elements necessary for theatrical digital projection (the digital cinema distribution master, or DCDM) in a compressed and encrypted digital file suitable for distribution for theatrical exhibition.

DCR *See* **degradation category rating.**

DCSS; Digital Cinema System Specification *See* **DCI.**

DCT; discrete cosine transform *See* **compression.**

DDD; Dynamic Digital Depth A developer of 2D to 3D conversion technology, originally established in Perth, Australia in May 1993. DDD products are available under the TriDef brand name as stand-alone computer applications for still and moving images, video game plug-ins, or embedded software for use by 3D display manufacturers including Hyundai, Samsung, and Sharp. The DDD Web site is www.ddd.com.

decimation A form of filtering that reduces undesirable artifacts when digitizing an analog signal by oversampling, processing, and then re-sampling the signal at the final output rate. For example, sound with a final sample frequency of 44.1 kHz may be sampled initially at 64 or 128 times 44.1 kHz, or roughly 2.8 to 5.6 MHz. Next, a low-pass filter removes all data above the Nyquist frequency. Finally, the data are re-sampled to produce a 44.1 kHz output stream. *Compare* **anti-aliasing filter; reconstruction filter; spatial decimation; temporal decimation.**

decoding Processing or transforming content to restore it to its original form or representation; reversing a previous process, as when decompressing a previously compressed media file. *Compare* **encoding; transcoding.**

decoding artifact A digital signal anomaly caused by the decoding process, generally the conversion of a received signal into a form that can be displayed to a viewer. *Also* **rendering artifact.** *See* **capture artifact; coding artifact; compressed depth artifact; display artifact; network artifact; production artifact.**

decorrelation Disconnecting accommodation from vergence when viewing a stereogram. *Compare* **accommodation/vergence reflex.**

degradation category rating; DCR A standardized method for measuring the subjective quality of a change made to a video signal using a five-point scale, ranging from "very annoying" to "imperceptible." Published as part of *ITU-T Recommendation P.910* in September 1999 by the International Telecommunication Union. Also published as the double-stimulus impairment scale or EBU method in *Recommendation ITU-R BT.500–12* in 2009.

Video sequences are presented to reviewers in a regular pattern: first the original, unaltered video sequence followed by a two second interval then the same video sequence altered by the process under review. Each test pair is separated by a longer interval (generally ≤ 10 seconds) during which the reviewers rate the positive or negative impact of the process. The same video sequence pair may be presented more than once during a test session to help ensure a more accurate result.

A variation on the DCR method allows for the simultaneous presentation of the "before" and "after" video sequences side-by-side on the same monitor.

Also **double-stimulus impairment scale; EBU method.** *Compare* **subjective test.**

delta The difference, or delta, between the near and far points in a stereogram; the total scene depth. Often expressed as a percentage of image width. *Compare* **2D+delta; depth range.**

depolarization The neutralization or elimination of polarity. With respect to polarized 3D systems, the loss of proper light polarization so that the left- and right-eye images in a polarized stereogram cannot be separated by the supplied eyewear. For example, if one projects a polarized image onto a white screen rather than a silver one, the reflected light will be depolarized.

depth The third dimension present in the natural world but absent in a flat 2D image.

The perception of binocular depth is simulated by stereoscopic systems, but not actually present in the individual 2D stereo views. Proper staging, lighting, motion, etc. can give traditional flat 2D images sufficient monocular depth cues to make them seem real enough to engage the viewer. Adding simulated depth through stereoscopic presentation can add additional visual texture and realism to a work, but 3D effects by themselves cannot redeem a poor quality work.

depth acquisition *See* **spatial capture.**

depth aliasing An undesirable visual artifact that occurs when ambiguous conjugate points are mismatched by the brain. When there are multiple possible matches for a particular conjugate point, other contextual cues will bias the brain's selection process leading to mismatched pairs that interfere with binocular depth perception. *Also* **binocular aliasing.**

depth balancing *See* **depth grading.**

depth bleeding When the depth information from one object carries over into neighboring objects. Generally occurs along object edges due to compression artifacts.

depth blend The reduction of the impact of Z-depth aliasing in a volumetric display. Just as traditional anti-aliasing is used to reduce stair step jumps along the X- and Y-axes of a 2D image, depth blending is used to reduce jumps along the Z-axis. The neighboring values of each image element (voxel) are examined and the element is adjusted as necessary to smooth the depth transitions. *Compare* **convergence animation.**

depth budget 1. Disparity limit or fusible range; the total range of depth that may be comfortably represented by a stereoscopic display system from maximum negative parallax (distance in front of the screen) to maximum positive parallax (distance behind the screen).

The depth budget may not be allocated symmetrically with respect to the screen, since the zone of comfort extends farther behind the screen than it does in front. As a convenience, however, the depth budget may be presented as a single number representing the total apparent distance from nearest to farthest points, as a plus/minus offset from the screen, or as percent of the total screen width or viewing distance.

If the depth budget is exceeded, then viewers will find it increasingly uncomfortable to view a

stereogram. Particularly large excesses will result in a double image as the viewer will be unable to fuse the left- and right-eye images into a single view. Since children have a smaller interocular distance than adults, they see an exaggerated stereoscopic effect and therefore have reduced depth budgets.

One can comfortably see more depth in a stereogram as the viewing angle (a function of screen size and viewing distance) increases. The average viewing angle for a nominal viewer is significantly different for IMAX, theatrical, home entertainment, and handheld environments. (Average home entertainment viewing angles are also different in the U.S. and Europe, since televisions in U.S. homes tend to be larger than those in Europe.) This leads to variable depth budgets for stereoscopic presentations based on the target presentation venue. Once the depth budget is known, the optimal interaxial distance (the space between the axes of the cameras' lenses) and toe-in angle (for cameras that are not set parallel) can be calculated for any given scene. A fixed interaxial distance may be used (some stereoscopic cameras cannot be adjusted), but this may exceed, or fail to take full advantage of, the available depth budget from one shot to the next.

2. The cumulative amount of depth information that may be depicted throughout a stereoscopic work. To avoid overexerting the audience, a limit may be placed on how much depth will be presented in a work so that one scene with a great deal of depicted depth is balanced by another scene elsewhere in the work with relatively little depicted depth. *Compare* **depth range; field of depth; interocular distance; parallax budget; Percival's zone.**

depth change stress Discomfort caused by repeated changes in image depth that are too abrupt, too great, or too fast. Generally caused by cutting between shots with significantly different depth characteristics or by the intemperate use of subtitles with variable Z-depths. *Compare* **absolute parallax transition limit; display parallax transition limit.**

depth conflict *See* **cue conflict.**

depth contouring *See* **aliasing; cardboarding.**

depth cue; perceptual ~ Information that helps the visual system determine depth and distance. *See* **binocular cue; monocular cue.**

depth cue confusion; depth cue rivalry *See* **cue conflict.**

depth curvature *See* **depth plane curvature.**

depth discontinuity An abrupt and unnatural change in perceived depth between neighboring or overlapping objects. *Compare* **aliasing; cardboarding.**

depth distortion *See* **depth non-linearity; distortion.**

depth effect The range of depth perceived when viewing a stereogram and fusing the conjugate points from each eye image into a representation of 3D space.

Conjugate point disparity in a captured image is primarily a function of interaxial distance, camera lens focal length, and the distance between camera and subject at that particular point. Perceived depth (the depth effect) when viewing a stereogram presented on a screen is further affected by the viewer's interocular distance and angle of view (display size plus viewing distance). When viewing a stereogram with a stereoscope, perceived depth is affected by the viewing lens focal length.

Compare **plasticity.**

depth grading The process of adjusting the visual depth cues in a stereoscopic work to reduce viewer eyestrain, emphasize a narrative point, achieve a particular aesthetic, etc. Similar in concept to *color grading* or *color timing*, the process of adjusting the color balance and exposure of each shot in a completed work to achieve a desired look. *Also* **depth balancing.**

depth jump cut An abrupt, unexpected change in image depth between shots in a stereoscopic work. The audience will require additional time to adjust to the new shot. *Also* **3D jump cut.** *Compare* **dashboard effect.**

depth keystone *See* **frustum effect.**

depth map A graphical depiction of the distance between the observer (usually, a camera) and each visible point in a scene. May be used when generating stereo views for 2D to 3D conversion or auto-stereoscopic displays. In many cases, storage space and transmission bandwidth can be saved by representing a stereogram as a single eye image and a depth map (2D+depth) rather than two full eye images.

NOTE: *Depth map* is often (incorrectly) used as a synonym for *difference map* and *disparity map*.

Also **displacement map.** *Compare* **difference map; disparity map; Z-buffer.**

depth mismatch When an object in a stereogram appears to be at the wrong depth given its surroundings. Generally caused during post-production compositing when mixing different elements with different depth characteristics into the same image or resulting from poor-quality 2D to 3D conversion. Most obvious where objects intersect, such as a chair sitting on the floor, an actor's hand grasping a virtual object, a window set in a wall, etc. *Compare* **partial pseudostereo.**

depth non-linearity A stereoscopic distortion where linear distances in the recorded scene are not perceived as linear in a stereogram: physical depth is recoded accurately at the screen plane (the point of zero parallax or image convergence), but increasingly stretched towards the viewer and increasingly compressed away from the viewer. This distorts motion as well as depth. For example, an object moving towards the camera will seem to accelerate even though it is moving at a constant speed.

depth of field; DOF The area between the nearest and farthest points from the camera that are in acceptably sharp focus. A function of the type of

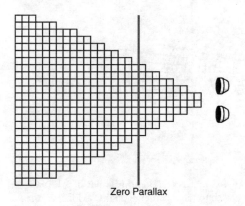

Zero Parallax

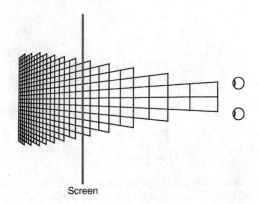

Screen

Depth non-linearity. A regular grid of squares before the camera (left) will appear distorted when viewed as a stereogram (right) (illustration by author; based on materials from Andrew Woods, www.andrewwoods3d.com).

lens, aperture setting, focal length, image area, and primary focus distance. If the depth of field is not matched in the lenses recording a stereogram, the eye images may not match, which will interfere with the 3D effect.

The depth of field for a given lens will increase as the aperture is reduced, decrease as the aperture is opened up. The depth of field also increases as the distance to the primary focal plane increases, which is how lenses can have an infinity (∞) setting. When a lens is focused on infinity, everything beyond a certain distance is presumed in focus. Wider (shorter) lenses have more depth of field than otherwise comparable longer lenses. Finally, there is more depth of field beyond the plane of focus than there is closer than the plane of focus (approximately ⅔ beyond and ⅓ in front). While T-stops are more accurate than *f*-stops in calculating exposure, *f*-stops are used more often in calculating depth of field.

NOTE: *Depth of field* and *field of depth* are unrelated concepts.

See **critical focus.** *Compare* **hyperfocal distance; rack focus.**

depth of field error When the depth of field is not the same in the lenses recording a stereogram,

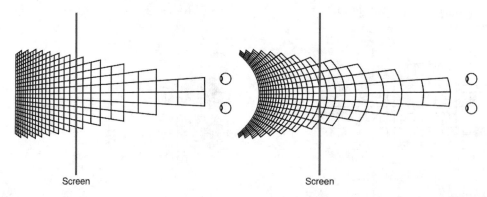

The effect of changing focal distance on the depth of field. Changing the lens focal length has an inverse effect on the depth of field — the longer the lens, the shorter the depth of field

resulting in differences in focus in the eye images interfering with the 3D effect.

depth perception The ability to register depth in a 3D image or judge distance between objects thanks to a combination of binocular depth cues (made possible by disparity and vergence) and monocular depth cues, such as the relative size of different objects, occlusion, geometric perspective, motion parallax, etc. *See* **stereopsis.**

depth plane curvature A stereoscopic distortion characteristic of toed-in cameras where points off the central axis of the display appear to be farther from the viewer than on-axis points recorded from the same physical distance. A side-effect of keystone distortion.

depth plot A document detailing the stereoscopic decisions in a work from one shot or scene to the next. Used when planning and producing a stereoscopic work. *Also* **depth script; depth storyboard.**

depth quantization noise A quantization artifact introduced when compressing a digital depth map. Significant quantization noise will interfere with proper depth representation in the associated stereogram.

depth ramp *See* **convergence ramp.**

depth range The distance from the physical or virtual stereoscopic cameras to the nearest and farthest points within the cameras' views or between points representing the maximum negative parallax and maximum positive parallax.

Depth range may be given as two

Deth plane curvature. A stereogram recorded with parallel cameras (left) exhibits flat depth planes, comparable to natural vision, while a stereogram recorded with toed-in cameras (right) exhibits noticeable curvature of the depth planes. As a result, points that were the same distance from the camera will appear to be farther from the view the farther they are from the central axis of the image (illustration by author; based on materials from Andrew Woods, www.andrewwoods3d.com).

numbers (the distance from the camera to the farthest visible point and the distance from the camera to the nearest visible point) or as a single number (the distance between the points that represent the maximum acceptable negative and positive parallax).

Correctly recording the full depth range in an image and representing it comfortably within the depth budget of a display system is a challenge unique to stereoscopic photography. Stereoscopic calculators exist to help calculate the optimal interaxial distance for the recording cameras given a set of image and display characteristics. *Compare* **depth budget; parallax budget; total scene depth.**

depth ringing A digital compression artifact affecting the edges between overlapping objects or areas of contrasting color, causing misinterpretation of depth information along the border, possibly resulting in alternating depths between one image frame and the next. *Compare* **color ringing; Gibbs phenomenon.**

depth script *See* **depth plot.**

depth-sensing *See* **spatial capture.**

depth shimmer Rapid fluctuations in perceived depth, such as those caused by raster aliasing or other digital compression artifacts. *Compare* **depth ringing.**

depth/size distortion; depth/size magnification 1. The altered perceptions of object size that result from hyperstereo and hypostereo. **2.** A stereoscopic malformation that results when presenting a stereogram in other than its intended viewing environment, causing image depth to be stretched or compressed. This effect is exaggerated when there is a non-linear relationship between object depth (as recorded in the natural world) and image depth (as represented in a stereogram).

Depth/size distortion is often thought of as occurring when viewing on a screen that is significantly larger or smaller than the one for which the stereogram was originally produced, but in fact relates to the change in viewing angle, which is a function of screen width and viewing distance. If the viewing angle is wider than anticipated (the screen takes up more of the visual field), then depth will be exaggerated, possibly exceeding the comfortable depth budget for that display environment and causing viewer discomfort. If the viewing angle is narrower than anticipated, then the perception of depth will be diminished and the images will appear unnaturally flat. In general, the narrower the viewing angle, the greater the

range of viewable parallax without discomfort or double vision. *Compare* **screen parallax.**

depth storyboard *See* **depth plot.**

depth warping Non-linear image disparity adjustments made within a stereogram that do not affect the horizontal boundaries. Coined in 2010 by Indian stereographer Clyde DeSouza.

A traditional horizontal image translation impacts the extent to which the left- and right-eye images overlap (either requiring the addition of material to the edges to maintain proper image overlap or clipping the non-overlapping material off the outside edges). Depth warping, on the other hand, does not affect the horizontal edges of the image, so the overlap remains constant. Instead, the disparity between conjugate points is variously compressed or expanded across the images so that only the depth characteristics of the inner portions of the stereogram are modified.

Also **volume reshaping.** *Compare* **convergence animation; horizontal image translation.**

depthies Stereoscopic motion pictures. Coined in imitation of "talkies," once used to distinguish sound movies from silent ones. *Compare* **flatties.**

Three Dimension Pictures' *Robot Monster* (1953), regularly voted one of the worst movies of all time, was one of the many depthies produced to take advantage of the 3D boom of the 1950s (courtesy Heritage Auctions, www.ha.com).

deviation A small, generally unintended and unnoticed, amount of relative displacement between conjugate points in a stereogram. *Compare* **disparity; parallax.**

dextrorotatory Rotating to the right or clockwise, as with circular polarized light. *Compare* **levorotatory.**

DFW; dynamic floating window *See* **floating window.**

dichoptic error *See* **retinal rivalry.**

dichroic filter; dichroic mirror; dichroic reflector A filter that does not simply absorb all but a certain type of light, but instead allows certain light to pass through and reflects back other types of light. This sort of filter does not heat up as much as a traditional absorptive filter, which converts the absorbed light into heat. *Compare* **absorptive filter; StereoJet.**

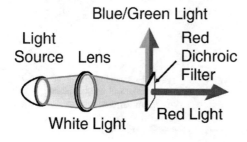

difference map A set of data that describes the visual differences between the left- and right-eye images in a stereogram. Since both eye images share more similarities than differences, a difference map can be much smaller than a full eye image and a stereogram may be more economically stored and transmitted as a single eye image and a difference map (2D+delta).

> NOTE: *Difference map* is often (incorrectly) used as a synonym for *depth map* and *disparity map*.

Compare **depth map; disparity map.**

differential distortion Visual distortions that do not affect both eye images in a stereogram to the same extent. This interferes with the 3D effect.

differential illumination Brightness levels that do not match in the left- and right-eye images, causing retinal rivalry and interfering with the 3D effect. A particular concern with dual-projector-based systems unless the projectors are carefully and regularly tuned.

differential keystoning Keystone distortion that affects the left- and right-eye images in different amounts, preventing conjugate points from aligning and interfering with the 3D effect.

digital billboard *See* **digital signage.**

digital cinema; dCinema; d-cinema Theatrical exhibition of high-resolution digital media using a digital projection system. Though not required, digital cinema may also include digital distribution (electronic content delivery rather than phys-

ical media delivery) and digital production (principal photography using digital cameras).

   The first digital cinema presentation in a commercial theater was the short film *La Cambrure* (*The Curve*) at the Cannes Film Festival in May 1999. Later in that year, the feature films *Star Wars: Episode I—The Phantom Menace* and *An Ideal Husband* were presented using digital projection at select theaters during their initial theatrical release. In 2000, *Titan A.E.* became the first major Hollywood production to be delivered via the Internet for digital presentation to theatrical audiences. In July 2005, a consortium of companies known as the Digital Cinema Initiative (DCI) announced that they had finalized a uniform, universal standard to guide digital cinema equipment manufacturers.

Also **e-cinema; electronic cinema.**

Twentieth Century–Fox's *Titan A.E.* (2000), the first digital feature film delivered to theaters via the Internet (courtesy Heritage Auctions, www.ha.com).

digital cinema distribution master *See* **DCDM.**

Digital Cinema Implementation Partners *See* **DCIP.**

Digital Cinema Initiatives *See* **DCI.**

digital cinema package *See* **DCP.**

Digital Cinema System Specification; DCSS *See* **DCI.**

digital home ecosystem *See* **home ecosystem.**

digital out of home; DOOH Digital signage (multimedia content display projector, video display, or electronic billboard) in public spaces, including airports, office buildings, restaurants, and retail outlets.

digital picture exchange *See* **DPX.**

digital signage Both a medium of delivery and a genre of audiovisual work, generally focused on commercial advertising, where video content is presented to viewers (with or without synchronous audio) in public places. Such displays range from a single video display in an information kiosk to giant screen displays (such as the 40m × 25m Sony Jumbotron) and video walls (a large grid of smaller displays). They can be found in airports, shopping malls, grocery stores, building lobbies, etc. They may attempt to inform or entertain, but generally have a marketing message to deliver that motivates their installation. *Also* **dynamic signage.**

Digital Video Broadcasting; ~ Project *See* **DVB.**

digitize; digitise To convert analog material into a digital form. *Compare* **quantization.**

dimensionalization The trade name for a 2D to 3D conversion process. The term was originally coined in 1999, and then trademarked by In-Three, Inc. in 2001. *Compare* **pixel shift; stereoscopic rendition.**

Clash of the Titans **was produced as a 2D feature film, but was then converted to 3D in only 10 weeks by Prime Focus so the studio could capitalize on the recent 3D success of** ***Avatar*** **(© 2010 Warner Bros.).**

diopter; dioptre A unit of measure of the refractive power of a lens, namely its ability to turn or bend light, equal to the reciprocal of the distance from the optical center of a lens to a focused object (1 divided by the distance), measured in meters. Each increase in diopter increases the apparent size of the image produced by the lens by 25 percent (for objects at the maximum focal distance from the lens).

Diopter	Lens Power	Object Magnification
-2	0.50 ×	-50%
-1	0.75 ×	-25%
0	1.00 ×	0%
1	1.25 ×	25%
2	1.50 ×	50%
3	1.75 ×	75%
4	2.00 ×	100%

diorama effect *See* **cardboarding.**

diplopia Double vision; when the separate images recorded by each eye fail to fuse into a single image and two images are perceived. Often a side-effect of convergence insufficiency where one is unable to maintain proper visual convergence when looking at a near object or when the left- and right-eye images in a stereogram contain too much disparity. *Compare* **accommodative insufficiency; amblyopia; aniseikonia; binocular suppression; convergence insufficiency; strabismus.**

direct view; ~ system A type of video display where the image is created on the surface of the device rather than being projected onto a distant surface, such as a movie screen. Most computer monitors and televisions are direct view devices, including CRTs, LCDs, plasma displays, etc.

direction of propagation *See* **propagation direction.**

dirty window; ~ artifact; ~ effect A digital compression artifact where a visible defect remains stationary while other objects in the scene continue to move, similar to viewing the world through a dirty window. Caused by digital compression schemes that use predictive or bi-directional frames (P- and B-frames in MPEG parlance) without allocating sufficient resources to residual error handling during the encoding process. The error will persist until the next complete frame (I-frame in MPEG) is presented. *Also* **sticky motion.**

discrete cosine transform; DCT *See* **compression.**

discrete rivalry Differences between left- and right-eye images that are the expected result of binocular vision, since each eye records the same scene from a slightly different position and angle.

In addition to horizontal image parallax, the relative positions of objects in each eye's view often means that more distant objects are blocked in one view but visible in another. These areas of exposed background occur naturally in a binocular image but must be re-created when performing a 2D to 3D conversion. If the differences are striking, such as rivalries that are particularly bright or large in a static shot, one may wish to remove them as a creative choice, even though they would have appeared in natural vision.
Compare **retinal rivalry.**

discrete view A scene presented from a single point of view outside of the viewer's control. Most audiovisual works present a discrete view selected by the work's creator. *Compare* **distributed views.**

discrete wavelet transform; DWT *See* **compression.**

discrimination The ability to perceive a difference between two elements. *Compare* **acuity.**

discrimination threshold The smallest reliably detectible difference between two similar things. *Also* **just noticeable difference.**

disocclusion The recreation of hidden parts of an object based on visual information in the neighboring areas. Often necessary in 2D to 3D conversion or when selectively adjusting depth information in a stereogram.

For example, if an object in the foreground is given negative parallax by moving it to the right for the left-eye image and vice versa, some portion of the background that was previously occluded by the object will be exposed. Rather than simply leave a hole in the resulting stereogram, the missing background elements are recreated to fill the gap.
Also **occluded surface reconstruction.**

disparate images The two separate but overlapping views (double vision) that are perceived when viewing a faulty stereogram where the left- and right-eye images fail to fuse into a single, 3D representation. *Compare* **fusion.**

disparity 1. binocular ~: The distance between conjugate points in a left- and right-eye image pair that makes up a stereogram. Only disparity in the same plane as the viewer's eyes (generally, horizontal disparity) contributes to depth perception. **2.** The apparent distance between an object and the plane of the screen, either closer to or farther from the viewer. **3.** A difference between left- and right-eye images that is not caused by parallax. Such differences conflict with the depth cues in the image pair. Minor disparities interfere with the 3D effect, while significant ones can cause physical discomfort in the viewer. *See* **retinal disparity; parallax.** *Compare* **crossed stereoscopic disparity; deviation; horizontal disparity; screen parallax.**

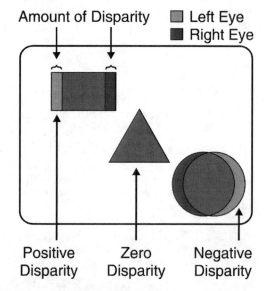

disparity difference The parallax calculated from the disparity between conjugate points in the left- and right-eye images of a stereogram, used in judging distance and depth perception.

disparity map A graphical depiction of the positional differences between conjugate points in the two images of a stereogram. Used to help identify camera misalignment, judge the relative distance separating different objects, highlight areas of positive or negative parallax, etc.

NOTE: *Disparity map* is often (incorrectly) used as a synonym for *depth map* and *difference map.*
Also Compare **depth map; difference map.**

dispersion 1. A change in an optical property linked to the wavelength of light. 2. The decrease in the index of refraction with an increase in the wavelength of light, and vice versa. This can be observed when a prism splits white light into a band of colors, since each wavelength is refracted (bent) by a slightly different amount on its way through the prism.

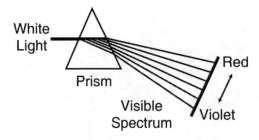

The relative amount of dispersion (v) for a particular material is characterized by its Abbe's number (also known as the v value or v number), which is based on the measured dispersion (n) of three specific wavelengths of visible light through the material (designated d, f, and c).

$$v = \frac{\left(n_d - 1\right)}{\left(n_f - n_c\right)}$$

The wavelengths selected are those generated by sodium and hydrogen atoms when they are heated until they glow (incandesce): yellow at the D line of the sodium spectrum (589.3 nm), blue at the F line of the hydrogen spectrum (486.1 nm), and red at the C line of the hydrogen spectrum (589.3 nm).

Glass with a v number ≥ 55 is considered to have low dispersion and is classified as crown glass, while glass with a v number < 55 is considered to have high dispersion and is classified as flint glass.

displacement The misalignment of conjugate points in the left- and right-eye images of a stereogram, generally caused by poor image registration.

displacement map *See* **depth map.**

display 1. An electronic device that produces a visual image, such as a CRT, LCD, plasma monitor, etc. 2. The information shown on a computer monitor or television screen.

display artifact A visual anomaly caused by the image presentation system. *See* **capture artifact; coding artifact; compressed depth artifact; decoding artifact; network artifact; production artifact.**

display parallax transition limit The maximum allowable amount of parallax change over time in an image stream when presented on a particular type of display. If the presented images exceed this limit, then the viewer will not be able to fuse the images to produce a 3D effect. The limit depends on a number of display characteristics including refresh rate and update frequency. *Compare* **absolute parallax transition limit; depth change stress; dZ/dt.**

display plane The set of conjugate points within a stereogram that have zero parallax (they are in the same position in the left- and right-eye images) and describe a 2D plane that appears to lie upon the surface of the screen. This plane lies between the audience space and the screen space.

All 2D images appear to lie upon the display plane. Stereograms may depict objects on the screen surface (zero parallax), in the audience space in front of the screen (negative parallax), or in the screen space behind the screen (positive parallax).
Also **screen plane.** *Compare* **audience space; screen space.**

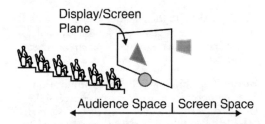

The circle is represented as being forward of the screen in the audience space, the triangle sits on the surface of the screen on the display plane, while the rectangle is behind the screen in the screen space.

display surface The physical surface upon which an electronic display creates its image. *Also* **screen.**

display/viewer space The area within which an image is viewed, as opposed to the camera/scene space where it is recorded. The intended display/viewer space should be known at the time a stereogram is recorded, since the display depth budget influences the selected interaxial distance and toe-in angles of the cameras. *Compare* **camera/scene space.**

display width *See* **screen width.**

disposable eyewear; disposable glasses Inexpensive stereoscopic spectacles designed to be used once and then thrown away, typically with cardboard frames printed with a promotional

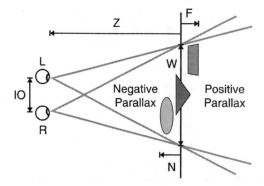

Display/viewer space. The intended display/ viewer should be considered when recording a stereogram. Key characteristics include the interocular (IO) distance, or the average space between the viewer's left (L) and right (R) eyes; the distance from the viewer to the display surface (Z); the width of the display (W); and the depth budget of the display, or the sum of the apparent distances from the display's surface to the nearest (N) and farthest (F) depths presented in the image.

message. Despite their name, they can be used more than once by the recipient, but are not re-used by commercial exhibitors. *Compare* **repeat-use eyewear.**

disruptive technology; disruptive innovation A new or improved business process or technology for which the market is not prepared. Generally classed as low-end (resulting in a significant cost reduction for an existing product) or new-market (appealing to consumers not served by products currently on the market). Examples of disruptive technologies include the steamship (in a market dominated by sail), television (in a market dominated by theatrical exhibition), and the home video recorder (further disrupting theatrical exhibition and also disrupting broadcast television). Coined in 1995 by Joseph L. Bower and Clayton M. Christensen in their article "Disruptive Technologies: Catching the Wave."

distortion 1. A material difference between an original subject (an image, a sound, etc.) and a recording of that subject (a film or video of an image, an audio recording of a sound, etc.). **2. depth ~:** An exaggerated representation of an object's depth in a stereogram, either compressed (too flat) or expanded (too deep); depth non-linearity.

distributed views A scene presented from multiple points of view, each one selectable by the viewer. Most virtual reality systems allow the user

to select any view desired (any direction, any angle, etc.) either from a list of pre-recorded views or by dynamically generating the requested view. *Compare* **discrete view; panorama; photo bubble; spinography.**

divergence 1. The coordinated outward turning of the eyes towards parallel when focusing on a far object or when adjusting one's gaze to a more distant point. **2.** The outward movement of left- and right-eye images beyond zero parallax, creating an increased sense of depth in the image. **3.** Positive image parallax in excess of the nominal viewer's interocular distance. *Compare* **convergence; vergence.**

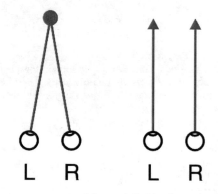

Eyes are converged inward (left) when viewing close objects and diverge towards parallel (right) when viewing more distant objects. For objects beyond 200 meters (stereo infinity), the eyes are set fully parallel and divergence is no longer useful in the estimation of depth.

divergence tolerance The maximum amount of positive parallax deemed acceptable in a stereoscopic work, generally limited to an outward angle of 0.5° per eye or 1° positive parallax in total. On large theatrical screens, this will result in image disparities that are far wider than the nominal viewer's interocular separation, but this will not cause a problem so long as people do not sit too close to the screen.

divergence viewing *See* **parallel viewing.**

diverging lens A lens that causes parallel beams of light to spread apart as they pass through the lens. The apparent focal point of the bent light rays is on the same side of the lens as the light source. In general, such a lens is thinner at its center than at its edge. *Also* **negative lens.** *Compare* **converging lens.**

DLP; digital light processing The trade name for the display system technology based on a dig-

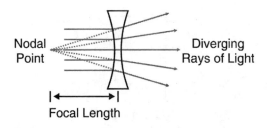

diverging lens

ital micromirror device (DMD) chip. DMD chips were originally designed in the 1970s for missile tracking systems, and later developed for use in high-resolution digital video projectors by Texas Instruments.

Commercial DLP-based projectors were first marketed as computer display devices for business presentations, but have since advanced to the point that they can be used as digital cinema projectors for theatrical exhibition. *Stars Wars: Episode II— The Attack of the Clones* (2002) was the first feature length, all-digital live-action movie, starting with Sony digital cameras on set, through digital editing and post-production, and ending with digital distribution and projection using DLP-based projectors. (Earlier digital live-action productions lacked the digital distribution necessary for a film to stay in the digital domain end-to-end. The animated work *Titan A.E.* (2000) was the first end-to-end digital feature film.)
Compare **LCD; LCoS; MEMS.**

DMD; digital micromirror device A semiconductor covered with a grid of several hundred thousand microscopic aluminum mirrors, each mirror representing a single pixel in an image display. Developed by Larry Hornbeck and William Nelson of Texas Instruments in 1987.

Each DMD mirror has independent motion control so it can be rotated to reflect light through a lens and onto a screen (pixel on) or off to one side and into a heat sink/light trap (pixel off). Shades of gray are achieved by quickly oscillating the mirror on and off, with the percentage of time in the on state equal to the desired intensity of the pixel. Colors are achieved by shining the reflected light through an appropriate color filter. Projectors with a single DMD use a spinning color wheel to create shades of red, green, and blue sequentially, while those with three DMDs have separate red, green, and blue filters whose images are combined optically to create a single full-color image. DMD projectors can be much brighter than traditional LCD projectors, which build up excessive heat due to light to heat conversion within the LCD panels.

Dolby A trade name referring either to Dolby Laboratories, Inc., one of the various analog or digital sound technologies developed by Dolby Labs and first introduced in 1975, or the Dolby/Infitec 3D system developed in 2006. The Dolby Web site is www.dolby.com.

Dolby 3D; Dolby anaglyph; ~ system The trade name for stereogram encoding process where the left- and right-eye images are color-coded using an interference filter and combined into a single image for presentation. The interference filter technology in the Dolby 3D is used system under license from its original developer, Infitec of Germany. The Infitec Web site is www.infitec.net.

Each image is recorded as a series of red, green, and blue (RGB) primary color values, much like a traditional RGB computer image. Different colors are produced by varying the intensity of the individual RGB values of each pixel. To encode the stereogram in a single image, specific wavelengths of each of the primary colors are used for each eye. When viewed through glasses with matching color filters, only the left-eye wavelength of red (629nm) is visible to the left eye, while only the right-eye wavelength of red (615nm) is visible to the right eye. Blue and green are similarly filtered. This causes some color distortion in the reconstructed image, but not nearly as much as a more traditional anaglyphic process. Since the projected images are not polarized, they can be presented using traditional white screens rather than the special silver screens required by polarized 3D systems. As with all interference filter-based 3D systems, the performance of Dolby 3D is very dependent on the color balance of the projector lamp, increasing the importance of proper projector maintenance.
Compare **Panavision 3D.** *See* **interference filter** diagram in color section.

dominant eye *See* **primary eye.**

DOOH *See* **digital out of home.**

double aperture A camera or projector configuration that uses two image apertures rather than the traditional one. Used to record or present two views of the same subject simultaneously. For example, in a double-aperture film camera, two synchronized strips of film are exposed through individual apertures at the same instant. This is not the same as interlocking two separate cameras to record the same scene, as is the case with many 3D rigs.

double-stimulus continuous-quality scale; DSCQS; ~ method A standardized method for measuring the subjective quality of changes made to a video signal using a continuous scale divided into five regions ranging from "bad" to "excellent." Published as part of *Recommendation ITU-*

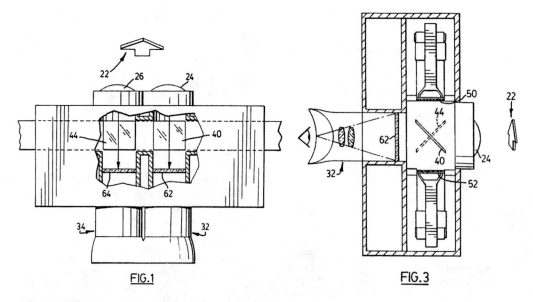

FIG.1   FIG.3

Double aperture. Top (Fig. 1) and right side (Fig. 3) views of a double aperture film camera. Item 24 at the front of the camera is the right lens, while item 32 is the right viewfinder. Incoming light from the subject (item 22) is redirected by the mirrors (40 and 44) to the two film apertures (50 and 52) inside the camera (U.S. Patent No. 4,993,828, issued February 19, 1991) (U.S. Patent and Trademark Office).

R BT.500–12 in 2009 by the International Telecommunication Union.

Sequences of unaltered and altered video are presented to reviewers in pairs, with the order of altered/unaltered randomly changed each time. Depending on the configuration, the sequences may be presented more than once. After reviewing the sequences, the reviewers rank both versions on the same scale. Allowing the reviewers to rank the unaltered content without realizing they are doing so provides a baseline for comparison.
Compare **subjective test.**

double-stimulus impairment scale; DSIS; ~ method *Also* **EBU method.** *See* **degradation category rating.**

double vision *See* **diplopia.**

downstream device One device that follows another in a data distribution chain. For example, in a cable TV system, the decoder in a subscriber's home is a downstream device with respect to the equipment at the cable company's headend. *Compare* **upstream device.** *See* diagram at **upstream device.**

downward scalability The ease with which a work's display size or resolution may be reduced, generally accompanied by a change in aspect ratio as well.

DPX file; .dpx A raster graphic file format for digital still images published as Society of Motion Picture and Television Engineers (SMPTE) standard 268M-2003. (DPX is an initialism of *Digital Picture eXchange*.) The DPX format was derived from the Kodak Cineon film scanner file format and is particularly well suited to recording images scanned from or destined to be recorded on film. As a result, it is commonly used in post-production and visual effects applications.

When rendering a motion picture using DPX, each individual frame is a separate file. This works out to about 130,000 DPX files for an average 90-minute feature film plus a separate file for audio (since the DPX format does not support synchronous sound recording). For convenience, longer works are often broken up into individual reels, or roughly 20-minute segments.

DPX supports a variety of encoding formats, but the most common is 10-bit uncompressed log encoding where each color channel (red, green, and blue) is represented by a separate 10-bit number (ranging from 0 to 1,023) on a logarithmic scale. Digital display devices use linear scales, but photographic film emulsions respond according to logarithmic scales, so the 10-bit log format offers a much more accurate representation of the colors that are actually recorded on film. Another key feature of the log format is its ability to record an extended dynamic range. In most digital formats 0 is black and 100 percent is white, but DPX allows custom black and white levels. The most common are 95 for black and 685 for white. This allows post-production color and exposure corrections without loss of image detail, since "pure black" still contains 95 levels of exposure in the shadows while "pure white" contains a further 338 levels in the highlights.

When viewed directly, a log format image will appear to have very little image contrast, so separate color lookup tables are necessary to translate the log values into appropriate color values for the target display device or media. *Compare* **EXR file; Targa file; TIFF file.**

drift *See* **convergence animation.**

drive-by shooting *See* **auto cha-cha.**

drop off; luminance ~ *Also* **fall off.** *See* **flatness of field.**

DSCQS *See* **double-stimulus continuous-quality scale.**

DSIS *See* **double-stimulus impairment scale.**

dt *See* **dZ/dt.**

dual-band 3D Stereoscopic material where the left- and right-eye images are recorded on separate strips of film, generally for polarized theatrical presentation using two projectors.

dual HD video *See* **full HD.**

dual-panel LCD 3D A type of polarized 3D display where the angle of polarization for each element of the stereogram presented on an LCD panel is controlled by a second LCD panel sandwiched on top of the first. This allows for full-resolution images (rather than the half-resolution images associated with micropolarizers) viewable with inexpensive polarized glasses (rather than more expensive, battery-operated active glasses). First released commercially by LG under the Cinema 3D brand in 2011. *Also* **active retarder; variable-polarization-angle display.** *Compare* **stacked display; ZScreen.**

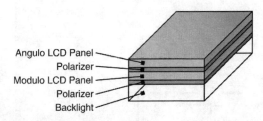

The brightness of each pixel is controlled by the modulo LCD panel while the polarization angle is controlled by the angulo panel.

dual-projector; ~ 3D; ~ system A stereogram presentation system where the left- and right-eye images are presented simultaneously using two interlocked film or video projectors, each generally filtered with a different polarizing lens matched to the corresponding lenses in the glasses worn by the viewers. The most common method employed for presenting theatrical 3D during the 1950s, though it is susceptible to stereogram misalignment (if the projectors or images get out of sync) and pseudostereo (if the content in the projectors is inadvertently switched, so the left-eye images are presented with the right-eye projector). *Compare* **single-projector.**

dual stream *Also* **frame-sequential.** *See* **time-sequential.**

Dubois anaglyph A full-color anaglyphic image where the colors in each eye view have been mathematically optimized to improve depth reproduction and minimize image crosstalk or ghosting. This method has traditionally been applied to red/cyan anaglyphs, but is equally suited to green/magenta or amber/blue anaglyphs. Developed by Canadian Professor of Electrical Engineering and Computer Science, Eric Dubois, and originally presented at the 2001 IEEE International Conference on Acoustics, Speech, and Signal Processing (ICASSP). *Compare* **optimized anaglyph.** *See* **Dubois anaglyph** images in the color section.

duration of comfort The amount of time during which one can view a stereoscopic work without experiencing discomfort.

DVD A 4¾" (12 cm) high-capacity optical disc standard, introduced in April 1997 as a video delivery format to replace the ubiquitous VHS tape. An initialism of *Digital Versatile Disc*.

DVDs commonly carry digital video compressed with the MPEG-2 codec. Even with the occasional digital compression artifact taken into account, a DVD provides a better motion picture recording format than its predecessors: a DVD can hold far more material than a CD or VCD (from 4.7 GB to 17 GB); DVD movies are recorded with more lines of image resolution (480 for NTSC-compatible discs) than videodiscs (≈425) or VHS tapes (≈250); and DVD audio (sampled at 96 kHz with 24-bits of data per sample) is superior to CD audio (44.1 kHz/16-bits).

- **DVD-5:** A single-sided, single-layer (SS/SL) DVD capable of holding 4.7 GB.
- **DVD-9:** A single-sided, dual-layer (SS/DL) DVD capable of holding 8.5 GB.
- **DVD-10:** A double-sided, single-layer (DS/SL) DVD capable of holding 9.4 GB. (One must generally flip the DVD over to read the second side.)
- **DVD-18:** A double-sided, dual-layer (DS/DL) DVD capable of holding 17 GB.

dwarfism *See* Lilliputism.

DWT; discrete wavelet transform *See* compression.

Dynamic Digital Depth *See* DDD.

dynamic signage *See* digital signage.

dynamic window; dynamic floating window *See* floating window. *Compare* edge violation.

dZ/dt Parallax change; the amount of change in the parallax of conjugate points in a stereogram over time, calculated by dividing the amount of change in image depth (dZ) by the elapsed time (dt). *Compare* absolute parallax transition limit; depth change stress; display parallax transition limit.

EBU method *See* double-stimulus impairment scale.

e-cinema; eCinema Electronic cinema. *See* digital cinema.

eclipse method A stereogram presentation technique where left- and right-eye images are presented in an alternating pattern while the viewer wears special glasses that open and close the lenses to block the view through the opposite-eye image. *Compare* active eyewear; polarized strip; Pulfrich.

edge distortion Anomalies in the depth information along an object's edges, generally due to compression artifacts.

edge violation; edge mismatch 1. When an object with negative parallax (seeming to extend out of the screen) is cut off by the edge of the screen. The brain does not know how to interpret this visual paradox. One expects far objects to be cut off by the edge of a window, but objects closer than the window should not also be cut off. This paradox leads to a visual/brain conflict and interferes with the 3D effect.

To avoid edge violations, it is best to keep objects with negative parallax away from the edge of the screen, even if they do not cross it. For example, home entertainment works may require a 10 percent border on all sides (restricting negative parallax to the interior 80 percent of the image). In general, vertical edge violations (affecting the left and right edges of the screen) are more severe than horizontal edge violations (affecting the top and bottom of the screen), so more care should be given to the vertical than the horizontal edges.

2. When an object lies within one of the monocular areas along the edge of a stereoscopic view. (It will be depicted in one eye view but not the other.) *Also* **breaking the frame; window violation.** *Compare* floating window.

electric vector The amplitude and direction of the electric field generated by an electromagnetic wave as it passes through space. The magnetic

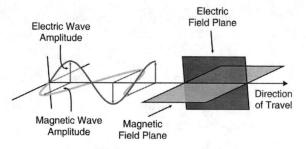

Electromagnetic waves, such as visible light, have both an electric and magnetic component. As an electric field passes through space, it creates a magnetic field of equal amplitude traveling in the same direction, but rotated 90°. As a magnetic field passes through space, it creates an electric field of equal amplitude traveling in the same direction, but rotated 90°. Thus, each creates the other. Since the electric component of an electromagnetic wave is generally easier to manipulate, electromagnetic waves are generally depicted by showing only the electric field.

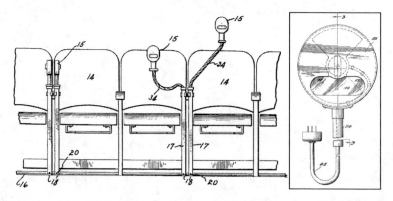

Eclipse method. From Laurens Hammond's U.S. patents for eclipse method eyewear with a mechanical shutter synchronized to twin projectors (Nos. 1,506,524, issued August 26, 1924, and 1,658,439, issued February 7, 1928) (U.S. Patent and Trademark Office).

vector is orthogonal (at a right angle) to the electric vector. Together, the electric and magnetic vectors define the direction, strength, and frequency of an electromagnetic wave. *Compare* **magnetic vector.**

electro-optical liquid crystal modulator *See* **polarization switch.**

elliptical polarization; EP An electromagnetic wave, such as visible light, that travels through space in an oblong corkscrew pattern. If the electric field vector of the light wave is measured against a flat plane fixed in space perpendicular to the direction of travel, then the tip of the electric field vector will describe an ellipse, rotating either clockwise (right-hand) or counterclockwise (left-hand) depending on the handedness of the EP wave.

> NOTE: In optics (and therefore most stereoscopic applications), the direction of EP spin is measured from the perspective of the viewer (right-handed for clockwise, left-handed for counterclockwise), while in electrical engineering, it is measured from the perspective of the source.

Elliptical polarization can be broken down into the sum of two linear polarized waves, where each wave has the same amplitude and travels along right angle planes (rotated 90° from each other). When these planar waves combine, they create a 3D wave that follows an elongated helix, or elliptical corkscrew, path through space over time.

The difference between height and width of the ellipse described by the tip of the wave's electric field vector depends on how far the two waves are out of phase. This results in two special cases:

- **Circular Polarization: CP:** The two waves are 90° out of phase, resulting in an ellipse where the height equals the width — namely, a circle.
- **Linear Polarization; LP:** The two waves are perfectly in phase, resulting in an ellipse with zero width — namely, a line.

Compare **circular polarization; linear polarization; polarization.**

emergence effect *See* **negative parallax.**

emissive display An electronic display where the image itself is luminous and does not require a separate light source to be seen, such as a CRT, LED, or plasma display. *Compare* **transmissive display.**

emitter An optical transmitter, such as the device that produces the IR light beam in an IR-based remote control. Most active display systems are linked to an IR emitter that produces the timing signal that keeps the active eyewear in sync with the display.

emmetripia Natural vision where a relaxed eye registers distant objects as clear images on the retina.

encoding Processing or transforming content into another form or representation; applying a reversible process to a signal, as when compressing a media file. *Also* **formatting.** *Compare* **decoding; transcoding.**

entrance pupil; entry pupil The opening in a compound lens through which light may pass when viewed from the front of the lens. (The *exit pupil* is viewed from the rear.)

The size of the physical lens opening is established by the diaphragm, or iris. When the diaphragm is viewed through the lens, the apparent pupil may differ in size and position from the physical diaphragm opening due to the optical properties of the lens elements. Depending on the lens design (and focal length in a varifocal, or zoom, lens), the entrance pupil may coincide with one of the lens nodal points or the diaphragm, but it need not.

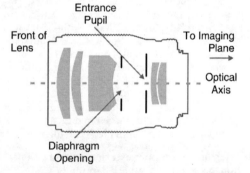

The intersection of the entrance pupil with the optical axis of the lens defines the center of perspective, or the rear focus point where the incoming light rays cross on their way to the imaging plane. For converging stereo cameras, the interaxial distance separating the stereo images may be measured between these centers of perspective. (Source: Paul van Walree.)

Compare **center of perspective; nodal points.**

EP *See* **elliptical polarization.**

epipolar 1. The geometry of binocular vision. **2.** Geometric differences between the images recorded by each eye that are explained by horizontal parallax. *See* **non-epipolar.**

equilibrioception The sense of balance, based on sensations registered by the vestibular system within the inner ear. *Compare* **cybersickness; motion sickness; proprioception; vection.**

ergonomics *See* **human factors.**

esotropia *See* **strabismus.**

essence *See* **audio essence; video essence.**

exit pupil *See* **entrance pupil.** *Compare* **center of perspective; nodal points.**

exotropia *See* **strabismus.**

expected size *See* **usual size.**

EXR file; .exr A high-dynamic-range graphic file format for digital still images developed by Industrial Light & Magic (ILM) in 1999 and made available to the public through OpenEXR in 2003. Supports lossy and lossless compression; 16-bit or 32-bit floating-point numbers or 32-bit integers per pixel per color channel; and an unlimited number of discrete channels. The OpenEXR Web site is www.openexr.com.

> The EXR format is commonly used to store lossless images with 16-bits per channel (1 sign bit, 5 exponent bits, and 10 mantissa bits) and 4 image channels (1 channel each for red, green, and blue color information and an alpha channel for transparency values, also known as RGBA). This gives each channel a dynamic range equivalent to 40 *f*-stops—30 at the high end without any loss of fidelity and another 10 at the low end with some loss of fidelity—and 1024 gradations per channel per *f*-stop. This compares to a standard 8-bit per pixel file format (32-bit RGBA) with 7–10 *f*-stops of exposure and 20–70 gradations per channel. 32-bit floating-point numbers may be used when more image dynamic range is required.

Compare **DPX file; Targa file; TIFF file.**

exterior orientation; exterior camera orientation *See* **extrinsic camera parameters.**

extinction Reduction of signal intensity, generally through absorption. In stereographic systems, the process carried out by the eyewear to block the alternate eye image from perception by the wrong eye. With anaglyphic and polarized eyewear, each lens absorbs (extinguishes) the off eye image.

extrastereoscopic cue *See* **monocular cue.**

extrinsic camera parameters The parameters that define the position (location and orientation) of a camera in relation to a world coordinate system: *T*, the translation (in X, Y, and Z space) necessary to align the world coordinate system's origin with the camera's principal point (the point where the optical axis of the lens intersects the image plane); and *R*, the rotation necessary to align the X, Y, and Z axes of the world coordinates with those of the camera coordinates. The extrinsic camera parameters change when the camera moves. Often used in computer vision applications or when reconstructing 3D objects from a series of 2D images. *Also* **exterior orientation.** *Compare* **intrinsic camera parameters.**

eye-dedicated display A stereoscopic display system where each eye sees a separate display. *See* **head-mounted display.**

eye fatigue *See* **asthenopia.**

eye fixation *See* **visual fixation.**

eye-image isolation *See* **ghosting.**

eyeline Where an on-screen actor is, or appears to be, looking.

> Eyelines are particularly important in close-ups and other shots where the camera does not show both the actor and where the actor is looking. Actors are often given something to look at off-camera that will have them looking in the proper direction when the different shots are edited together. This ensures a consistent eyeline between takes. In 3D works, eyeline mismatches are more obvious to the viewer than in 2D works, so greater care must be taken to ensure they line up.

eye poke An object (often something sharp and pointy) moving rapidly and directly at the viewer in the audience space to (hopefully) cause the audience to flinch or duck. A classic example appears near the beginning of *House of Wax* (1953) when a barker for the wax museum shoots a paddle ball at the audience. This same gag is repeated as an homage at the beginning of *Monsters vs. Aliens* (2009). *Compare* **flinch factor.**

eye separation *See* **interocular distance.**

eye-sequential; ~ 3D *See* **time-sequential.**

eyestrain; eye strain *See* **visual discomfort.**

eye tracking Monitoring the position and orientation of the viewer's eyes. Common to virtual reality and certain auto-stereoscopic display systems. May be used to adjust the display to help ensure that each eye receives the correct image. *Compare* **head tracking; tracking.**

eyewear A device worn by the viewer in front of the eyes. This includes head-mounted displays (HMDs) typical of virtual reality systems and the more familiar spectacles (commonly, glasses) equipped with special lenses for anaglyph, polarized, or active stereo viewing. *Compare* **virtual retinal display.**

fall off; luminance ~ *Also* **drop off.** *See* **flatness of field.**

false contouring *See* **aliasing; cardboarding.**

false depth When all or part of an object in a stereogram appears to be the wrong distance from the viewer given the other depth cues. Often the result of incorrect or insufficient segmentation during 2D to 3D conversion.

false edges *See* **aliasing; cardboarding.**

far disparity *See* **positive parallax.**

far plane The 2D surface perpendicular to the camera's lens axis that contains the far point. *Compare* **near plane.**

far point 1. The conjugate points in a stereogram that appear to be farthest from the viewer. The far point can change from frame to frame, but should not exceed the maximum allowable distance defined by the depth budget. **2.** The farthest distance that can be seen clearly. *Compare* **near point.**

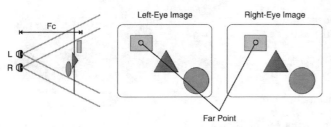

The farthest point from the camera with discernable depth information (*Fc*, left) corresponds to the far point depicted in the stereogram pair (right). Objects that are more distant may be recorded in the same image, but after a certain distance (generally 200 meters), there is no longer sufficient binocular disparity to convey depth information.

far point distance; FPD The space from the camera to the most distant object visible in a stereogram.

far point of accommodation The most distant point at which the eyes can focus. For people with normal vision, this is infinity. *Compare* **near point of accommodation.**

farsighted *See* **hypermetropia.** *Compare* **myopia.**

feathering A gradual reduction in effect moving outwards towards the edges, used in computer graphics to help blend one area into another. This results in a smooth visual transition but can have the effect of causing the edges of an object to

blend into the background contrary to the natural behavior of a 3D object.

field *See* **image field.**

field inversion Interlaced video fields presented in the wrong order — the odd numbered field is presented on the even lines and vice versa. This has the effect of switching both the vertical relationship (what was supposed to be the top line is presented on the bottom) and the time order (one field is recorded earlier in time than the other, inverting them will cause the later field to display first).

field of depth; FOD The range of depth that a stereoscopic display can physically produce given a particular voxel size and the angular resolution of the anticipated viewer.

> NOTE: *Field of depth* and *depth of field* are un-related concepts.

Compare **depth budget.**

field of view; FOV The largest solid angle that can fit within one's vision or can be captured by a camera lens, generally measured as a certain number of degrees from side to side (less often from top to bottom). An important factor in stereoscopic calculations.

Human vision has a horizontal field of view of about 180° (each eye covers about 150°— 60° inward towards the nose, 90° to the side — with about 120° of overlap in the center). A feeling of immersion arises when the FOV is greater than roughly 60°–90°. All else being equal, the greater the field of view, the more immersive the viewing experience. However, if one simply sits closer to the screen in order to increase the field of view, at a certain point the individual film grains or video pixels in the image become apparent and the visual appeal diminishes. Studies indicate that humans can perceive pixels as small as 1/60 of 1° (one

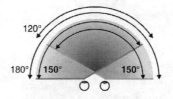 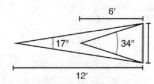

The typical human vision field of view (left) shows how the field of view of each eye overlaps. Binocular depth perception is limited to the 120° span in the center where the two eyes overlap. The right diagram shows how much of the field of view would be filled by the image on a 52" diagonal (44" wide) 16:9 television when sitting 6' away (34°) or 12' away (17°).

minute of arc, or 0.017°), so if one wants to view a 16:9 television image with a 100° angle of view, there must be more than 6,000 pixels in each scan line, leading to the UHDTV (ultra-high-definition television) standard of 7,680 pixels per line.
Compare **angle of view; viewing angle.**

field replication Presenting each row of an interlaced video field more than once, as with basic line doubling where each scan line is presented twice to fill a high-resolution screen with a low-resolution image.

field-sequential; ~ 3D *See* **time-sequential.**

fields per second The rate at which individual fields are recorded or presented in a display system, generally twice the frame rate. Each interlaced video frame is made up of two fields, so if the nominal frame rate is 30 frames per second, the field rate is 60 fields per second. Time-sequential 3D systems present the left- and right-eye images that make up a complete stereoscopic frame one at a time, resulting in a field rate that is twice the frame rate.

> NOTE: Contemporary 3D video displays designed for use with active eyewear using a time-sequential format are often described as running at 120 Hz or 240 Hz, giving the impression that the displays are presenting 120 or 240 images per second. This is the display refresh rate, not the image frame rate. To avoid perceptible flicker, each video image is refreshed more than once. For example, when presenting a time-sequential program recorded at 30 frames per second on a display running at 120 Hz, there will be 60 unique images presented each second (30 for the left eye and 30 for the right eye) and each one will be presented twice. On a 240 Hz display, each one would be presented 4 times.

film A thin sheet of flexible material.
> Films with special optical characteristics may be used to coat a surface to achieve a particular effect, such as the polarization of light, filtering or bending certain colors of light, reflecting light, etc. Photographic film consists of a clear, flexible base coated with a light sensitive emulsion that records the image.

film chip *See* **chip.**

film image width *See* **imaging sensor width.**

first surface mirror *See* **front silvered mirror.**

fisheye effect *See* **barrel distortion.**

fixation *See* **visual fixation.**

fixation conflict; fixation point conflict A scene with an excess of points of visual interest, causing the viewer's gaze to move rapidly from point to point across the screen. *Also* **reference point conflict.** *Compare* **focus-fixation mismatch.**

fixation distance The space from the center of an observer's gaze to the point where the ocular axes cross when the eyes are turned inward from parallel. *Compare* **vergence.**

fixation-focus conflict When the viewer's gaze is drawn to an object that is not in focus. *Also* **focus-fixation mismatch.**

fixed interaxial An integrated stereoscopic camera that simultaneously records both eye-images of a stereogram using a set stereo base (the separation between the images is not adjustable). May use a single- or twin-lens design recording to one or two imaging devices.

The CP-31, a twin-lens, twin-CMOS 1920 × 1080p imaging chip 3D digital camcorder with a fixed interaxial distance (65mm standard, 55mm optional) and adjustable vergence angles (0°–3.6°) (courtesy 3D-one B.V., www.3d-one.com).

flash LIDAR *See* **3D flash LIDAR.**

flat 1. A non-3D image (namely, a standard image with only two dimensions) on film or screen. **2.** A non-anamorphic (un-squeezed) image; filmed with a spherical lens. For most contemporary theatrical productions, this equates to a 1.85:1 aspect ratio.

flat image *Also* **2-dimensional image.** *See* **planar image.**

flatness of field A relative measure of the overall evenness of the distribution of light intensity in a projected image.
> Ideally, all areas on the screen should have the same light intensity. In practice, there is a luminance drop off where the center of the screen has the maximum light intensity with the light level diminishing as the distance from the center increases. Luminance drop off is greatest in the corners (since they are farthest from the center) and

more severe with high-gain screens, where there is often a perceptible hotspot in the image. (The exact position of the hot spot on a high-gain screen will vary depending on the position of the observer.)

flat panel display; FPD A video display device that is significantly thinner (and lighter) than a traditional cathode ray tube (CRT) display of comparable height and width. Common FPD technologies include LCD, LED, and plasma displays.

flatties Traditional 2D motion pictures. Coined in imitation of "talkies," once used to distinguish sound movies from silent ones. *Compare* **depthies.**

flicker An unsteady wavering; a perceptible visual artifact of alternating light and dark, commonly caused when a film or video work is presented at a low frame rate or when too much ambient light spills onto the screen.

To prevent flicker, the typical theatrical film runs at 24 frames per second with each frame projected twice using a two-blade shutter for an effective rate of 48 images per second. Video images are typically presented at 25 to 30 frames per second. To prevent flicker, interlaced video images divide each frame into two fields and present 50 to 60 fields per second. High-definition progressive video displays often present each image multiple times to reduce flicker, resulting in refresh rates of 120 Hz or 240 Hz.

Compare **color flicker; luminance flicker.**

flicker frequency; flicker rate The speed with which a projected image switches from light to dark. In theatrical projection and high-frequency digital televisions, the same image is shown more than once so that the flicker frequency is a multiple of the frame rate. *Compare* **critical fusion frequency.**

flinch factor A subjective measure of the likelihood and degree of audience physical reaction (ducking or flinching) to an object that appears to be coming directly at them. *Compare* **eye poke.**

floating edge When a fore window image (something that seems to extend out of the screen and into the audience space) is cut off by the edge of the display, resulting in an unnatural and abrupt end to the object. This leads to a visual/brain conflict that may interfere with the 3D effect. *Compare* **edge violation.**

floating image An image that appears to be floating in space before the viewer's eyes, rather than fixed to a display surface.

floating window An adjustment to the size or shape of the stereo window, generally asymmetrical expansions and contractions to the right and left edges of a stereogram to reduce depth cue confusion or avoid edge violations. May be prerecorded (made a permanent part of the image) or generated during presentation (by providing suitable metadata to the display system).

Static floating windows (fixed for the duration of a work) are generally attributed to British stereographers Nigel and Raymond Spottiswoode, who used them in the sort film *Black Swan* (1952). Dynamic floating windows (which adjust at intervals throughout a presentation) are credited to American stereographer Brian Gardner, who first used them as a creative storytelling technique in *Meet the Robinsons* (2007).

In theatrical applications, the screen must be wider than the projected image to allow space for horizontal framing adjustments. Projectionists often incorrectly bring the side curtains in tight to the projected image without leaving room on the sides for the floating window. Not generally used in home entertainment applications as the display bezel provides a fixed frame surrounding the image and the black pillar-bars that would be necessary to allow space for the floating window might distract the viewer.

Also **dynamic window.** *Compare* **edge violation.**

focal length The distance from the optical center of a lens focused on infinity to the focal plane where the image comes into sharp focus, usually expressed in millimeters; an inverse measure of how strongly a lens bends (converges or diverges) light (the shorter the focal length, the greater the light bending power of the lens).

Since lens focal length affects both image magnification (the longer the focal length, the greater the magnification) and 2D depth cues (the shorter the focal length, the greater the perceived relative distance between objects), if the focal lengths of the left- and right-eye images in a stereogram are not matched exactly, binocular image distortions will occur that may interfere with the 3D effect.

focal length mismatch Differing amounts of magnification in the left- and right-eye images of a stereogram. May be static (the same throughout a shot) or dynamic (a zoom mismatch, where the focal length is not synchronized during a zoom shot, or the result of unintended focal length drift during a shot). If both lenses do not have exactly the same focal length at all times, or if there is an optical mismatch between the lenses to begin with, the two images recorded for a stereogram will not align properly, interfering with image fusion and the 3D effect.

NOTE: Two seemingly identical lenses (same

make and model) are not necessarily identical enough for stereography. It is vital that the cameras' lenses are perfectly matched prior to shooting.
Compare **focus mismatch.**

focal plane **1.** The flat surface in space inside a camera where a lens forms an acceptably sharp image (critical focus) when focused at infinity.

The camera gate is positioned to hold film in the focal plane. For video cameras, the imaging device sits at the focal plane.

> NOTE: When the lens is focused at a point closer than infinity, what is commonly called the *focal plane* is more correctly called the *image plane*, though few people make this distinction.

2. The area before the camera that is in perfect focus in the resulting image, often thought of as a flat plane perpendicular to and out a certain distance from, the lens. The area nearer to and farther from the lens than the focal plane that is still in acceptable focus bounds the image depth of field. *See* **film plane.** *Compare* **image plane.**

focal point *See* **rear focal point.**

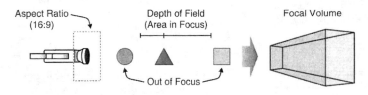

focal volume The area within a scene that is in focus. When recorded by a camera, this is taken to be a truncated pyramid with the sides established by the image aspect ratio and depth equal to the depth of field. *Compare* **horopter.**

focus **1.** The relative clarity of an image, typically ranging from soft to sharp. **2.** The process of collecting light that starts at a single point in space and directing it into a single point in an image. **3.** One of the parameters of binocular symmetry. In a stereogram, the left- and right-eye images differ due to horizontal disparity (parallax), but may share a number of other characteristics, including color, geometry, illumination, registration, and temporal symmetry.

focus accommodation *See* **accommodation.**

focus-fixation mismatch *See* **fixation-focus conflict.**

focus mismatch Differing levels of image sharpness (focus) in the left- and right-eye images of a stereogram, because either the camera lenses were not focused properly before recording the images or the focus was adjusted during a shot and both lenses were not adjusted in perfect synchronization. This can interfere with image fusion and the 3D effect. *Compare* **focal length mismatch.**

FOD *See* **field of depth.**

folded cone method A technique for calculating the size, location, and orientation of the bounce mirror(s) when constructing a rear-projection mirror rig.

The throw distance is first calculated to produce the desired width image given a particular projector (and lens). These measurements describe a conical projection beam that will produce the desired image, which can be represented in two dimensions as an isosceles triangle with the base equal to the image width, the height equal to the throw distance, and the narrow point originating at the optical center of the projection lens. Next, this triangle is cut out of paper at a reduced scale and folded as necessary to connect the projector to the screen using a matching scale diagram of the available space, bypassing any physical obstacles that might be in the way.

Each fold in the triangle represents a mirror, with the angle and length of the fold describing the mirror's angle and size, respectively. The mirrors need not be at 45° to the central axis of the pro-

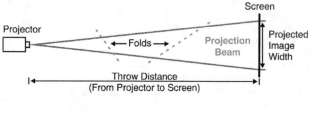

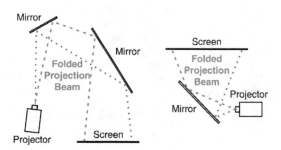

jection beam and can be rotated along two axes simultaneously to position the final image above or below the projector. *Compare* **bounce mirror; mirror rig.**

folding frequency *See* **Nyquist frequency.**

foot lambert; footlambert A measure of reflected light volume (the light reflected from a diffusing surface such as a theatrical movie screen); one lumen per square foot.

Common foot-lambert readings include:
- Consumer-grade 27" CRT-based television: maximum 30 foot lamberts without blooming.
- Consumer-grade projection video system: about 10 foot lamberts.
- Standard (2D) film projector on a white screen: 16 foot lamberts with an open gate.
- Digital cinema projection system on a white screen: 14 foot lamberts.
- Passive polarized 3D theatrical projection system: 35–60 foot lamberts with an open gate, 3.5–5.5 with the polarized filters in place (depending on the 3D system employed).

force feedback A physical sense of resistance to a virtual reality system user's actions, including strength, direction, and torque. *Compare* **haptic; tactile feedback.**

forced perspective An in-camera effect that makes objects appear larger or smaller than they actually are by adjusting their size and distance from the camera. Binocular depth cues generally conflict with forced perspective, limiting its use in stereoscopic works.

fore window image A visual element in a stereogram that appears to be within the audience space in front of the screen. If a fore window image is cut off by the edge of the screen, this may interfere with the 3D effect. *Compare* **floating edge.**

format A standard for analog or digital data recording, transmission, and display such as ATSC, D1, IMAX, etc. *Compare* **3D format.**

formatting *See* **encoding.**

4D; 4-D A 3D work presented with live, in-theater special effects to enhance the viewing experience. The live effects are synchronized with the 3D presentation, such as the smoke and laser light effects that accompanied *Captain EO* (1986), to the water, air, and rat-tail effects that accompany *R.L. Stine's Haunted Lighthouse* (2003). For *Haunted Lighthouse*, the rat tail is a thin rubber tube that extends from under each chair, whipping back and forth against the back of each audience member's legs to simulate the feel of a rat's tail during a segment when a hoard of rats appears on screen.

4K Digital video with a maximum resolution of 4,096 horizontal pixels and 3,112 vertical pixels (when scanned from 35mm film), or 4096 × 2160 for digital cinema. *Compare* **2K.**

4-perf; four-perf; ~ film stock The traditional 35mm film arrangement with four perforations (sprocket holes) per image frame. The film image may be of any aspect ratio and filmed with spherical or anamorphic lenses. *Compare* **2-perf.**

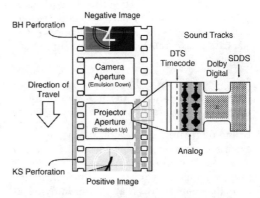

The traditional arrangement of 35mm Academy aperture 4-perf film. Note that the sound track areas are empty in the camera original negative.

45/135; 45/225 The most common orthogonal angles for cross-angled polarization, with one eye's polarization angle set at 45° off the vertical and the other eye rotated clockwise 90° to 135°. (May also be expressed as being rotated counterclockwise to 225°.)

FOV *See* **field of view.**

fovea; ~ centralis; retinal ~ A small depression in the retina at the center of the macula containing closely-packed cones, covering about 3° of the full visual field but responsible for ½ of all of the visual information registered by the eye; the portion of the eye that registers sharp, full-color images. The fovea is used to register images while reading, watching movies, whacking things that you want to eat with a rock, etc. *Compare* **macula.**

FPD *See* **far point distance; flat panel display.**

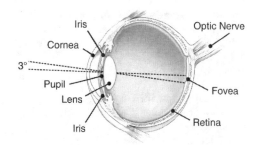

Fovea. National Eye Institute, National Institutes of Health).

FPS; fps *See* **fields per second; frames per second.**

fractal *See* **compression.**

frame-compatible; ~ 3D; ~ encoding A stereogram recording format that allows both the left- and right-eye images to be presented in a single standard image frame. *See* **anaglyph; half-resolution.**

frame magnification The ratio of screen width to image sensor width. An important factor in stereoscopic calculations.

frame of reference The objects in an image against which motion is judged. Since all motion is relative, to register that an object is moving, it must be compared to other elements in the visual field that appear to be at rest or moving at different rates or directions than the object of interest.

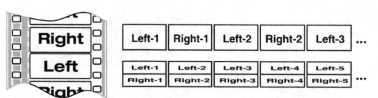

The left/right frame pair in a 35mm film-based over/under format (left) and the conceptual sequence of left/right video frames in a frame-sequential format (top right) compared to a frame-compatible over/under video sequence (bottom right).

frame pair The two frames that make up a stereogram when the left- and right-eye images are recorded in consecutive frames rather than combined and presented in a single frame.

frame rate The number of times complete image frames are recorded or presented each second in a display system, expressed in frames per second or fps. *Compare* **refresh rate.**

frame-sequential; ~ 3D *See* **time-sequential.**

frame splitter *See* **beam splitter.**

frames per second; fps The rate at which complete images are recorded or presented in a display system.

The threshold in human vision where a series of flashing images appears to deliver steady motion is around 50 images per second, depending on the amount of ambient light present. For sound film, the most common speed is 24 fps. To avoid visible flicker, film projectors generally employ two- or three-blade shutters so that each single frame is flashed on screen two or three times in a row to deliver 48 or 72 images per second. Contemporary progressive scan video displays often present the same frame multiple times in a row, leading to refresh rates of 120 Hz or 240 Hz even though the content is still only running at 30 frames per second.

Also **frame rate.** *Compare* **fields per second.**

free-viewing; freevision; binocular ~ A method for perceiving depth in a stereogram without special eyewear by adjusting the vergence of one's eyes.

There are two different methods of free-viewing: cross-eyed and parallel. In cross-eyed viewing, two separate images are prepared so the left-eye image is to the right and the right-eye image is to the left. The viewer crosses her eyes until the two images align and 3D depth is perceived. (If one uses the cross-eyed method on traditional stereograms, their depths will be reversed — far objects will be brought near and near objects will appear far.) In parallel viewing, the images are prepared so the left- and right-eye images are offset left and right, respectively. To perceive 3D depth, the viewer de-focuses her eyes to bring them parallel to each other, as if looking at a distant object beyond the surface of the image. Parallel free-viewing was made famous in the 1990s by Magic Eye, Inc., which holds a patent on the process for producing a planar image that contains a hidden 3D image that can only be seen by parallel or cross-eyed free-viewing.

French tissue *See* **tissue stereocard.**

frequency of light The number of complete light waves that pass a fixed point in one second. The perceived color of light is derived from its frequency, ranging from approximately 405–480

THz (red) to 689–789 THz (violet), where a THz (terahertz) is equal to 10^{12} (1,000,000,000,000) cycles per second.

Visible light is the portion of the electromagnetic spectrum that can be registered with the human eye and interpreted by the brain as light. Visible light ranges in color from violet (with a wavelength of 380–435 nanometers, measured in a vacuum) to red (with a wavelength of 625–740 nanometers) with shades of blue, cyan, green, yellow, and orange in between. Electromagnetic energy outside the visible spectrum includes radio waves, microwaves, gamma rays, ultraviolet (black light — just above the visible spectrum), and infrared (just below the visible spectrum).

NOTE: The exact range of the visible spectrum is subjective and depends on the quality of the observer's vision. Similarly, the frequency ranges of the named colors, violet through red, are also subjective and vary from one published source to the next. The frequencies provided here are approximate, and were calculated from the wavelengths according to the formula f equals c divided by λ, where f is the frequency, c is the speed of light (299,792,458 meters/second), and λ is the wavelength.

See **visible light** diagram in the color section.

front projection An image projection configuration where the projector and audience are both on the same side of the screen and the audience views a reflected image. All else being equal, front projection is brighter than rear screen projection and is the most common arrangement for theatrical exhibition.

Any object that comes between the projector and the screen will occlude the light beam path and cast a shadow on the screen, so front projection may not be suitable for certain public space, theme park, or virtual reality applications. In polarized 3D applications, the front projection screen surface must not change the polarization state of the reflected light, so silver screens are used in place of standard white screens. With circular polarized light, the reflected light will have the opposite handedness of the projected light — projected left circular polarization becomes reflected right circular polarization — which must be taken into account when matching the polarized lenses in the viewer's eyewear to the polar-

ization of the projection system. Linear polarized light is not affected.
Compare **rear projection.**

front silvered mirror; front surface mirror A mirror with the reflective material applied to the side from which it is viewed, rather than on the back side as is the case with traditional household mirrors. This produces an optically precise mirror and avoids the slight double images that are common with rear-silvered mirrors (caused when light is reflected off both the top glass surface and the lower reflective surface). Front silvered mirrors are particularly susceptible to damage and difficult to clean. To maintain optimal performance, such mirrors may have to be resurfaced periodically. *Also* **first surface mirror.**

frustum A three-dimensional slice between two parallel planes taken from a cone or pyramid. *See* **perspective frustum; view frustum.**

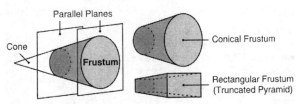

The focal volume of a recorded image is described by a rectangular frustum where the shape of the base is determined by the image aspect ratio and the near and far planes are the near and far edges of the depth of field.

frustum effect A type of Z-depth keystone distortion where objects appear to grow larger with increasing distance. The near side of a cube parallel to the stereo base will appear smaller than the far side, contrary to the normal rules of perspective.

full-color anaglyph *See* **anaglyph, full-color.**

full-frame stereo; full-resolution; ~ 3D; ~ encoding A stereoscopic system that records and presents separate high-definition images for each eye — generally progressively scanned video images with 1,080 lines of resolution per eye image (2 × 1080p) or 35mm motion picture film where each stereoscopic image pair spans eight perforations rather than the standard four. *Compare* **half-resolution; time-sequential.**

full HD; ~ 3D; ~ encoding Full-frame stereo where each eye image is recorded in high-definition video, generally 1920 × 1080 pixels each.

full reverse stereo *See* **pseudostereo.**

fundamental disparity The fact that when viewing a stereoscopic work, accommodation (focal distance) is held constant while vergence (the inward turning of the eyes to track objects at different distances) changes, contrary to natural vision where the two change together. *Compare* **accommodation/vergence reflex.**

fused views *See* **fusion.** *Compare* **irregular fusion.**

fusible range *See* **depth budget.**

fusion; binocular ~ The process performed by the brain that combines separate but overlapping 2D left- and right-eye images into a single 3D representation. Binocular fusion can be divided into sensoric fusion, the neural process performed on images registered near the center of the retina, and motoric fusion, the physical movement of the eyes (vergence) to align images of interest with the center of the retina. *Compare* **irregular fusion; Panum's fusion area.**

fusional reserves Excess convergence and divergence capacity within an individual's vision system leading to the ability to maintain image fusion and focus over time without experiencing discomfort. Low reserves can lead to difficulty concentrating on close work and may cause headaches, inspiring one to avoid close viewing. May affect adults, though children are particularly susceptible.

gain A signal amplification factor measured as the ratio of the output signal level to the input signal level, expressed either in decibels or as a percentage of a standard reference value, where 1.00 equates to zero gain. Gain is usually measured at a single frequency and assumed to be level throughout the operational band.

gaze *See* **viewer's gaze.**

GB3D *See* **glasses-based 3D display.**

genlock error A timing mismatch between the cameras' shutters when recording a motion stereogram resulting in the left and right shutters not opening and closing in perfect synchronization. *Compare* **sync error.**

geometric camera parameters *See* **camera parameters.**

geometric distortion Unequal magnification or reduction across an image, including barrel, keystone, mustache, and pincushion distortion.
  Stereoscopic keystone distortion is a common side effect of using toed-in cameras. This distortion may be corrected in post-production to avoid

image fusion issues when the stereogram is presented for viewing.
See **geometric distortion** images in the color section

geometric perspective *Also* **linear perspective.** *See* **perspective.** *Compare* **monocular cue.**

geometrical mismatch A failure for the shapes of objects viewed by each eye to align properly when they are viewed as a stereogram, excluding differences that can be accounted for by image parallax. *See* **geometric distortion.**

geometry 1. Collectively, the size, shape, and position of an object. 2. One of the parameters of binocular symmetry. In a stereogram, the left- and right-eye images differ due to horizontal disparity (parallax), but may share a number of other characteristics, including color, focus, illumination, registration, and temporal symmetry.

gesture A hand motion that can be interpreted by a virtual reality system as a sign, signal, or symbol.

ghost busting The process of adjusting a stereoscopic recording during post-production or presentation to eliminate ghosting.

ghost edge; ghost area *See* **monocular area.**

ghosting When one eye inadvertently sees some part of a stereoscopic image intended for the other eye, resulting in an apparent double exposure; a subjective measure of crosstalk. May be caused by incomplete channel separation during stereoscopic encoding, presentation (a problem with projection or display), or reception (a defect in the selection device, such as an active eyewear lens that remains open too long during each cycle). Most noticeable around areas of sharp contrast, such as the bright highlights caused by streetlamps at night or sunlight reflecting off metal. *Compare* **channel separation; crosstalk; stereo extinction ratio.**

Gibbs phenomenon A mathematical property of Fourier series (common to many digital compression algorithms) that contributes to ringing artifacts. *Compare* **color ringing; depth ringing.**

gigantism; giantism A stereoscopic effect where an object appears unnaturally large. Caused by recording an image with too narrow an interaxial distance (the separation between the cameras' lens axes) given the lens focal length. Tools exist to help calculate the optimal interaxial distance for the recording cameras given a set of image and display characteristics. *Compare* **hypostereo; Lilliputism; stereomacroscopy.**

gimmick movie A pejorative for a work that lacks originality and/or creativity and survives because of its marketing, such as many of the 3D movies from the 1950s.

William Castle was known for his gimmick movies, such as *The Tingler* (1959), where theater seats vibrated when the titular Tingler appeared on screen; *Macabre* (1958), when audience members were insured for $1,000 with Lloyds of London in the event that they suffered death by fright; and *13 Ghosts* (1960), which included hidden images that could only be seen using the provided hand-held viewer. *13 Ghosts* did not include stereoscopic effects, though Castle did produced three 3D films in his career: *Fort Ti* (1953), *Jesse James vs. the Daltons* (1954), and *Drums of Tahiti* (1954) (courtesy Heritage Auctions, www.ha. com).

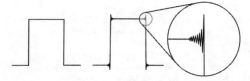

Gibbs phenomenon. When a signal with a jump discontinuity (as may be caused by the abrupt change from one color to another in a digital image) is processed using a Fourier series, the resulting representation overshoots the jump and oscillates briefly before settling at the new level. The greater the amount of discontinuity, the greater the amount of overshoot. In this example, a square wave (left) is represented by a Fourier series (right). The enlarged area shows the signal aberration caused by the Gibbs phenomenon.

glasses Spectacles worn for stereoscopic viewing equipped with special lenses for anaglyph, polarized, or active stereo viewing. *Compare* **eyewear; head-mounted display.**

glasses-based 3D display; GB3D The general class of stereoscopic displays that require the use of special eyewear to perceive the 3D effect, including passive eyewear (such as anaglyph, polarized, and ChromaDepth) and active eyewear (such as liquid crystal shutters). *Compare* **auto-stereoscopic.**

glasses-free; glassless *Also* **non-glasses-based 3D display.** *See* **auto-stereoscopic.**

glitter *See* **sparkle.**

global shutter An image acquisition scheme where the entire image is exposed at a single instant in time rather than recording individual scan lines in sequence. Typical of CCD-based video cameras and most film cameras. *Compare* **rolling shutter.**

go with the flow A rough rule of thumb for use when recording sequential stereograms to help reduce unwanted image differences due to motion in the recorded scene. Generally, sequential stereograms (produced using a single camera to record first the left-eye image then the right-eye image, or vice versa) only work if there is no motion in the scene (such as with stop-motion photography, where the technique is used extensively). However, if there are slow moving objects in the scene (such as clouds in the sky), the negative effects can be diminished by moving the camera in the direction of the movement between exposures.

GPU *See* **graphics processing unit.**

graininess A speckled or mottled effect made up of small, random variations in luminance or chrominance typical of the irregularly sized clumps of metallic silver in developed photographic film. Since grain is inconsistent from one image frame to the next and between the different eye images in a stereogram, it can interfere with the perception of fine gradations in depth.

graphical overlay Visual material added to an image at display time, such as pop-up menus in a home entertainment playback system. With stereoscopic playback, graphical overlays should be adjusted for depth so they do not obstruct objects that extend into the audience space.

graphics processing unit; GPU A microprocessor dedicated to the mathematically intense calculations associated with the visual presentation of computer-generated imagery and so-phisticated 2D or 3D image manipulation, generally located on a video display adapter or graphics accelerator. A dedicated GPU frees up the primary processor in an electronic device (the central processing unit, or CPU) for other tasks. *Also* **visual processing unit.**

H.264 The ITU-T (International Telecommunications Union) designation for the digital video encoding standard jointly developed with ISO/IEC, first released in 2003. *See* **MPEG-4 AVC.** *Compare* **VC-1.**

half-color anaglyph *See* anaglyph, half-color. *Compare* optimized anaglyph.

half-gain viewing angle The angle with respect to the surface of a screen at which the reflected light level is half its peak value when measured at an angle perpendicular to the screen. Someone watching a projected image at the half-gain viewing angle will see an image that is half as bright as a viewer sitting directly in front of the screen. Low-gain screens have wider half-gain viewing angles than high-gain screens, which translates into a larger acceptable viewing area. *Compare* **peak gain at zero degrees viewing axis.**

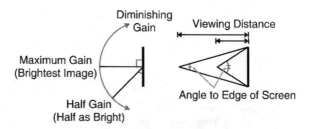

Half-gain viewing angle. As the angle of view moves away from the perpendicular, the brightness diminishes (left), until the half-gain viewing angle is reached. The exact angle is dependent on the type of screen. This can limit how far from center one may wish to site with a high-gain screen. The screen gain also differs across the surface of the screen (right), with the brightest area directly in front of the viewer and then falling off as the angle increases towards the edges of the screen. The closer one is to the screen and the higher the screen gain, the greater the angle and the more pronounced the difference in illumination across the surface. This can limit how close one sits to a high-gain screen.

half-resolution; ~ 3D; ~ encoding An image that only uses half of the available horizontal or vertical frame; stereoscopic encoding where the left- and right-eye images are both included in a single frame with each eye image taking up only half of the available space. This allows both left- and right-eye information to be encoded in a format that can be processed, recorded, and trans-

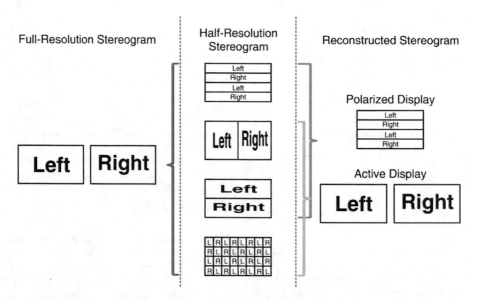

Full-resolution stereograms are most commonly encoded as (from top to bottom in the center column) row-interleaved, side-by-side, over/under, and checkerboard. Row-interleaved is best suited to polarized displays and checkerboard to active displays, while side-by-side and over/under can be used with either polarized or active displays.

mitted using standard 2D systems and techniques, though a specialized display is required for final stereogram presentation. *Also* **split-resolution.** *See* **frame-compatible.** *Compare* **full HD; interlaced; mux/demux workflow.**

hand-held media Audiovisual content that is intended to be viewed on a device that can be held in the user's hand, such as a cell phone or PDA.

handedness *Also* **chirality.** *See* **polarization handedness.**

handover The process of making visual adjustments to smooth the transition between shots at a cut point. *See* **convergence animation.**

haptic Pertaining to the sense of touch. *Compare* **force feedback; tactile feedback.**

hard window violation An edge violation involving a visually distinctive object with negative parallax intersecting the stereo window edge. *Compare* **legal window violation; soft window violation.**

HD *See* **hi-def.**

HDMI High-Definition Multimedia Interface, a secure digital interface standard using a single all-in-one connector for audiovisual devices that supports video, audio, and data. Supplanted DVI (digital video interface) in the consumer electronics industry. In Europe, HDMI is often called "digital SCART" in reference to its replacement of the analog SCART interface. When connecting a Blu-ray 3D player to a display device, HDMI 1.4 (released in June 2009) or newer is required for the presentation of full-resolution stereoscopic images. The HDMI Web site is www.hdmi.org.

head box The volume of space within which a viewer's head must be placed in order to perceive

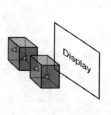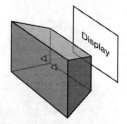

A stereoscopic display with two distinct head boxes (left) as might be found with an auto-stereoscopic display and a display with a single, large head box as might be found with an active display.

a full stereoscopic effect; the sweet spot. A particular display technology may have one or more separate head boxes.

head-mounted display; helmet-mounted display; HMD; head-mounted binocular display; HMBD A stereoscopic imaging device that ensures that the two separate left- and right-eye images are sent to the correct eye by mounting a separate display in front of each eye. The displays are attached to a pair of glasses or to a helmet worn by the viewer. Often used with virtual reality simulation systems, though the long-term close vision accommodation required by HMDs can lead to visual fatigue. *Compare* **glasses.**

head-on shot A shot composed so that the action moves directly towards the camera. Popular in 3D photography as it shows off the 3D effect and gives the filmmaker an opportunity to startle the audience. The Lumières' 2D actuality *Arrivée d'un Train en Gare* (*Arrival of a Train at the Station*, 1896) may represent the first use of a head-on shot.

head tilt The angle of a viewer's head with respect to the horizontal. With certain linear polarization and auto-stereoscopic systems, the 3D effect can be lost if viewers tilt their heads too far to the side. Cross-angled linear polarization is less susceptible to head tilt than strictly vertical/horizontal linear polarization, but circular polarization is immune to head tilt, so it is generally preferred over linear polarization even though it does not deliver as sharp an image. Note, however, that as viewers tilt their heads, horizontal parallax translates into vertical parallax and the 3D effect is lost even though each eye is still receiving the correct image.

head tracking Monitoring the position and orientation of the viewer's head. Common to virtual reality and certain auto-stereoscopic display systems. May be used to adjust the display's sweet spot for improved viewing. *Compare* **eye tracking; tracking.**

head-up display *See* **HUD.**

headset *See* **head-mounted display.**

height error *See* **vertical disparity.**

helmet-mounted display *See* **head-mounted display.**

hemianopia The loss of half of the field of vision in one or both eyes.

hero eye *See* **primary eye.**

hi-def; HD High definition; audiovisual image resolution or fidelity that is a significant improvement over the present industry standard. Today's standard definition was yesterday's high definition. For contemporary video, high definition implies significantly greater than the NTSC or PAL standards of 480 or 576 lines of active picture resolution, respectively–generally 720–1080 lines with a 16 × 9 aspect ratio. *Also* **high resolution.**

high contrast A significant and abrupt change in brightness levels between adjacent areas within an image. Areas of high contrast and non-zero parallax in a stereogram often cause ghosting in the perceived image, with the brighter areas from one eye image appearing over the darker areas in the alternate eye.

high-gain screen A screen that reflects significantly more projected light than a standard reference white surface coated with magnesium oxide. The standard reference has a screen gain of 1.0, so anything above 1.0 should be high gain, but screens do not generally exhibit the visual artifacts associated with high gain until they exceed 1.3 (30 percent more reflected light than the standard), so high gain tends to be anything over 1.3.

High-gain screens reflect more light in a narrower angle than low-gain screens, so they produce brighter images but have smaller viewing areas. They also tend to show a visible drop in illumination moving out from the center of the projected area, which may result in a noticeable hot spot, and do not generally reflect all wavelengths of light evenly, causing a visible color shift when viewed from different angles.

Because of their drawbacks, high-gain screens are limited to special applications that require bright images, including venues with high levels of ambient light, such as classrooms, and polarized stereoscopic projection, where each eye is only receiving half the projected light. *Compare* **screen gain; silver screen.**

high-mode *See* **over-slung.** *Compare* **under-slung.**

high resolution *See* **hi-def.**

HIT *See* **horizontal image translation.**

HIT point *See* **zero disparity plane.**

HMBD *See* **head-mounted binocular display.**

HMD *See* **head-mounted display.**

HOE *See* **holographic optical element.**

Holmes; ~ card; ~ format; ~ stereocard; ~ stereoview An arrangement for presenting side-by-side still image stereograms, developed by American physician Oliver Wendell Holmes, Sr. c. 1860. Holmes format stereocards are typically 7" × 3½" with nearly square stereo images that are classically, but not necessarily, cropped into an arch along their upper edge. Less common Holmes formats include cabinet cards (4" tall), deluxe cards (4½" tall), and imperial cards 4¾"–5" tall). Because the image centers are farther apart than the average human eyes, Holmes stereoscopes include (generally prismatic) lenses to bend light and reposition the images for viewing.

A Holmes format stereocard with images by Stanley J. Morrow, featuring three Hidatsa Indians. Most likely taken on the Fort Berthold Reservation, North Dakota between 1868 and 1881 (courtesy Heritage Auctions, www.ha.com).

Holmes stereoscope; Holmes/Bates stereoscope A hand-held, open-framework stereoscope design originally developed by American physician Oliver Wendell Holmes, Sr. in 1861 and later improved upon by American merchant Joseph L. Bates. Most examples include prismatic lenses

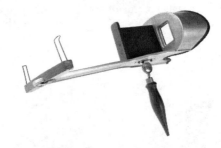

A Holmes/Bates stereoscope produced for the Paris Exposition Universelle of 1900. Key features added by Bates to the original Holmes design included the sliding card holder (left) to allow focus adjustments and the eye hood (right) to block ambient light (courtesy Heritage Auctions, www.ha.com).

that bend light, allowing one to view stereograms with centers wider than the distance between an average pair of human eyes.

hologram A single image recording of a 3D subject based on light-wave interference patterns. Unlike stereograms, holograms do not present separate left- and right-eye images. Holograms may be classed as auto-stereoscopic images since they represent depth without requiring special eyewear, but they do require special lighting and have a relatively narrow viewing angle. *Compare* **reflective hologram.**

holographic display An auto-stereoscopic device where the images presented are holograms. True holographic displays remain experimental and do not yet represent a practical technology. Some auto-stereoscopic systems may employ a holographic optical element (HOE), replacing a more complex optical component. *Compare* **3D display.**

holographic optical element; HOE A lens (transmission hologram) or mirror (reflection hologram) that can focus light, produced by rendering a holographic diffraction as a modulation pattern throughout the thickness of a thin film or as a surface relief on a thicker solid. HOEs can perform multiple functions at once, such as acting as a combined lens, filter, and diffuser. HOEs are relatively inexpensive and easy to produce compared to a conventional lens or mirror with the same optical properties.

holographic screen A projection screen with numerous, small holographic optical elements (HOEs) covering its surface.

holography; laser ~ The process used to produce a hologram; a type of 3D photography where laser light diffraction is used to produce a 3D picture on a 2D photographic plate.

A holographic image is composed of light-wave interference patterns. The interference patterns are created by splitting the beam from a laser, sending half to the subject (the object beam) and half directly to the photographic plate (the reference beam). The light reflected off the subject recombines with the light that went directly to the plate, creating a unique pattern of light-wave interference. After the recorded image is processed, the appearance of a 3D subject can be recreated by illuminating the photographic image with another laser beam.

HoloVizio The trade name for a line of auto-stereoscopic (glasses-free) 3D displays produced by Holografika Ltd. of Budapest, Hungary. HoloVizio displays support multiple, simultane-ous viewers over a wide field of view. The image voxels (three-dimensional pixels) project beams of light of different colors and intensity in different directions, providing multiple angles of view of the same scene that change based on the position of the observer. The Holografika Web site is www.holografika.com.

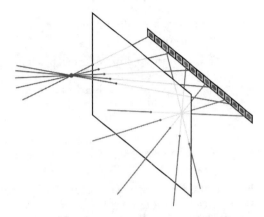

A particular light emitter may illuminate one or more voxels at a time, while each voxel is generally illuminated by more than one emitter at a time. This combination produces images of an object as it would appear when viewed from multiple angles and the perception of three-dimensional depth without special viewing glasses.

home ecosystem A completely integrated system of electronic devices and communications networks within the home, including home automation, lighting control, security, communications, appliances, and entertainment systems.

home 3D The consumer-focused market for in-home stereoscopic viewing, including display systems and content.

home use Intended for use at home by the normal circle of a family and its social acquaintances.

homologous points; homologues *See* **conjugate points.**

horizontal disparity; horizontal parallax The horizontal distance between conjugate points in the left- and right-eye image pair that makes up a stereogram. Only disparity in the same plane as the viewer's eyes (generally assumed to be horizontal) contributes to depth perception. Too much horizontal disparity can interfere with 3D image fusion, leading to viewer discomfort and double vision. *See* **parallax.** *See* **horizontal disparity** diagram in color section.

horizontal image translation; HIT A change in the relative horizontal position of the left- and right-eye images that make up a stereogram, performed to change the distance between conjugate points and thereby adjust the perceived depth in the images. Affects all conjugate points in the image by an equal amount.

> NOTE: *Convergence* is often used to mean *horizontal image translation.*

Compare **convergence animation; convergence ramp; depth warping.**

horizontal overscan Surplus horizontal pixels in a digital image. If each eye image in a recorded stereogram is wider than the finished aspect ratio, then the surplus width may be used to adjust the image disparity.

horizontal scale factor The distance between pixel columns in an imaging grid; the width of a pixel. *Compare* **intrinsic camera parameters.**

horizontal viewing angle The figure formed by extending a line from the center of the viewer's gaze to the surface of the screen, measured in relation to its horizontal offset from a line perpendicular to the surface of the screen. For simplicity, generally measured from the center of the viewer's gaze to the center of the screen. Certain 3D display technologies, such as lenticular displays, have a limited horizontal viewing angle, while others, such as line-interlaced polarized displays, have a limited vertical viewing angle. *See* diagram at **vertical viewing angle.**

horizontally interlaced display *Also* **line-interlaced display.** *See* **polarized display.** *Compare* **row-interleaved.**

horopter The curved surface within a binocular field of view where the two images from an object fall on corresponding locations on the two retinas, resulting in a region of zero image disparity and parallax.

> The physical size and position of the horopter depends on the vergence of the observer's eyes. When the eyes are directed at a near object, disparity increases rapidly with distance, narrowing the horopter to a curved plane. When the eyes are directed at a distant object, disparity increases slowly with distance, extending the horopter into a 3D volume.

See **Vieth-Müller circle.** *Compare* **focal volume; Panum's fusion area.**

hot spot An area within an image that is noticeably brighter than the surrounding area, such as is often found in the center of high-gain screens. The intensity of reflected light varies with the angle of reflection, so the hot spot on a high-gain

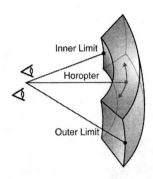

The horopter extends vertically and horizontally in front of the eyes, creating a roughly spherical surface of zero parallax in front of the head. Surrounding the horopter is the region of clear single binocular vision (Panum's fusion area), where left- and right-eye images are fused by the brain to create a single image. Any closer or farther away and the individual eye images cannot be fused, resulting in double vision. (If the eyes are set parallel, then there is no outer limit and the single vision region extends to infinity.)

screen will move based on the relative position of the observer. *Compare* **screen gain.**

hourglass distortion; hourglassing A type of pincushion distortion where straight lines bow inward toward the center of the image more in the horizontal direction than vertical, deforming squares into the shape of an hourglass. The amount of hourglass distortion is generally expressed as a percentage of the overall picture width.

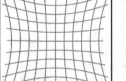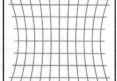

Pincushion distortion (left) compared to hourglass distortion (right).

HUD; head-up display A system that creates an image that seems to float in space before the viewer. The projected image is generally not three-dimensional, but instead overlays and is seen along with the natural 3D world. Originally developed for military aviation to allow pilots to see flight status information without looking down at the instrument panel. Now found in some passenger cars, where instrument data seem to float in space beyond the windshield. *Compare* **augmented reality; holographic display.**

hue The shade of a particular color independent of brightness and saturation. Determined by the dominant wavelength of visible light and judged according to its similarity to one of the perceived colors red, yellow, green, and blue, or some combination. The shades of gray, ranging from black to white, do not have hue. *Also* **tint.** *Compare* **saturation; value.** *See* **color** diagram in the color section.

human factors The application of physical and psychological human capabilities and limitations to the design, construction, and implementation of devices, systems, and services. *Also* **ergonomics.**

human vision *See* **binocular vision.**

human vision system; HVS The components of the human body that receive light and interpret it as images, principally the eyes, optic nerves, and the vision centers of the brain.

hunting time *See* **stereoscopic latency.**

hybrid eyewear; hybrid glasses Spectacles that can be used to view both polarized and time-sequential stereograms. Essentially, a pair of active (shutter) spectacles with appropriately polarized lenses. *Compare* **active eyewear; passive eyewear; spectral eyewear.**

hyper-convergence When an object in a stereogram is too close to the viewer (too much negative parallax) for proper image fusion, requiring the eyes to converge excessively (cross-eyed) and resulting in visual discomfort or double vision — generally anything closer than half the distance from the viewer to the screen. Most often caused by recording objects set too close to the camera or by using too sharp an angle of convergence with toed-in cameras. *Compare* **stereo distance.**

hyper-divergence When an object in a stereogram is too far from the viewer (too much positive parallax) for proper image fusion, requiring the eyes to diverge more than 1° beyond parallel (wall-eyed) and resulting in visual discomfort or double vision — generally anything farther than twice the distance from the viewer to the screen. Most often caused by using too much divergence with toed-in cameras or by using a very long focal length lens. *Compare* **stereo distance.**

hyperfocal distance The space from the imaging plane to the nearest object in acceptably sharp focus when the lens' focal distance is set to infinity. All objects at or beyond the hyperfocal distance will be in focus at the same time. An important factor when establishing image depth of field.

hypermetropia The ability to focus clearly on distant objects but not on close objects. *Also* **far sighted.** *Compare* **myopia; presbyopia.**

hyperphoria *See* **strabismus.**

hyperstereo; hyper Using an interaxial distance that is larger than the interocular distance of the nominal viewer when recording a stereogram. This enhances stereo depth while reducing apparent image scale, causing objects to appear as if they are unusually small. May be used when recording landscapes or to draw attention to depth details in architectural applications. *Compare* **hypostereo; Lilliputism.**

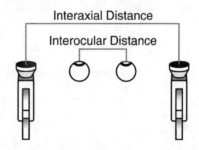

With hyperstereo, the interaxial distance is greater than the average interocular distance.

hypostereo; hypo Using an interaxial distance that is smaller than the interocular distance of the nominal viewer when recording a stereogram. This increases apparent image scale, causing objects to appear as if they are unusually large. May be used when filming miniatures to make them appear full scale. *Also* **macro stereo.** *Compare* **gigantism; hyperstereo; stereomacroscopy.**

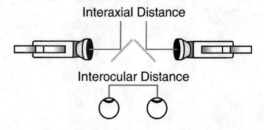

With hypostereo, the interaxial distance is smaller than the average interocular distance.

IA *See* **interaxial.** *Compare* **interocular.**

IAD *See* **interaxial distance.** *Compare* **interocular distance.**

IDR pulse A visual anomaly caused when an MPEG-4 AVC digital video decoder restarts itself in response to an instantaneous decoder refresh (IDR) instruction, such as when switching from one video source to another. An IDR pulse is always followed by a new I-frame. The decoder takes longer to process the frame following an IDR pulse than normal, causing a slight glitch in the smooth visual flow that is most visible in areas with relatively little motion. Generally more severe than I-frame breathing.

I-frame breathing Periodic visual anomalies that may occur when a digital video decoder processes an I-frame. I-frames take longer to process than P- or B-frames, which may cause a slight glitch in the smooth visual flow that is most visible in areas with relatively little motion. Generally not as severe as an IDR pulse.

IL; interleaved. *See* **row-interleaved.**

illumination 1. Lighting, both natural and artificial. **2.** One of the parameters of binocular symmetry. In a stereogram, the left- and right-eye images differ due to horizontal disparity (parallax), but may share a number of other characteristics, including color, focus, geometry, registration, and temporal symmetry. Proper balance between left- and right-eye stereogram image illumination helps reduce eye fatigue.

image A visual recording of an instant in time (a photograph on film, a frame recorded by a video process, a synthetic scene created by a computer graphics system, etc.) or a presentation of such a recording on a surface (on a movie screen, a television, a computer monitor, etc.). Motion pictures, whether recorded on film or video, are made up of a series of still images presented in quick succession that the brain interprets as being in motion. A 3D image recorded using a stereoscopic process is actually two (or more) separate left- and right-eye images that the brain fuses into a single 3D image.

image curvature *See* **depth plane curvature.**

image distortion *See* **stereoscopic distortion.** *Compare* **depth non-linearity, depth plane curvature, depth/size distortion, keystone distortion, shear distortion.**

image field A discrete portion of a single 2D image frame. A single image frame may be divided into two or more fields. The most common image fields are the odd and even fields that comprise an interlaced image, divided so that the odd scan lines are in one field and the even scan lines are in the other.

image flipping The quick transition from correct stereo to pseudostereo that may occur when the observer moves outside the viewing zone of certain auto-stereoscopic or polarized displays, causing the left-eye image to be seen by the right eye and vice versa. With auto-stereoscopic displays, this may be caused by moving too far to one side, while with certain polarized displays this may be caused by moving too high or low. *Also* **left/right inversion.**

image format The standard specification for the electronic representation of an image, particularly a computer image when saved to disk or residing in memory.

image frame A complete representation of a single 2D image. A film image frame is exposed in a single instant of time. A video image frame is divided into scan lines, which may be recorded and presented sequentially. A video image frame may be further divided into image fields.

image pair The set of 2D left- and right-eye images that make up a single stereoscopic view. *Also* **stereo pair.** *Compare* **stereogram; stereoscopic image pair.**

image parallax The horizontal angle between conjugate points when a stereoscopic image is presented on a particular size screen. An important factor in stereoscopic calculations.

image plane The flat surface in space where a lens forms an acceptably sharp image (critical focus) when focused at a point closer than infinity.
   NOTE: When the lens is focused at infinity, the *image plane* is more correctly called the *focal plane*. *Also* **imaging plane.** *Compare* **focal plane.**

image space The area that is perceived to be within a stereoscopic image as presented on a particular display. *Compare* **object space.**

image splitter *See* **beam splitter.**

imaging sensor width The horizontal dimension of a camera's image recording area. An important factor in stereoscopic calculations. For digital cameras, this is the width of the image sensor. For film cameras, this is the width of the exposed image on the film as defined by the camera's gate.

IMAX The trade name for a large-screen process originally developed using special 65mm film cameras and 70mm projectors with horizontal movements, now evolving towards digital image capture and presentation. The IMAX Web site is www.imax.com.
   Film-based IMAX uses frames 15 perforations wide (15/70) — 3 times larger than the standard

70mm film frame (5/70) and nearly 9 times larger than a 35mm film frame. The camera aperture aspect ratio (shooting on 65mm film) is 1.36:1, while the projector aperture is 1.43:1. IMAX theaters contain the largest fixed screens in use for theatrical presentations. The traditional IMAX installation includes a multi-story screen facing a stadium-style auditorium with the seats set on a 30°–45° slope to ensure each audience member has an unobstructed view.

More complex installations include the Magic Carpet Theater at the Futuroscope theme park outside Paris, France with one IMAX screen in front of the audience and an even larger IMAX screen beneath the audience, visible through the glass floor of the theater, delivering what was billed as a 180° view that immersed the audience in the program. The world's first 3D IMAX simulation ride, *Race for Atlantis* (1998), was projected on a 9-story tall hemispherical screen at Caesars Palace in Las Vegas, Nevada using a single projector 3D system and active eyewear. Other IMAX 3D programs use a more traditional polarized light system. *Compare* **OMNIMAX.**

immersive A 3D image that appears to surround the viewer, as with many virtual reality systems. A feeling of immersion arises when the field of view is greater than roughly 60°–90°. Often accomplished by using particularly large screens (to fill the visual field) or head-mounted displays (to change the image as the viewer moves his head). Theme park and virtual reality systems may achieve full immersion using wrap-around screens that surround the viewer. Such screens may be smoothly curved or composed of segmented flat surfaces.

immersive projected 3D *See* **virtual reality.**

impinge To make physical contact or collide with sharply. Often used to describe light striking (impinging upon) an object.

in phase Waves with the same frequency traveling in time with their peaks and troughs aligned. When waves combine in phase, the effect is additive, with the amplitude of the combined wave equal to the sum of the individual wave amplitudes. *Compare* **out of phase.**

induced effect An illusory slant that may be perceived in the Z-depth of an object's surface presented in a stereogram with vertical parallax.

infinity *See* **stereo infinity.**

Infitec *See* **Dolby 3D.** *Compare* **Panavision 3D.**

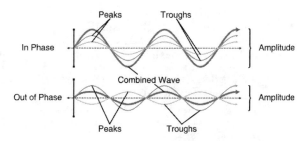

In phase. The same two waves are combined in each example. When they travel in phase (top), they combine to create a taller wave (their amplitudes add). When out of phase (bottom), they combine as a shorter wave (one wave subtracts from the other).

infrared; IR; ~ light Invisible energy in the infrared band of the electromagnetic spectrum (wavelengths ranging from 0.7 to 1,000 microns), located just below the red end of the visible spectrum and experienced to some extent as heat. Many wireless remote control units (such as traditional television remotes) use IR light signals to communicate with the device they control. *Compare* **ultraviolet; visible light.** *See* **infrared** diagram in color section.

ingest To bring media (audio, video, or metadata) into a digital system. This may include an analog to digital data conversion, transfer from tape- to disc-based storage, conversion from one digital format to another, etc.

inner orientation *See* **intrinsic camera parameters.**

instantaneous decoder refresh; instantaneous decoding refresh *See* **IDR pulse.**

integral display An auto-stereoscopic display where multiple pairs of left- and right-eye images are presented so that as the viewer moves vertically or horizontally, a different but valid pair of images is presented. This is far more complex than a multi-view display, where only horizontal viewing motion is supported, but more closely approximates a natural viewing experience. May use lenses to direct the images to the correct eye or parallax slit barriers to block the left image from the right eye and vice versa. *Compare* **3D display.**

inter-camera distance *See* **interaxial distance.**

inter-eye distance *See* **interocular distance.**

inter-lens separation *See* **interaxial distance.**

inter-optical center distance Interaxial distance. Coined in 2010 by French stereographer Bernard

Mendiburu to avoid confusion over the difference between *interaxial distance* (the separation between camera lenses) and *interocular distance* (the separation between the eyes).

interaxial; IA Literally, between axes. A comparison of some characteristic between two lenses, usually the interaxial distance in a stereoscopic camera system (the distance separating the optical axes of the two lenses).

Measuring the interaxial distance between stereoscopic camera lenses is easiest when the cameras are parallel: every point along the optical axes has the same IA. However, if the lenses are not parallel, then the IA will differ based on where it is measured. Optimal results are realized when measuring between the centers of the lenses' entrance pupils or rear focal points. This can be challenging as these positions differ for each lens design and move when the focal length is adjusted on a varifocal (zoom) lens.
Compare **interocular.**

interaxial convergence The point in space where the optical axes of two lenses in a stereoscopic camera system meet and beyond which begin to diverge when the lenses are toed-in from parallel.

The point of convergence is carefully controlled and, along with the interaxial distance, adjusted according to the focal length of the lenses, the distance to the subject, and the apparent scale desired. Interaxial convergence can cause geometric distortions in the recorded images, which must be corrected in post-production, but gives greater control over the presentation of depth than using parallel lenses. When presented, the point of interaxial convergence generally corresponds to the plane of the screen — objects closer to the camera than the point of convergence will appear to be between the viewer and the screen, while objects farther than the point of convergence will appear to be behind the screen.
Compare **plane of convergence.**

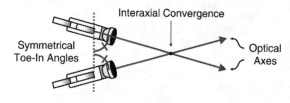

interaxial distance; IAD; IA; interaxial separation The horizontal space between the left and right cameras recording a stereogram. An important factor in stereoscopic calculations.

On average, the IAD is set between 50–70mm, or about 65mm/2½" (the approximate distance be-

tween the centers of the left and right eyes in an adult), though this is often adjusted depending on the distance between camera and subject and the focal length of the lenses.

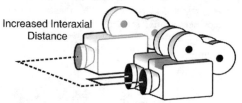

For parallel 3D camera systems, the IA is measured between the centers (optical axes) of the lenses. If the cameras' optical axes are not parallel, then the IAD is more accurately measured between the centers of the lenses' entrance pupils or rear focal points. The actual IA employed will vary depending on the subject being filmed. Long lenses tend to diminish the 3D effect, so to compensate, one typically increases the IA. For example, an aerial shot may use a 22" IA. One may also increase the IA in order to decrease the apparent sense of scale. For example, an entire city skyline can be given the feel of a miniature set by using a 6' IA.

NOTE: *Interocular distance* is often used synonymously with *interaxial distance*, but the two are technically different. Interocular refers to the distance between the eyes, while interaxial refers to the distance between the lenses in a stereoscopic system.

When using two interlinked cameras to record stereoscopic imagery, the physical size of the cameras and lenses may prevent achieving the proper IA. In such situations, one typically employs a beam splitter (50/50 two-way mirror) to divide the incoming image between two cameras. With this arrangement, the IA can be set to any desired size down to zero (images perfectly aligned).
Also **inter-lens separation; stereo base.** *Compare* **interocular distance; zero interaxial.**

interference filter A complex optical filter that blocks two or more color bands and passes the others.

The lenses in anaglyphic glasses are simple band-pass filters where each passes a single color band (in general, red or cyan). The Infitec filters used in Dolby 3D, however, are more complex interference filters where the left lens passes 629nm (red), 532nm (green), and 446nm (blue) light, absorbing or reflecting all other wavelengths, while the right lens passes 615nm (red), 518nm (green), and 432nm (blue) light. The performance of interference filter-based 3D systems is very dependent on the color balance of the projector lamp, increasing the importance of proper projector maintenance.

Also **spectral filtration; wavelength interference.** *Compare* **comb filter; Dolby 3D; Panavision 3D.** *See* **inference filler** diagram in color section.

interior orientation *See* **intrinsic camera parameters.**

interlace distortion Image aliasing visible in a progressive scan display that results from inadequate interlaced to progressive scan video conversion.

Simple de-interlacing combines the scan lines from the odd and even fields of interlaced video into a single progressive frame. However, if there is motion in the frame, then the image will change between the odd and even fields. When the two are combined, they will not line up, leading to jagged edges in the final image. More sophisticated de-interlacing examines the changes between frames over time and interpolates what a progressive scan image would have looked like, thus avoiding most interlace distortion.

interlaced A video image scanning pattern where half the image detail is captured or presented at a time, generally the odd numbered lines (the odd field) followed by the even numbered lines (the even field). This results in two fields per image frame.

Interlaced video equipment is generally easier to construct than progressive scan equipment and interlacing helps reduce visible flicker. However, since the subject may have moved during the time it takes to scan the two separate fields that make up each frame (field-level movement), interlaced video does not compress well and exhibits increased motion artifacts. As a result, most contemporary digital formats use progressive scan techniques.

In interlaced video, the first field for each frame contains the odd numbered scan lines from top to bottom of the image (1 through 525 for NTSC) while the second field contains the even numbered lines from top to bottom (2 through 524 for NTSC). When displaying video, an NTSC display draws one field approximately every 1/60 of a second. A PAL display draws one field every 1/50 of a second. (Video cameras follow a similar process when capturing the original images.)

Persistence of vision causes the human brain to combine the two alternating fields to create 29.97 whole NTSC frames per second (or 25 whole PAL frames). Again, persistence of vision causes the individual frames to blend together and create the illusion of motion.

Interlaced technology may also be used to present stereograms, where the first field carries the left-eye image and the second field carries the right-eye image or where alternating lines in progressive video carry the left- and right-eye images. This has the advantage of fitting the full stereogram in the same video bandwidth as a standard flat image (allowing the use of standard storage and delivery technologies), but each eye image has half the vertical resolution of the full composite image, thereby delivering reduced image quality when compared to full-resolution progressive scan techniques.
Compare **half-resolution.**

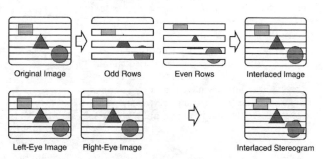

Original Image   Odd Rows   Even Rows   Interlaced Image

Left-Eye Image   Right-Eye Image   Interlaced Stereogram

In the first example (top row), a standard two-dimensional image is divided into scan lines then split into two fields — one with all the odd numbered rows and another with the even numbered rows. In the final display, the two fields are recombined to create an interlaced image. In the second example (bottom row), the two halves of a stereogram are divided into scan lines. More sophisticated image processing methods may be employed, but conceptually, the odd numbered rows are taken from one eye image while the even numbered rows are taken from the other. When the two are recombined for display, the disparity between left- and right-eye images is apparent.

interleaved; IL *See* **row-interleaved.**

interocular; IO Literally, between the eyes. Generally taken to be a comparison of some characteristic between the eyes of an animal with binocular vision or between the two optical elements in a binocular viewing device, such as a stereoscope.

> **NOTE:** Some may limit the use of *interocular* to comparisons between a pair of optical viewing devices and use *interpupillary* specifically for comparisons between a pair of eyes.

Also **interpupillary.** *Compare* **interaxial.**

interocular adjustment A change in the distance between the lenses in a stereo viewer. *Compare* **3D adjustment.**

interocular convergence In binocular vision, the point in space where the optical axes of the eyes meet when they are turned inward from parallel. *Compare* **interaxial convergence.**

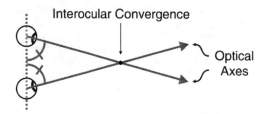

Interocular Convergence

Optical Axes

interocular distance; IOD; IO; interocular separation The physical space between the optical centers of the eyes in binocular vision or between the optical axes of a binocular viewing device, such as a stereoscope. An important factor in stereoscopic calculations.

Generally measured with the optical axes set parallel, such as when the eyes are focused on infinity. The average adult interocular distance ranges between 50–70mm, while children old enough to wear eyeglasses tend to range between 40–55mm. The average IOD is about 65mm (or about 2½").

L

R

L   R

NOTE: *Interocular distance* is often used synonymously with *interaxial distance*, but the two are technically different. Interocular refers to the distance between the eyes or between optical viewing elements, while interaxial refers to the distance between the cameras' lenses or resulting images in a stereoscopic imaging system.

Interocular distance may also be used synonymously with *interpupillary distance*, the distance between the centers of the pupils, but only when the eyes are set parallel. When they eyes converge in, the distance between the pupils differs from the distance between the optical centers of the eyes.

Also **interocular separation; pupillary distance.** *Compare* **interaxial distance.**

interposition *See* **kinetic interposition; static interposition.** *Compare* **monocular cue.**

interpupillary *See* **interocular.**

interpupillary distance; IPD; interpupillary separation *See* **interocular distance.**

intrinsic camera parameters The factors that determine how a particular camera and lens combination maps a 3D image onto the camera's 2D image plane, including focal length, the principal point (the point where the optical axis of the lens intersects the image plane), the vertical and horizontal scale factors (the height and width of an image pixel, or the distance between each row and column), and the geometric distortion introduced by the lens. Often used in computer vision applications or when reconstructing 3D objects from a series of 2D images. *Also* **interior orientation; inner orientation.** *Compare* **extrinsic camera parameters.**

inversion; inverted stereo *Also* **reverse stereo.** *See* **pseudostereo.**

inversion, point of *See* **point of inversion; rear focal point.**

IO *See* **interocular.**

IOD *See* **interocular distance.**

IP; interpupillary *See* **interocular.**

IPD; interpupillary distance *See* **interocular distance.**

IPTV Internet protocol television; a technology standard that allows for the delivery of digital television programming to the home viewer via private broadband Internet protocol (IP) data networks. IPTV may not actually use the Internet, since timely delivery of content cannot be guaranteed, and so video would not stream evenly. Instead, IPTV generally uses private networks that deliver broadband services to the home, including Internet connectivity, telephone services, etc. IPTV streams only the content being viewed at that time, so it requires less bandwidth at the receiving end than traditional cable or satellite TV, which delivers all channels simultaneously, even when no one in the home is watching television.

IR *See* **infrared.**

IR emitter; IR transmitter A device that sends a synchronizing signal to the active eyewear used in most contemporary sequential 3D systems. This ensures that the left-eye shutter is open in the eyewear when the left-eye image is displayed on screen, and vice versa.

iridescence *See* **sparkle.**

irregular fusion The fusion of two nonconjugate points into a single image that does not represent a correct 3D view.

jaggies *Also* **outline aliasing; spatial aliasing; staircase artifact.** *See* **aliasing.**

Java 3D An extension of the Java programming language developed by Sun Microsystems, designed for the development of Internet-based 3D graphics applications and virtual reality systems. *Compare* **VRML; X3D.**

jitter 1. Unsteady image registration in a film projector's gate.

As film moves through a projector, it is held stationary for a moment while the image is projected on the screen. Any variation in the precise positioning of the image frame at this moment will appear on screen as jitter: horizontal movement may be called "weave," while vertical movement may be called "jump." This tends to be most obvious when static white credits are presented against a dark background. This can disrupt the 3D effect in film-based projection systems where the two images do not move in lock step, such as when using a dual-projector setup or when using side-by-side images that are not oriented the same direction (as with the original Oculus3D system).

2. Small, rapid variations in a waveform; slight deviation in or displacement of the high-frequency pulses in a digital signal from their ideal positions, affecting amplitude, width, or phase timing. May be perceived as image flicker or audio clicks in a digital video signal.

JND; just noticeable difference *See* **discrimination threshold.**

JPEG file; .jpg: A still image compression standard published in 1992. The standard uses the DCT (discrete cosine transfer) image compression algorithm to reduce the amount of data necessary to represent digital images, achieving compression ratios of from 2:1 to 30:1, depending on image type and required image quality. JPEG compression is generally lossy and suffers from ringing artifacts (blurring or halos at edge boundaries) and macro-blocking artifacts (visible color blocks due to the 8 × 8 pixel blocks used during compression).

JPEG compression works by filtering out an image's high-frequency information to reduce the overall volume of data and then shrinking the reduced data with a compression algorithm. Low-frequency information does more to define the characteristics of an image, so losing some high-frequency information does not necessarily affect the image quality. JPEG images retain a high degree of color fidelity during compression making it an ideal format for photographic images.

JPEG is an acronym of *Joint Photographic Experts Group*, a joint committee of the International Organization for Standardization (ISO) and International Electrotechnical Commission (IEC) established in 1982 and technically known as ISO/IEC JTC1 SC29 WG1. The JPEG committee administers international standards primarily di-

rected at continuous-tone, still-image compression. The JPEG Web site is www.jpeg.org. *Compare* **Motion JPEG; MPEG.**

JPEG 2000; .jp2; .jpx A still image compression standard published in 2000. The standard uses a wavelet-based image compression algorithm to reduce the amount of data necessary to represent digital images. JPEG 2000 compression can be lossy or lossless and may suffer from ringing artifacts. The lossless compression feature of JPEG 2000 makes it an important image compression format for digital cinema and archival storage. *Compare* **JPEG file; Motion JPEG 2000; MPEG.**

JPS file; .jps A variation on the JPEG digital image compression standard that stores both the left- and right-eye images for a stereogram in the same digital file. *Also* **stereoscopic JPEG.**

jump *See* **jitter.**

just noticeable difference; JND *See* **discrimination threshold.**

jutter Interruptions in a steady image playback rate, may be caused by video bandwidth limitations, buffering issues, image decoding delays, etc. Particularly problematic for stereo presentations as it may affect left- and right-eye image synchronization.

keystone distortion An image malformation caused when the optical axis of the camera or projector lens is not perpendicular to the surface of the subject or screen, respectively. When these elements are out of alignment in a camera, the portion of the image that is closest to the lens will be abnormally large while the portion of the image farthest from the lens will be abnormally small, causing the shape of the image to resemble the keystone of an arch. In a projector, the effect is reversed (close is small, far is large). May rarely be caused by a misalignment between the imaging plane and the lens.

With parallel stereoscopic cameras, both images will keystone in the same direction and stereoscopic alignment will be preserved. With converging (toed-in) stereoscopic cameras, the imaging grids do not lie in the same plane, so the images will keystone in opposite directions causing vertical parallax in which the conjugate points do not align properly, preventing their fusion into a single 3D image. Vertical parallax tends to be greatest in the image corners and increases with increased toe-in angle or decreased focal length. Keystoning also causes a horizontal parallax distortion, resulting in depth plane curvature.

Also **trapezoidal magnification disparity.** *Com-*

pare **corner mismatch; frustum effect.** *See* **keystone distortion** diagram in color section.

killer application; killer app A product that is so desirable that it drives the sales of the device(s) required to use it. Originally applied to computer programs that were so popular that they caused an immediate increase in sales of the computers upon which they ran. Examples include *VisiCalc* and the Apple II computer, *Lotus 1-2-3* and the IBM PC, *Space Invaders* and the Atari 2600 game console, and *Wii Sports* and the Wii gaming system. When new technology platforms are introduced to slow initial sales, industry pundits often look for a killer app that will cause sales to soar. For example, while 3D display systems have been available for home use for several years, the industry is still waiting for a killer app that will advance 3D from a novelty to a necessity.

kinetic interposition A motion depth cue where a nearer object temporarily obscures or casts a shadow upon a farther object as an object or the observer moves, allowing the observer to interpret the relative depths of the objects. *Compare* **static interposition; monocular cue; motion parallax.**

LADAR *See* **3D flash LIDAR.**

lamp 1. A source of artificial light; a light bulb or globe. **2. projector ~:** The light source in a motion picture projector.

lamp house; lamphouse A structure that holds and provides protection for a lamp, such as the lamp housing in a projector, generally incorporating a light source, a reflector, and a condenser lens. In early motion picture projectors, the lamp house was a separate unit, but in contemporary video and narrow-gauge film projectors, it is integrated into the projector case.

LANC A bi-direction device control system for camcorders and edit controllers developed by Sony and also available from Canon, Nikon, Ricoh, and Yashica. May be used to control multiple camcorders for synchronous stereoscopic recording. Since the protocol is only available on camcorders and cannot maintain camera sync for more than a minute or two, it is best suited for short shots and 3D previz. An acronym of *Local ApplicatioN Control.*

The LANC control protocol encodes data into 64 bits (8, 8-bit bytes), transmitted in sync with each video frame using a serial interface operating at 9600 bits/second. Physical LANC connectors are either 5-pin mini–DIN or 2.5mm TRS (3-conductor phone plug). Sony's Control–S interface is essentially a uni-directional LANC, allowing camera control, but with no feedback information

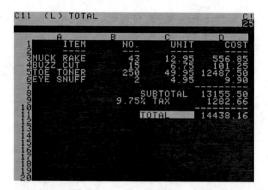

Killer application. The original killer app: *Visi-Calc* running on an Apple II computer (© 2010 Apple II History, www.apple2history.org).

Kinetic interposition. As the pyramid moves to the left, it passes through the box's shadow and is then partially occluded by the box, indicating that the pyramid is farther from the observer than the box. This is, admittedly, unusual behavior for a pyramid, but this example also points out another interesting phenomenon of vision: The pyramid may seem to be getting smaller when it actually remains the same size throughout. Humans are programmed to expect more distant objects to be smaller than near objects, so as it becomes clear that the pyramid is behind the box, the pyramid seems to diminish in size.

Lamp house. Early film projectors featured a physically separate lamp house, as with this home-built model c. 1915. Theatrical film projectors retain this same basic layout.

from the camera. Newer camcorders include an AV/R interface rather than LANC, but adapters are available to connect AV/R camcorders to LANC interfaces.

Also **Control-L.** *Compare* **AV/R; ste-fra LANC.**

Akumira anaglyph. "Martian Surface at an Angle," a multi-exposure panorama of the Martian surface taken by the Mars Exploration Rover *Spirit* in 2004. From top to bottom: the original 2D panorama, a 2D to 3D conversion in standard anaglyph, an Akumira anaglyph (3D images courtesy Brightland Corporation, www.brightland.com; 2D image courtesy NASA/JPL).

Top, left: Anaglyph, black-and-white. A black-and-white anaglyph encoded with red and cyan filters (red eye left). *Above:* Anaglyph, full-color. A full-color anaglyph encoded with red and cyan filters (red eye left). The red elements of the tricycle appear in both eye images. Since red is also one of the filter colors, the resulting anaglyph suffers from noticeable retinal rivalry. *Left:* Anaglyph, half-color. A half-color anaglyph encoded with red and cyan filters (red eye left). The shades of red have been removed from both eye images, eliminating retinal rivalry but distorting the natural colors of the stereogram (© Boris Starosta).

Anti-aliasing. The enlarged area shows how anti-aliasing adjusts each pixel so the image appears smoother, avoiding abrupt jumps between light and dark areas, and blending one color into another (photograph by Shahla Omar, www.shahlaomarphoto.com).

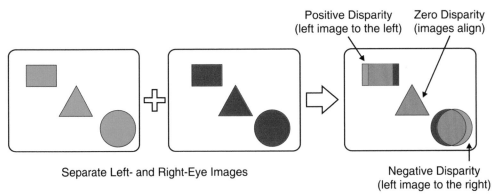

Positive Disparity (left image to the left) Zero Disparity (images align)

Separate Left- and Right-Eye Images

Negative Disparity (left image to the right)

Binocular disparity. The binocular disparity recorded in the two eye images from a stereogram (left) becomes apparent when the images are superimposed (right).

Color. A particular color can be described in many different ways. Using the Munsell color system (developed by American painter Albert H. Munsell, c. 1905), each color is a unique combination of hue (the primary wavelength of light), saturation (the extent to which the color differs from an equally bright shade of gray), and value (a shade of equally bright gray, ranging from black to white). Hues are

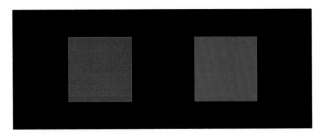

divided first into red, yellow, green, blue, and purple (the five principal hues). Halfway between each principle hue is an intermediate hue. The 10 principal and intermediate hues are each divided into 10 gradations, resulting in 100 identified hues. Values range from 0 (black) at the bottom of the diagram to 10 (white) at the top.

Chromostereopsis. In this example, both the red and blue boxes are the same size, but the red box appears to be slightly closer or larger than the blue box.

ColorCode 3-D. The left half of a stereogram (top, left) compared to a traditional red/cyan anaglyph (top, right). Note the poor color rendition of the red car. The ColorCode 3-D encoded stereogram (bottom) reproduces colors with much greater accuracy (courtesy Eric Dubois).

C4

Full Color Image

Red Channel

Green Channel

Blue Channel

Color separation. A full color image (top, left) divided into its constituent RGB (red, green, and blue) color channels (left to right) (photograph by Melanie B. Kroon).

Dubois anaglyph. The effect of Dubois' process can be seen when comparing an original image (the left half of a stereogram, shown in the upper left) to optimized Dubois anaglyphs (moving clockwise): red/cyan, green/magenta (TrioScopics 3D), and amber/blue (ColorCode 3-D). Proper reproduction of the color red (the car in this scene) is a particular challenge for red-based anaglyphs (such as red/cyan and green/magenta) (courtesy Eric Dubois).

Horizontal Disparity
Interpreted as Depth

Vertical Disparity
Disrupts Illusion of Depth

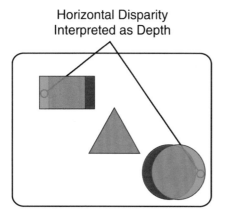

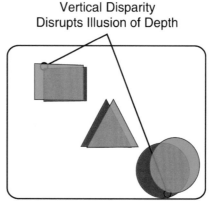

Correct Stereogram Alignment

Effect of Geometric Distortion

Geometric distortion. A stereogram recorded with parallel cameras (left) shows proper alignment of the left- and right-eye images. If, instead, the cameras are toed-in (right), the geometry of the left eye does not match that of the right eye, resulting in variable vertical misalignment and disrupting the stereoscopic illusion.

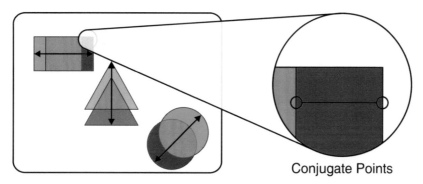

Conjugate Points

Horizontal disparity. Moving left to right in the main diagram, the rectangle in the anaglyphic stereogram shows horizontal disparity, conveying depth information to the viewer. (The enlarged section shows the actual disparity between the conjugate points in the left- and right-eye images that make up the stereogram.) The triangle shows vertical disparity. This does not convey any depth information and simply appears to the viewer as a double image. The circle shows both horizontal and vertical disparity. Conjugate points in the stereogram will not align properly, resulting in a distorted sense of depth (if any) and double images.

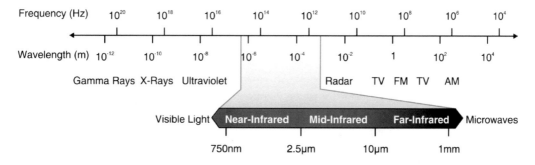

Infrared. The infrared portion of the electromagnetic spectrum, lying between visible light and microwaves and generally divided into near-, mid-, and far-infrared, based on the distance from the visible spectrum.

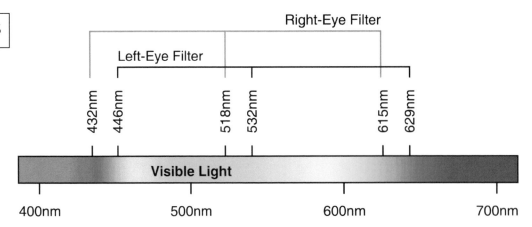

Interference filter. The three-band interference filters used in Infitec/Dolby 3D. A similar arrangement is used for Panavision 3D. In both systems, each eye is viewed through a different three-band interference filter.

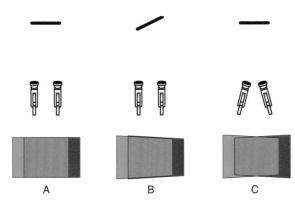

Keystone distortion. Overlapping stereogram images with the left eye cyan and the right eye red show proper geometric alignment when a perpendicular surface is recorded with parallel cameras (A), matching keystone distortions when an angled surface is recorded with parallel cameras (B), and misaligned keystone distortions when a surface is recorded with toed-in cameras (C).

Right: Raster. An enlarged area of an LCD monitor image showing the raster grid: a row marked in red, a column marked in cyan, with a single pixel is at the intersection of the two. This also shows a 4 × 3 image displayed on a 16 × 9 screen with gray pillar bars surrounding the active area (photograph by Shahla Omar, www.shahlaomarphoto.com). *Below:* Screen parallax. The larger the display size, the larger the screen parallax for any given stereogram. For example, on a 47" television screen, the disparity between the conjugate points above would translate into a screen parallax of 1.4", or 0.6° when viewed from 12' away. The same image viewed on a 70' movie screen would have a screen parallax of 22.4", or 1.1° when viewed from 100'.

16x9 Monitor Display Area (gray)

4x3 Active Area (black)

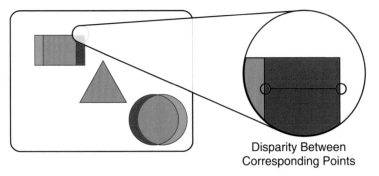

Disparity Between Corresponding Points

Sub-pixel. The sub-pixels of a plasma display, showing how separate red, green, and blue phosphor cells are grouped in sets of three to produce a single, full-color pixel.

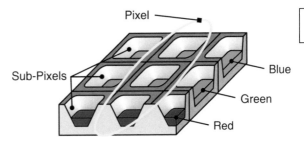

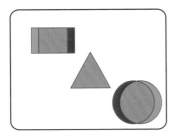 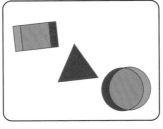 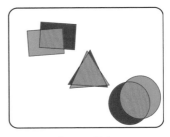

Correct Camera Alignment   Camera Tilt   Camera Twist

Tilt and twist. A stereogram with the two eye images overlapping in the same frame showing correct image orientation (left); tilt, where the images are rotated with respect to the horizon (center); and twist, where one image is rotated with respect to the other (right).

TrioScopics 3D. A TrioScopics 3D green/magenta encoded anaglyph (courtesy Eric Dubois).

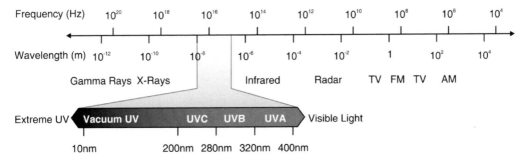

Ultraviolet. The ultraviolet portion of the electromagnetic spectrum, lying between visible light and X-rays and generally divided into UVA (black light), UVB, and UVC. Vacuum UV is blocked by the atmosphere and so is generally used inside a vacuum.

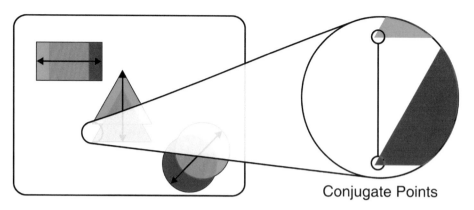

Conjugate Points

Vertical disparity. Moving left to right in the main diagram, the rectangle in the anaglyphic stereogram shows horizontal disparity, conveying depth information to the viewer. The triangle shows vertical disparity. (The enlarged section shows the actual disparity between the conjugate points in the left- and right-eye images that make up the stereogram.) This does not convey any depth information and simply appears to the viewer as a double image. The circle shows both horizontal and vertical disparity. Conjugate points in the stereogram will not align properly, resulting in a distorted sense of depth (if any) and double images.

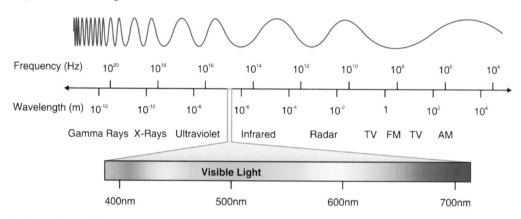

Visible light. The frequencies and wavelengths of the electromagnetic spectrum, showing the portion of the spectrum received by the eyes and interpreted by the brain as visible light in greater detail. Different wavelengths are registered as different colors, ranging from violet (with the shortest wavelength/highest frequency) to red (with the longest wavelength/lowest frequency).

Wimmer anaglyph. In the original anaglyph (left), the red shirt causes visual anomalies. These are corrected in the Wimmer anaglyph (right), though the shirt is no longer red (courtesy Peter Wimmer, www.3dtv.at).

LANC Shepherd The trade name for a wired LANC stereoscopic camera controller developed by Ledametrix for use with Sony or Cannon camcorders and Sony still cameras. The LANC Shepherd provides remote synchronization and operation of a pair of matching still cameras or camcorders, including power on/off, camera start/stop, zoom, focus, and interval exposure for time-lapse photography. The Ledametrix Web site is www.ledametrix.com. *Compare* ste-fra LANC.

(**Courtesy Ledametrix, www.ledametrix.com.**)

laser A device that emits a highly focused, pure beam of light (technically, coherent electromagnetic radiation in or near the visible spectrum). Lasers are commonly used in fiber optic systems, optical disc players (CD, DVD, Blu-ray, etc.), and holography (3D imaging that does not require special eyewear).

> NOTE: Laser was originally coined as an acronym of *Light Amplification by Stimulated Emission of Radiation*, but is now treated as a standard noun.

laser holography *See* holography.

last opportunity position; last reasonable position The point closest to a projected image where a polarizer may be effectively placed within the projected beam of light. The last opportunity position is a function of the size of the projected image and the number of bounce mirrors that may lie in the light path between the polarizer's selected position and the projected image.

> When light rays reflect off a surface, they are slightly depolarized. If a beam of polarized light is reflected several times, this effect is cumulative. This depolarization can lead to an increase in cross talk between the left- and right-eye images in a polarized stereogram, disrupting the desired 3D effect. Therefore, the last opportunity position is chosen to maximize the image quality of the final 3D image.

latency The time delay between initiating and completing a process. In virtual reality systems, there is often a small amount of latency (in the order of a few hundred milliseconds) between initiating a head move and updating the visual presentation. This can be enough to cause a visuo-vestibular conflict and induce motion sickness. *Compare* **cybersickness.**

layered display *Also* **multi-plane display.** *See* **volumetric 3D.**

lazy eye *See* **amblyopia; strabismus.**

LBE *See* **location-based entertainment.**

LC *See* **left circular polarized light.**

LCD Liquid-crystal display or device; a technology employed in flat panel displays such as digital watches and television monitors and in the active eyewear often used with sequential 3D systems.

> Liquid crystals twist when electricity is applied. This fact can be used to create a display grid that is generally transparent, but that turns dark in selective areas as electricity is applied to individual crystals, much like opening and closing a series of tiny shutters. This makes LCDs transmissive, not emissive (they can pass or block light, but do not generate any light of their own). In displays, the LCD grid is typically sandwiched between two layers of polarized glass with a light source (a fluorescent light or bank of LEDs — light-emitting diodes) behind the grid. When activated, the crystals block or unblock the light, creating a luminous image. The brightness and viewing angle of an LCD screen is limited, much like a projection television. In active 3D eyewear, each lens is a separate LCD grid that can be turned on or off to allow or block light in time with the presentation of time-sequential stereograms.

LCD shutter eyewear; LCS eyewear Spectacles with lenses made from a liquid crystal material sandwiched between a pair of crossed polarization elements. In one state of the liquid crystal material, light passes through both polarization elements. In the other state, light is blocked by the crossed polarization elements. When viewing a stereoscopic work, the lenses are opened in time with the presentation of left- and right-eye images in the stereogram. *See* **active eyewear.**

LCoS Liquid crystal on silicon; a device where liquid crystals are mounted directly to the silicon chip that controls their orientation.

> Silicon is opaque, so light cannot be shown through the LCoS chip. Instead, the pixel electrodes on the silicon chip are coated with mirror-grade aluminum. Light directed at the LCoS chip can then be selectively allowed through the

An HED-5216 color sequential LCoS micro-display. This device has a 0.55" diagonal active display area (shown to the left) containing 1280 × 768 pixels. The ribbon cable (extending to the right) connects the LCoS chip to its controller (courtesy HOLOEYE, www.holoeye.com).

crystals and reflected by the electrodes according to the amount of power applied by the silicon chip. The reflected light passes through the liquid crystal layer twice (once on its way into the mirrors and once on its way back out), changing its polarization state with an applied electrical field. This architecture makes LCoS display devices very light efficient and allows inter pixel spacing of approximately 350nm (0.000014 inches). *See* **DLP; MEMS.**

LCS eyewear *See* **LCD shutter eyewear.**

LE The left eye half of a stereogram.

leakage The amount of left eye information from a stereogram accidentally observed by the right eye, and vice versa. Typically, active shutter glasses have the least leakage, while polarized glasses have the most. *See* **crosstalk.** *Compare* **stereo extinction ratio.**

LED Light-emitting diode; a semiconductor diode (a device with two electrical connectors that passes electricity more freely in one direction than the other) that converts electricity into light. LEDs are very efficient and produce a large amount of light with relatively little heat compared to more traditional electric light sources. Commercial LEDs were originally limited to red, but can now be produced to output all wavelengths of light from ultraviolet (UV) to infrared (IR). Infrared LEDs are commonly used in television remote controls. Visible light LEDs may be used in a variety of applications, including the construction of television monitors.

left circular polarized light; LC Polarized light that travels through space in a counterclockwise corkscrew pattern with the electric vector completing a full rotation around the axis of propa-

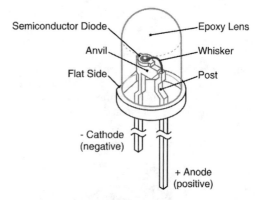

LED. A typical 5mm round LED. An LED's color is principally determined by the composition of the semiconductor diode. Positive power is applied to the diode by the whisker wire attached to the anode. The diode's negative lead is connected to the cathode through the anvil. The epoxy resin enclosure acts as a lens and protects the LED from the elements.

gation in the time it takes the light ray to move forward exactly one wavelength.

The electric vector of circular polarized light is not constrained to a single plane of vibration. The wave can be broken down into the sum of two linear polarized waves, where each wave has the same amplitude, is 90° out of phase from its companion, and travels along right angle planes (rotated 90° from each other). When these planar waves combine, they create a 3D wave that follows a helix, or corkscrew, path through space. When measured at a specific point, the tip of the passing LC wave's electric field vector travels in a counterclockwise circle, completing one full rotation around the axis of propagation in the time it takes the wave to move forward one wavelength.

NOTE: In optics (and therefore most stereoscopic applications), the direction of circular polarized light spin is measured from the perspective of the viewer, while in electrical engineering, it is measured from the perspective of the source.

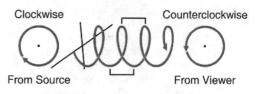

Left circular polarized light

left eye; LE The left half of a stereo image pair; the image intended to be viewed by the left eye.

left eye dominance Using the left as the starting eye for a sequential 3D application.

left field Information from a stereogram intended for the left eye only. *See* **image field.**

left homologue A point in a left-eye image that corresponds to a point in the matching right-eye image. *Compare* **conjugate points.**

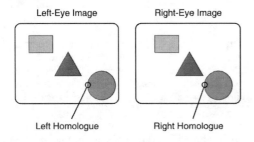

left/right inversion *See* **image flipping; pseudostereo.**

legal window violation An object with negative parallax that does not intersect the stereo window edge. Technically, there is no violation here, only a visual intrusion into the audience space. *Compare* **hard window violation; soft window violation.**

lens An optical device that focuses light and is commonly composed of several pieces of ground glass housed in a metal cylinder. In a camera, light coming through the lens is focused on the film or imaging plane. In a projector, light is focused by the lens on the screen.

lens convergence The extent to which a lens with a positive focal length focuses, or converges, light passing through it.

Each side of a lens may be curved inward (concave), curved outward (convex), or flat (plano),

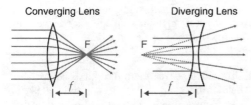

Light coming into the converging lens (left) is focused at a point beyond the lens, F. The distance between the optical center of the lens and Point F is the focal distance, *f*. With a converging lens, this point is beyond the lens, so it is treated as a positive distance. Light coming into a diverging lens (right) is dispersed outwards. Tracing the outward rays back through the lens defines the lens' focal point. Since this is in front of the lens, it is treated as a negative focal length.

resulting in six different combinations, including plano-concave (flat on one side, curved inward on the other) and convexo-convex (curving outward on both sides). If the lens is thicker in the center than at its edges, it will converge light (a converging, or positive, lens). If it is thicker at its edges, it will diverge light (a diverging, or negative, lens).
Compare **convergence.**

lens distortion; lens radial distortion Image malformation caused by the fact that spherical lenses have slightly different focal lengths moving outward from the center of the lens, resulting in optical distortions that are (approximately) symmetric radially. Pincushion distortion results when the focal length increases moving outward, while barrel distortion results when the focal length decreases moving outward. Complex, or mustache, distortion results when pincushion and barrel distortions affect different portions of the same lens. These distortions tend to be more pronounced in shorter focal length lenses and may be corrected by using an aspherical lens.

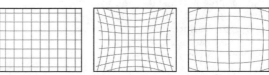

The effects of radial lens distortion (left to right): an undistorted grid; the grid with pincushion distortion; and the grid with barrel distortion.

lens focal length *See* **focal length.**

lens memory A function of theatrical digital video projectors that retains various lens settings (amount of zoom, left/right position, up/down position, etc.) for a particular show. These settings are typically determined by experimentation and observation during the initial show setup, and then saved as part of the title file for future use. *Compare* **title.**

lens shading A digital filter applied to a recorded image to correct optical vignetting (slight darkening around the edges) and help ensure even illumination across the entire image.

lenticular A type of device that makes use of multiple, half-cylindrical or half-spherical lenses to control the angle of reflected or transmitted light. Each lenticular lens is curved on one side, flat on the other, and thickest in the middle (plano-convex) and long, like a cylinder split in half lengthwise.

Lenticular lenses may be used to produce auto-stereoscopic images. When arranged vertically and placed over a set of stereoscopic images that have been arranged as alternating vertical strips, the lenticular lenses control which eye sees which image, creating the illusion of depth. The development of the lenticular stereoscope c. 1850 is generally credited to Sir David Brewster (perhaps best known for inventing the kaleidoscope), who expanded upon the work of Charles Wheatstone, the inventor of the stereoscope in 1832. Auto-stereoscopic displays need more than two eye images, or views, per frame to support multiple viewing positions, so lenticular displays may support 2–25 views per frame.

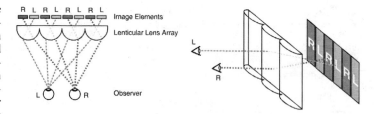

An array of lenticular lenses arranged in front of an interleaved array of left- and right-eye image strips — left, viewed from above; right, viewed from the side. Both diagrams are exaggerated for effect. Note that because of the way the lenticular lenses bend light, the images corresponding to the right eye are to the left of the images for the left eye.

Lenticular lenses may also be used on rear-projection television screens to help focus the light into a more horizontal beam, thus improving image brightness. Front-projection screens may use lenticular mirrors, rather than lenses, to help focus the light back to the viewer.
Compare **parallax barrier.**

lenticular barrier A series of regularly spaced lenticular lenses arranged flat side down to create a parallax barrier. *Compare* **simple wall barrier.**

lenticular screen A projection or display screen where the surface is covered with an array of lenticular lenses or mirrors.

Le/Re Left eye/Right eye; the two views of a single scene that make up a stereogram.

level of detail *See* **LOD.**

levorotatory Rotating to the left, or counterclockwise, as with circular polarized light. *Compare* **dextrorotatory.**

LIDAR *See* **3D flash LIDAR.**

light adaptation The decrease in light sensitivity of the human visual system that occurs over time as illumination levels increase. *See* **dark adaptation.**

light doubler A method of recycling the light normally wasted by a polarized light 3D presentation system, nearly doubling the amount of light produced by a polarized projector.

In a standard polarized 3D projection system, approximately 70 percent of the incident light directed at the polarizer is discarded, either reflected off to the side (and into a light trap) or absorbed by the polarizer (and converted into heat). The actual transmission through the system is somewhere between 32 percent and 42 percent of the incident light intensity. With a light doubler, the incident light that is reflected off the back side of the polarizer is redirected and processed to match the polarization characteristics of the light transmitted through the original polarizer. This creates a second beam of polarized light. When the two beams are recombined, there is a dramatic increase in the total amount of useable light passed through the system.
Compare **RealD 3D.**

light-emitting diode *See* **LED.**

light engine 1. A device that produces a controlled amount of light that can be sustained over time, ranging from common incandescent light bulbs to high-intensity LED clusters. **2.** The part of a digital video projector that encodes the image and focuses the light. For a three LCD or three micro-mirror projector, the light engine does not include the lamp, the cold mirror, or the integrating rod. Typically, the light engine can take light from any source, use it to image-encode the light stream, and then project the image out through the lens.

light field The treatment of light as comprising a field, rather than viewing it as individual particles or waves, much like the traditional view of a magnetic field.

A ray of light can be described by a position in space that defines an origin (X, Y, and Z coordinates) and a pair of angles that defines its direction (θ and φ) along with its wavelength, polarization angle, and behavior over time. If one then considers all the rays of light, traveling in free space from all possible directions, and passing through all possible points, one has a light field. A planar photograph captures a 2D slice of the light field.

To create a three-dimensional representation, one needs at least two slices of the light field — more to produce a 360° virtual reality view, particularly if viewers are not restricted in their direction or angle of view. Computer graphics systems may use a light field to more accurately represent the behavior of light within a scene, though this is computationally complex. Ray tracing, where one calculates the path and interactions of each ray of light in a scene, is generally limited to those rays of light that strike the virtual camera lens. If this is extended to encompass all rays of light within a defined space, one can approximate the complete light field.

The concept of the light field was first proposed by the British physicist Michael Faraday in 1846, patterned after his experiments with magnetic fields, but the term itself was coined by Russian physicist Alexander Gershun in his 1936 paper, "The Light Field" (first published in English translation in 1939).

light to heat conversion When an object absorbs light, it is converted into heat. Since optical devices are not 100 percent efficient, a certain amount of light is always absorbed. With high levels of concentrated light, such as those required by projectors, optical efficiency and heat generation become a significant concern.

Polarized light systems are particularly susceptible to light to heat conversion since, by their nature, they do not pass all of the incoming light — they only pass that portion that is oriented in the desired direction. The residual light must be diverted elsewhere (generally reflected into a light trap, where it is converted into heat) or absorbed directly by the polarizer (which tends to shorten the useful life of the polarizer). Traditional 35mm over/under 3D projection systems and LCD projection systems use absorptive polarizers in the light beam path. Such filters typically transmit less than 50 percent of the incident light and absorb the rest, essentially acting as light energy to heat converters.

lighting cue A monocular depth cue based on the effects of lighting and shadows on 3D objects. For example, the varying amounts of illumination on the different sides of an object help identify its 3D shape, while the shadow cast by one object onto another indicates that the first object is closer to the light source than the second object. *Compare* **monocular cue.**

Lilliputism A stereoscopic effect where objects appear unnaturally small. Generally caused by recording an image with too wide an interaxial distance (the separation between the cameras' lenses) given the lens focal length. May also be simulated by adjusting the depth of field to mimic

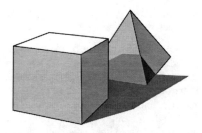

Lighting cue. The shading on the cube and pyramid help define their shapes, while the shadow cast by the cube helps define the relative position of and distance between the objects.

Lemuel Gulliver in the land of Lilliput, from Part I of *Travels into Several Remote Nations of the World* (1726), better known as *Gulliver's Travels* (illustration by Louis Rhead, from the 1913 edition of *Gulliver's Travels* published by Harper & Brothers, New York).

miniature photography on a much larger scale using a tilt lens or digital post-production image manipulation. Tools exist to help calculate the optimal interaxial distance for a set of image and display characteristics. The term was coined in reference to the land of Lilliput, a parody of English politics that appears in Jonathan Swift's *Gulliver's Travels* (1726). *Also* **dwarfism; miniaturization; puppet effect.** *Compare* **gigantism; hyperstereo.**

linear perspective *Also* **geometric perspective.** *See* **perspective.** *Compare* **monocular cue.**

linear polarization; LP An electromagnetic wave, such as visible light, that travels through space vibrating within a single plane, defined by the direction of the electric field of the light wave (the electric field vector).

Natural light is composed of an infinite number of linearly polarized light rays, each with its own plane of vibration. A linear polarizing filter blocks light rays that are not vibrating in planes substantially parallel to the plane of polarization of the filter (also called the plane of transmission). If two linear polarizers are positioned so their planes of transmission are orthogonal (offset by 90°), then no light will pass through the polarizer stack. Taken another way, light polarized horizontally will not pass through a vertically oriented polarizer, and vice versa.

The left- and right-eye images in a stereogram

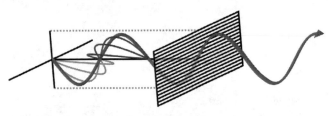

This diagram may seem slightly counter-intuitive. Often, linear polarization is depicted with the filtered ray parallel to the grid, as if it had squeezed sideways through the gap in a picket fence. In reality, the ray is perpendicular to the polarization grid, as shown. This is because a linear polarizer extinguishes (absorbs or reflects) light waves with electric vectors parallel to the grid and passes only those waves with electric vectors perpendicular to the grid.

BattleTech combat simulators from Virtual World Entertainment (www.virtualworld.com) arranged at a location-based entertainment facility in Kirkland, Washington (photograph by Tim Batzel, courtesy The Airlock, www.the-airlock.com).

can be encoded with linear polarization filters offset by 90° (generally, horizontally and vertically or at 45° diagonals) then presented together as a single image on screen. Eyewear with matching LP lenses can decode the combined image for stereoscopic viewing. Since the angle of the viewing lenses must closely match that of the presented image, the 3D effect is lost if the viewer tilts her head too far out of alignment. With circular polarization, the separation of the two images is not angle dependent, but handedness dependent, so viewers can tilt their heads from side to side without affecting image separation. However, viewing a stereogram from off the horizontal introduces vertical parallax, which requires vertical vergence eye movements and causes fatigue.
Compare **circular polarization; polarization.**

line-by-line; line-interlaced; line-interleaved *See* **row-interleaved 3D; polarized display.**

linger longer A summary of the unique aesthetic required by stereoscopic works compared to traditional 2D works; images are composed with wider lens angles, camera movements are slower, and individual shots are kept on screen longer to allow the action to unfold before the viewer rather than creating motion through fast camera moves and editing. Coined by the European satellite broadcaster BSkyB.

liquid crystal device; liquid crystal display *See* **LCD.**

liquid crystal on silicon *See* **LCoS.**

liquid crystal shutter; liquid crystal switch; LCS *Also* **valve.** *See* **active eyewear; LCD shutter eyewear.**

local application control; ~ bus system *See* **LANC.**

location-based entertainment; LBE Out-of-home entertainment facilities. Often a single venue theme park, themed experience, or themed ride, focused on small group experiences, such as 3D or virtual reality simulators. Examples include BattleTech multiplayer virtual combat centers, the DisneyQuest Indoor Interactive

Theme Park, and laser tag centers. *Compare* **special venue.**

locking focus and convergence Adjusting camera convergence along with focus so that the focal point of each shot coincides with the point of convergence. This ensures that objects at the screen plane (zero parallax) will always be in focus, but can lead to some visually odd (and often physically uncomfortable) results. *Compare* **convergence tracking.**

LOD Level of detail; the amount of visual complexity displayed in an image.

Look3D An Australian manufacturer of stereoscopic polarized glasses. The Look3D line includes single-use and reusable glasses. In 2011, Look3D (in cooperation with Oculus3D) released a line of RealD-certified, eco friendly, biodegradable glasses made from plant-based resins. The Look3D Web site is www.look3d.com.

lorgnette A pair of glasses with a handle so they can be held in front of the eyes with one hand. A common configuration for stereoscopic eyewear intended for viewing still images or motion pictures with intermittent 3D effects.

Back and front views of the souvenir lorgnette given out for Warner Bros.' release of *The Mask* (1961). Only portions of the film were presented in 3D, so the audience was instructed, "Each time the man in the picture puts on his mask you look through this for the shock of your life! REMEMBER! You cannot see the thrills of 'THE MASK' unless you wear this mask!" The handle is oriented so the glasses can be held with the right hand (from the Todd Franklin collection).

lossless compression; lossy compression *See* **compression.**

low-gain screen A screen that reflects less projected light than a standard reference white surface coated with magnesium oxide. The standard reference has a screen gain of 1.0, so anything below 1.0 should be low gain, but screens with gains as high as 1.3 (30 percent more reflective than the standard) may be included in the low-gain category because they do not generally exhibit the visual artifacts associated with a high-gain screen.

Low-gain screens reflect light more evenly over a wider angle than high-gain screens, so they tend to have less bright, but more accurate, images over a larger viewing angle. Most theatrical exhibition screens are white (low gain), with silver (high gain) generally limited to polarized stereoscopic projection. Home theater projection screens may be white (typically 1.3 to 0.65) or gray (typically 0.9 to 0.45), with gray screens producing the most even illumination over the largest area, but requiring special darkened viewing environments to make up for their reduced image brightness. *Compare* **screen gain.**

low-mode *See* **under-slung.** *Compare* **overslung.**

LP *See* **linear polarization.**

LR independent A stereoscopic system that provides a separate, full-resolution image for each eye. *Compare* **full HD; half-resolution.**

luma mismatch *See* **luminance rivalry.**

luminance differences A measure of the reflected light off a surface, usually in foot-lamberts, as the value changes from the center of the screen to the edges of the screen.
- **Drop Off:** The absolute value of the luminance change across the surface of a screen.
- **Flatness of Field:** A relative measure of the drop-off value for screen luminance — the lower the drop off, the flatter the field. Digital cinema systems have a naturally flatter field than traditional 35mm film projectors.
- **Hot Spot:** The brightest point on the screen, based on screen and projector geometry.
  - On low-gain screens, there is a single hot spot.
  - On high-gain screens, every observer experiences a slightly different hot spot depending on their angle of view.
- **Vignetting:** Illumination drop-off moving out from the center of a lens. Digital cameras may employ lens shading to correct for this.

luminance drop off; luminance fall off *See* **flatness of field.**

luminance error *See* **luminance rivalry.**

luminance flicker Repeated variations in the brightness of conjugate points in a stereogram. This can interfere with the 3D effect. *Compare* **color flicker.**

luminance rivalry When there is a significant difference in brightness between conjugate points in a stereogram that is not explained by the available depth cues, leading to contradictory depth information in the fused image. Common to anaglyphs and film-based polarized 3D systems. The two separate film images that combine to form a polarized stereogram may not be equally bright if the projector is misconfigured or unbalanced light is passed through the two chambers of an over/under or side-by-side lens. *Also* **luma mismatch; luminance error.** *Compare* **color rivalry; cue conflict; retinal rivalry.**

M-3DI A standard for active shutter 3D glasses developed to promote compatibility across TVs, computers, home projectors, and in theaters, proposed by Panasonic and XpanD in 2011.

M-JPEG *See* **Motion JPEG.**

macro stereo; macrostereo *See* **stereomacroscopy.** *Compare* **gigantism; hypostereo.**

macula An oval-shaped region in the center of the retina containing the highest concentration of cone cells in the eye, covering about 13° of the visual field and responsible for detailed color vision. The macula is surrounded by the peripheral vision area, mostly populated by rod cells and responsible for motion detection and night vision. *Compare* **fovea.**

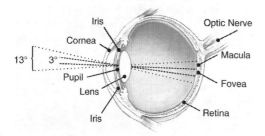

(National Eye Institute, National Institutes of Health)

Magic Eye method The trade name for the patented process of creating advanced, full-color auto-stereograms that appear to depict a repeating 2D pattern but that, when viewed using parallel or cross-eyed free-viewing (depending on the image design), resolve into complex, 3D images.

The Magic Eye method was developed in 1991 by Tom Baccei, Cheri Smith, and Bob Salitsky, based in part on the earlier work of Dr. Bela Julesz (who developed the computer-generated black-and-white random dot stereogram in 1959) and Christopher Tyler and Maureen Clarke (who developed the black-and-white, single-image random dot stereogram in 1979). Magic Eye images are comprised of various full-color shapes, not dots, and, unlike traditional black-and-white random dot stereograms, combine complex two- and 3D images in a single presentation. In addition to their aesthetic attributes, Magic Eye images are also used therapeutically. Images configured for parallel free-viewing can help strengthen the eye muscles used for distance viewing, while images configured for cross-eyed free-viewing can help strengthen the muscles for close viewing. *Compare* **random dot stereogram.**

magnetic vector The amplitude and direction of the magnetic field generated by an electromagnetic wave as it passes through space. The electric vector is orthogonal (at a right angle) to the magnetic vector. Together, the electric and magnetic vectors define the direction, strength, and frequency of an electromagnetic wave. *Compare* **electric vector.**

MAOFD; maximum allowable on-film deviation *See* **depth budget.** *Compare* **depth range.**

MasterImage analog for film projection A static (non-rotating) filter designed to present over/under formatted 35mm film images with the correct polarization handedness (direction of circular polarization) and plane of polarization for viewing with a pair of MasterImage polarized glasses.

MasterImage configuration glasses Spectacles with circular polarized lenses that match the handedness and plane of polarization of a MasterImage-formatted stereogram (typically right eye right circular and left eye left circular with the plane of polarization parallel to the ground, though MasterImage has used at least two different configurations for their glasses).

MasterImage 3D; MI The trade name for a digital cinema polarized stereoscopic projection system. The MasterImage Web site is www.masterimage3d.com.

The MasterImage system uses a rotating disk of polarization material placed in the path of the light coming out of the projector. The disk is synced with the projector so the left eye information is circularly polarized with one handedness, while the right eye information is circularly polarized with the other handedness. As with all polarized projection systems, MasterImage 3D requires a silver screen to maintain the proper polarization in the reflected image.

Originally founded in 2004 in Seoul, Korea, MasterImage is now headquartered in Burbank, California. Its first digital cinema 3D system was installed in 2006; by 2009 it had installed 1,000 systems. The company also produced the first commercial auto-stereoscopic LCD screen for use in a cell phone (released in Japan with the Hitachi Wooo H001 in February 2009). *Compare* **RealD 3D.**

maximum allowable on-film deviation; MAOFD *See* **depth budget.** *Compare* **depth range.**

MCGD file A digital cinema projector data file that describes the current color output of the projector (based on colorimeter measurements entered into the MCGD by the operator) in terms of chromaticity (hue and saturation independent of brightness) and white point (the particular color characteristics of what is presented as white). These data are compared by the projector to the specified color space of the material to be projected, and automatic adjustments are made to ensure the image is presented correctly without color distortion. MCGD is an initialism of *Measured Color Gamut Data.*

mean opinion score; MOS The arithmetic mean (average) of the scores from multiple subjective image quality evaluations such as absolute category rating (ACR), degradation category rating (DCR), double-stimulus continuous-quality scale (DCSQS), and pair comparison method (PC). *Compare* **predicted mean opinion score.**

mean square error; MSE An objective measure of system accuracy or signal fidelity calculated by taking the average of the squared sample differences between two data sets. These could be the differences between predicted and actual values, between signal-to-noise ratios for input and output signals, between original and compressed images, etc. For video signals, this is typically applied to a pixel-by-pixel comparison of a single attribute, such as the pixel's hue, saturation, or value. This can be calculated using the equation at right, where n is the number of samples in the data set, X is the value of a sample from one set and X' is the corresponding value from the other set.

$$\frac{\sum_{i=1}^{n}\left(X_i - X_i'\right)^2}{n}$$

(Since the difference between the sets is squared, it does not matter which one is subtracted from the other.) *Compare* **root mean squared error.**

MEMS A microelectromechanical system. A device composed of a series of microscopic moving parts that are controlled by the electric current running through the silicon substrate to which they are attached. *Compare* **DLP; LCoS.**

metamer **1.** A color that appears identical to another color (together, metamers or a metameric pair) under one set of lighting conditions, but different under another. For example, two objects could appear to be the same color under fluorescent light but appear to be different colors under sunlight. **2.** Two different light sources that stimulate the same set of cones in the eye (and so are registered as being the same). Interference filter-based stereoscopic systems such as Dolby 3D/ Infitec and Panavision 3D rely on metamers to register the same colors in each eye using two sets of wavelengths.

MI *See* **MasterImage 3D.**

micro-display; microdisplay A very small display device, typically less than 2" on the diagonal. Micro-displays are used in head-mounted display systems (where each eye has its own display) and digital video projection systems (either transmissive, where light is shown through the display to project an image onto the screen, or reflective, where mirrors on the surface of the display create an image by controlling the light that is reflected onto the screen). Head-mounted displays can produce an immersive 3D experience when coupled with a virtual world engine. Both eyes receive full-resolution images without shutter interruptions, leading to very smooth and rich 3D images.

An LE-750A HMD (helmet-mounted display) equipped with a translucent micro-display, creating an augmented reality that superimposes enhanced imagery over the wearer's view of the natural world (courtesy Liteye Systems, www.liteye.com).

micro-electromechanical system *See* **MEMS.**

micro-polarizer; micropolarizer; µPol A very small polarizer, typically a circular polarizer one pixel tall running the width of a display. Polarized

3D displays have an alternating array of orthogonal micro-polarizers covering their surface, generally in an alternating left circular/right circular pattern to match the polarized glasses worn by the viewer. The eye images are row-interleaved (spatially multiplexed) and presented simultaneously with one eye image on the odd rows and the other eye image on the even rows. This technique was originally developed by Sadeg Faris, founder of Reveo, Inc., c. 1994. *Also* **passive retarder.** *Compare* **Xpol.**

miniaturization *See* **Lilliputism.**

MIO; ~ 3D *See* **multiple interocular.**

miosis A contraction of the pupil, as in response to a bright light. Also accompanies accommodation and vergence when focusing the eyes on a near object. This has the effect of increasing the visual depth of field and decreasing the amount of effort that must be dedicated to accommodation, since less focal precision is required with the greater depth of field.

mirror rig **1.** A mechanical framework designed to support two identical cameras set at right angles to each other with a 45° beam-splitter (50/50 two-way mirror) between them.

With a mirror rig, one camera shoots through the beam-splitter while the other records the reflection. (The reflected image must be flipped left-for-right before it can be used.) This arrangement allows one to shoot the two views of a stereogram with variable interaxial distances as small as zero (with the two lenses aligned through the mirror). In this configuration, one camera points directly at the action while the second camera is above and

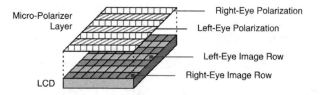

Micro-Polarizer Layer — Right-Eye Polarization — Left-Eye Polarization — Left-Eye Image Row — Right-Eye Image Row — LCD

Micro-polarizer. When a micro-polarizer is applied to an LCD, there is a small, but significant, gap separating the two. As a result, if the viewing angle is too high or too low, the right-eye micro-polarizer may align with all or part of the left-eye image row, and vice versa. This can lead to image ghosting or pseudo-stereo in extreme situations.

pointing down (over-slung), below and pointing up (under-slung), or off to one side.

Beam-splitting mirrors act as linear polarizers, delivering polarized light in the reflected image. This creates unwanted visual differences between the recorded images. Adding a ¼ wave retarder to the front of the beam splitter prevents linear polarized light from entering the rig and helps ensure that both cameras record comparable images. Mirrors are not optically perfect, giving the reflected image a slight blue color-cast when compared to the transmitted image, which can lead to retinal rivalry in the stereogram. Various techniques exist to minimize this in rig design and camera settings. This color-mismatch can be quite difficult to correct in post-production, particularly in the color gradients found in a shot of the sky and reflections off water, metal, and skin.

The characteristics to consider when selecting a mirror rig include:
- The quality of the glass used for the mirror (affects both the reflected and transmitted images)
- The alignment of the glass and cameras (to avoid keystone distortions in the reflected image)
- Rigidity of the rig (so the cameras and glass remain properly aligned)
- Orientation of the reflected camera (a reversed mount avoids top-for-bottom image flipping and rolling shutter issues)
- Light contamination (stray light entering the mirror box and affecting the transmitted or reflected images)
- Mirror protection (an open framework holding the mirror or a sealed box protecting mirror from damage) and the opportunity for physical contamination (dust, water, etc. on the mirror or lenses)
- Physical size (the weight and bulk of a rig could prevent its use in certain situations)

2. A projector configuration that allows for greater image magnification than is otherwise possible given the distance between projector and screen.

Two views of a Stereotec 3D Live mirror rig: a side view without cameras (left) and a three-quarter front view with two Panasonic VariCam digital cinema cameras (right) (courtesy Stereoscopic Technologies GmbH, www.stereotec.com).

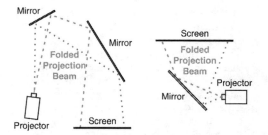

With a mirror rig, the throw distance of the projector exceeds the line of sight distance between the projector and the projection surface. This is useful for rear-projection, such as a DLP-based rear-projection television, where there is sufficient volume for mirror placement. The bounce mirrors can affect the quality of polarization, so polarization filters must be carefully positioned in systems used to present polarized stereograms to ensure that a proper 3D effect is achieved.

3. A traditional, now rarely used, stereoscopic camera arrangement where the cameras face each other and record their images off 45° angled mirrors. *Also* **beam-splitter rig.** *Compare* **side-by-side rig.**

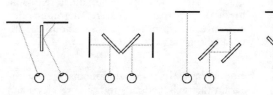

Recorded Action

45° Mirrors

mirror stereoscope A stereoscope design employing one, two, or four flat mirrors, but generally no lenses. First developed by English scientist Charles Wheatstone in 1832.

The principal advantage of mirror stereoscopes is

that they can be used to view very large stereograms (with image centers significantly farther apart than the average interocular distance). When constructed with high-quality, front-silvered mirrors (and no lenses), they offer distortion- and aberration-free viewing. Contemporary mirror stereoscopes are often used in industrial and scientific applications, such as analysis of aerial geological stereograms, and for fine art presentations.

mirror-viewing A stereogram viewing technique where one eye image is presented normally and the other is placed next to it, but reversed left-

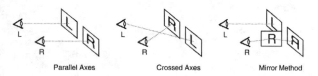

Parallel Axes   Crossed Axes   Mirror Method

In mirror-viewing, the left eye looks directly at the left-eye image while the right eye looks at a mirror image of the right-eye image. This is an inconvenient method of free-viewing (for example, you must provide your own mirror), but requires fewer ocular gymnastics than either parallel or cross-eyed viewing methods. If done correctly, the circle should appear in front of the triangle with the rectangle in the background

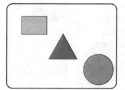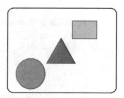

for-right (a mirror image). One views the stereogram by placing a mirror between and at a right angle to the two images with the reflective side of the mirror facing the reversed image. One image is seen directly while the reflection of the other is seen in the mirror. Mirror-viewing qualifies as a free-viewing method because it does not require spectacles or a stereoscope, though single-mirror stereoscopes, such as the MirScope, do exist. Mirror-viewing has the advantage of not requiring the eye muscle coordination necessary for other free-viewing methods, but it is still rather cumber-

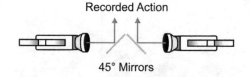

Mirror stereoscopes configured with one, two (the original Wheatstone configuration), two (in an unusual "one eye" configuration), and four mirrors (left to right). In the first two variants, the images viewed in the mirrors must be reversed left-for-right so their mirror images read correctly. Since the images in the second two-mirror and the four-mirror variants are viewed as double reflections, they do not need to be reversed. The two-mirror/one-eye configuration can be used to view side-by-side or over/under arrangements, but the image viewed with the mirrors must be larger or brought closer (as shown) so that it appears the same size as the image viewed directly.

some to perform without a stereoscope. *Compare* **cross-eyed viewing; free-viewing; parallel-viewing.**

MirScope The trade name for a line of single-mirror stereoscopes developed in 2006 by American stereographer, John Hart. MirScopes can accommodate images up to 13" × 19".

misalignment When conjugate points are offset vertically so they do not properly fuse into a single image. This can cause double vision and eyestrain. *Compare* **tilt; twist.**

mixed resolution coding; MRC *See* **asymmetric coding.**

MJ2; MJP2 *See* **Motion JPEG 2000.**

mobile media Audiovisual material designed for presentation on a hand-held device such as a cell phone, PDA (personal digital assistant), or dedicated media player (such as an iPod).

There are five different methods commonly employed to deliver audiovisual content to mobile media devices:

- **Unicast:** A one-to-one live transmission using a cellular telephone network where a unique signal is sent to each receiver — essentially the same process used for delivering phone calls to a cell phone. Used for low-resolution video-on-demand applications.
- **Multicast:** A one-to-many live transmission using a cellular telephone network where a single signal is sent to multiple receivers. This uses less network bandwidth than unicast, but is still not optimized for high-quality video.
- **Broadcast:** A one-to-many live transmission using a dedicated broadcast network. Broadcast bandwidth is not constrained by the limitations of the voice (telephone) network and so supports high-quality video.
- **Background Download:** A variation on the unicast approach where the content is not transmitted live (in real time), but is instead transmitted over longer periods of time (transmission speeds can be adapted to compensate for network congestion). Once the file has been downloaded, it can be played back at the user's convenience.
- **Wired Connection:** A variation on the background download approach where the mobile device is physically connected to a computer so the content can be transferred at high speed (generally faster than real time).

Also **portable media.** *Compare* **PMP.**

moiré effect; moiré pattern A wavy or rippled distortion that appears in images affected by harmonic distortion or when lines are so close together the imaging system has difficulty differentiating them.

Since standard-definition video generally has lower resolution than high-definition video or film, images that look fine during original filming may show a moiré pattern when down-converted or transferred to video. Striped clothing and Venetian blinds are common sources of moiré patterns. In video, lines that are only slightly off the horizontal (and to a lesser extent, vertical) are more likely to show moiré patterns than those with greater angles.

Theatrical projection screens are covered with a series of small holes to allow improved sound transmission from the center channel speakers traditionally located behind the screen. Digital image pixel patterns can combine with the screen's hole pattern to create a beat frequency that appears as a series of parallel lines running through the video image, usually at a slight angle to the horizontal.

monocular area A region within a stereogram that appears in only one of the views. This can occur naturally for points in space beyond the plane of convergence (in the screen space), but generally represents an edge violation when it occurs in the audience space. *Also* **ghost edge.** *Compare* **perspective frustum; sensor axial offset.**

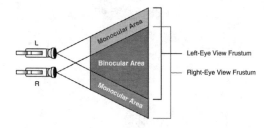

A stereoscopic image composed of left- and right-eye views (shown from above) has monocular areas to the left and right of the stereoscopic binocular area in the center. The monocular areas are more pronounced when shooting with parallel cameras.

monocular artifact A visual anomaly in a stereogram that exists equally in both eye views and therefore may be perceived using only one eye. *Compare* **binocular artifact.**

monocular blur A lack of image clarity in one eye view of a stereogram as compared to the other. Often the result of asymmetric coding, where the eye view that was subjected to increased compression (the dependent view) does not have the same image fidelity as the eye view with the lower compression rate (the base view).

monocular cue; monocular depth cue Depth information that can be interpreted from a single image or sequence of images, such as when looking through one eye or viewing traditional 2D film images. Monocular cues include static depth cues (atmospheric perspective, blur gradient, linear perspective, geometric perspective, relative height, relative size, shadows and lighting cues, static interposition, and texture gradient) and motion depth cues (kinetic interposition and motion parallax). For example, if two similar objects appear to be different sizes, the smaller one is assumed farther away; as the observer moves, nearer objects will appear to move faster than more distant objects; a near object may block part of a far object, etc. *Also* **extrastereoscopic cue.** *See* **depth cue; motion parallax.** *Compare* **binocular cue.**

monocular vision Visual perception based on individual eyes working independently of one another. Monocular vision with two eyes provides a much wider visual field than binocular vision (since the eyes do not have sufficient overlap to support stereopsis) but reduced depth perception (since only monocular depth cues are available). This tradeoff is most advantageous to prey animals, which tend to have their eyes on opposite sides of their heads to help them spot and avoid predators.

People with the use of only one eye naturally lack binocular vision and must rely solely on monocular depth cues, but not everyone with two eyes has sufficient binocular vision to appreciate the 3D effect in a stereoscopic presentation. Approximately 3 percent of the population in completely incapable of binocular vision, while a further 7 percent has a measurable defect impacting their binocular vision. For the 90 percent of the population with "normal" binocular vision, there is still a wide variation in stereo ability. A key factor in this equation is the distance between an individual's eyes, which is significantly different for children and adults.
Compare **binocular vision.**

monoscopic... *See* **monocular...**

MOS *See* **mean opinion score.**

mosaic artifact *See* **pixelation.**

mosquito noise An undesirable visual artifact found along object edges in digitally compressed images.

Mosquito noise is technically described as "a time dependent video compression impairment in which the high frequency spatial detail in video images having crisp edges is aliased intermittently." In other words, it is a type of visual distortion where sharp edges (abrupt transitions from one color to another) that do not follow a line of pixels (and therefore must be aliased to appear smooth) are aliased in one way in one frame and a slightly different way in another frame. This leads to a slight visual buzzing along the edge of the object. Mosquito noise is most common when an object is in motion. Since each eye image will normally have differing noise patterns, mosquito noise interferes with the 3D effect.
Compare **quantization artifact.**

motion aliasing *Also* **temporal aliasing.** *See* **aliasing.**

motion artifact A visual defect in a moving image caused by motion that is faster than the sampling rate or smaller than the image resolution. The former is most obvious with fast rotating objects (mostly propellers and wheels) that seem to spin in different directions or speeds. The latter is the opposite extreme and occurs when an object moves at sub-pixel rates from frame to frame. For example, with vertical movement, the imaging system will have trouble deciding which lines are occupied by the object, resulting in jagged motion as the image snaps forward to the next line, pauses for a time, then snaps forward again to the next line.

motion blur The image smearing that accompanies recordings of objects in motion, proportional to the speed difference between object and observer and dependent on the camera's shutter speed — the slower the shutter and faster the motion, the more motion blur.

If one views a single frame of film or video, a hummingbird's body may be sharp and clear but the wings may be an indistinct blur due to their much higher rate of motion. A high-speed camera, with a much faster shutter speed, may be able to capture even the hummingbird's wings in sharp focus. Because the eye is trained to expect a certain amount of blur from objects in motion, moving objects that lack motion blur look fake. This problem most often presents itself in stop-motion animation (addressed to some extent by using go-motion photography instead) and photorealistic computer animation (wherein motion blur can be created mathematically). Traditional hand-drawn animation does not incorporate motion blur, but viewers have been trained not to expect it, so it is not missed.

motion-control rig; moco rig A mechanical framework with computer-controlled electric motors. Designed to support and precisely control the movement and operation of a camera. Stereoscopic motion-control rigs may hold two or more cameras. For stop-motion stereography, a single still image camera may be employed with the motion-control rig shifting the camera left and right (and possibly adjusting convergence with each shot) to record the two halves of a stereogram. *Compare* **sequential stereogram.**

motion depth cue *See* **motion parallax.**

Motion JPEG; M-JPEG A digital video encoding format that uses JPEG to compress each frame or interlaced field. Similar in concept to I-frame only MPEG encoding, which uses only intraframe compression. Originally developed for PC multimedia applications, now also used by digital video cameras, non-linear editing systems, and game consoles. Unlike JPEG and MPEG, Motion JPEG is not an international standard, so different implementations are not necessarily compatible. *Compare* **JPEG file; MPEG.**

Motion JPEG 2000; MJ2; MJP2 A digital video encoding standard published in 2001. It uses JPEG 2000 to compress each digital video frame or interlaced field. Similar in concept to I-frame only MPEG encoding, which uses only intraframe compression. Motion JPEG 2000 was designed for high-quality digital video recording and editing, digital cinema, digital still cameras (when recording video clips), and medical and satellite imagery. The JPEG Web site is www.jpeg.org. *Compare* **JPEG 2000; MPEG.**

motion parallax A monocular depth cue used to estimate the depth in a scene by comparing the relative motion of objects as the viewer or the objects move (closer objects will appear to move faster than distant ones). Motion depth cues are particularly important in human vision. According to noted American psychologist James Jerome Gibson, "...a moving point of observation is necessary for any adequate acquaintance of environment. So we must perceive in order to move, but also move in order to perceive." *Also* **non-pictorial depth cue.** *Compare* **kinetic interposition; monocular cue; static depth cue.**

motion sickness A disturbance of the inner ear or conflicting sensory input that disrupts the sense of balance and equilibrium, causing dizziness, nausea, sweating, and vomiting. Motion sickness is most often caused by slow, repeated, complex motions (such as the motion of ocean waves). If the eyes record motion but the inner ear does not, the sensory conflict can result in a false sense of physical motion (vection). The full symptoms of motion sickness can also be induced by an immersive virtual reality environment (such as one using a head-mounted display) or motion simulator (such as those used in pilot training). These particular types of motion sickness may be called cybersickness or simulator sickness, respectively.

motoric fusion; motor fusion The muscular adjustments to the orientation of the eyes (vergence) undertaken to align the conjugate points of an object of interest with the fovea at the center of the retina so that sensoric fusion can combine them into a 3D representation. **Panum's fusion area; sensoric fusion.**

mount The substrate and frame that supports a stereo pair in the correct orientation for convenient viewing with a stereoscope.

mounting The process of aligning and fixing the individual images in a stereo pair to a mount, creating a stereocard for viewing with a stereoscope.

mounting jig A device that holds and correctly aligns the images in a stereo pair when producing a stereocard.

moustache distortion *See* **mustache distortion.**

MPEG; .mpg: One of several digital format standards for moving images with synchronized audio and associated metadata.

MPEG is an acronym of *Moving Picture Experts Group*, a joint committee of the International Organisation for Standardisation (ISO) and International Electrotechnical Commission (IEC) established in 1988 and technically known as ISO/IEC JTC1 SC29 WG11. The MPEG committee administers international standards primarily directed at digital audiovisual data compression. *Compare* **JPEG file.**

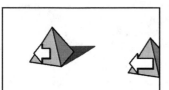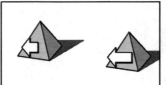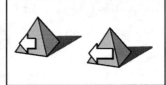

Motion parallax. Both pyramids are moving to the left, but the right-most pyramid is moving faster than the other. All things being equal (including the average linear velocity of a pyramid), one would presume that the faster pyramid is closer to the observer than the slower pyramid.

MPEG-2 The digital video compression standard defined in ISO/IEC 13818 and used in DVDs and digital broadcast television; a progressive scanned or interlaced digital video format based on MPEG-1 (ISO/IEC 11172). MPEG-2 was originally published in 1995 and supports image resolutions of 720 × 480 (720 pixels on each of 480 lines) and 1280 × 720 at up to 60 fields per second (30 frames per second) with full CD-quality digital audio. MPEG-2 supports video rates from 1.5 Mb to 15 Mb per second and has more than four times the image resolution of the original MPEG-1.

MPEG-4 The digital video compression standard defined in ISO/IEC 14496. Originally published in 1998, intended for use in low bandwidth environments such as Internet video streaming, mobile wireless device broadcasting, gaming, and other multimedia applications that require moving images with synchronized audio. The development of MPEG-4 was heavily influenced by Apple's QuickTime format, based on object-based compression. Individual objects within a scene are tracked separately and compressed together to create an MPEG-4 file. This results in very efficient and scalable compression, ranging from very low to very high bit rates. It also allows developers to control objects independently within a scene, and therefore introduce interactivity.

MPEG-4 AVC; advanced video coding A variation on the MPEG-4 video compression standard suitable for diverse applications ranging from cell phones to high-definition video. Developed and maintained jointly by ITU-T Video Coding Experts Group (VCEG) and the ISO/IEC Moving Picture Experts Group (MPEG). First published in 2003 as Part 10 of the H.264/MPEG-4 standard. AVC is the video encoding standard most often used for Blu-ray discs. *Also* **H.264**. *Compare* **VC1**.

MPEG-4 MVC; multiview video coding A multi-stream variant of MPEG-4 AVC that supports multiple, full-resolution video streams, officially released in 2009 as Annex H of the H.264/MPEG-4 AVC standard. Can be used to record two high-definition stereoscopic video streams (left and right eyes) on Blu-ray discs. MVC video, if properly encoded, can play on AVC equipment, allowing a 3D disc to play as a single view (in 2D) on AVC equipment that does not directly support MVC, such as older 2D Blu-ray players.

MPEG-4 SVC; scalable video coding A variant of MPEG-4 AVC that supports multiple resolutions derived from the same video stream, published in 2007 as Annex G of the H.264/MPEG-4

AVC standard. With SVC, reduced bandwidth (lower-resolution) video streams are derived from the original high-quality video stream by dropping packets. The resulting SVC video streams may have lower spatial resolution (suitable for smaller displays), lower temporal resolution (fewer frames per second), reduced video quality (higher rates of compression), or any combination of the three.

MPPP *See* **multiple pixels per point.**

MRC; mixed resolution coding *See* **asymmetric coding.**

MSE *See* **mean square error.**

M3D *See* **multiscopic.**

multi-picture JPEG *Also* **stereoscopic JPEG.** *See* **JPS file.**

multi-rig camera A technique for applying different stereoscopic settings to different objects or regions in an image. For example, stereo depth may be highlighted in the foreground for an object of interest, such as the main character, and reduced in the background where there is less visual interest. Requires advanced camera software and post-production techniques, so is limited to situations where compositional flexibility is very important.

multi-view; multiview; multi-stereo A stereogram with multiple pairs of left- and right-eye images or a series of images where any two neighboring images can act as a left- and right-eye pair.

    With a multi-view display, as the viewer moves horizontally, a different pair of images is presented. This also allows multiple viewers to use a multi-view display at the same time, with each viewer receiving a different pair of images. The two most common technologies in a multi-view display are lenticular, where special lenses direct the images to the left and right eyes, and parallax slit barriers, where the barrier blocks the left image from the right eye and vice versa. Multi-view displays often use up to 9 or 10 simultaneous views, though there are designs that can generate more than 100 views, significantly extending the horizontal viewing area, though usually at the cost of reduced image resolution.
Compare **3D display; integral display; super multi-view; two-view display.**

multi-view video coding; MVC *See* **MPEG-4 MVC.**

multiplane camera; multi-plane camera; multiplane; 3-D ~ An animation camera rig designed to give an illusion of depth from flat images by recording multiple images in a single exposure, each placed a different distance from the camera and allowed to move at different speeds according to their perceived distance from the observer.

Developed by Ub Iwerks of Walt Disney Productions c. 1937. Originally used drawings on clear acetate sheets placed on glass plates at different distances from the camera lens. When combined with a narrow depth of field, a 3D multiplane camera produces foreground and background objects that are out of focus, while the principal subject is sandwiched between these overlapping elements and is in sharp focus. This simulates a natural 3D world using only 2D drawings. First used for the short film *The Old Mill* (1937). *Compare* **parallax process.**

An Australian daybill promoting Disney's Academy Award–winning cartoon short *The Old Mill* (1937) (courtesy Heritage Auctions, www.ha. com).

multiplane display; multi-plane display *Also* **layered display.** *See* **volumetric 3D.**

multiple interocular; multi IO; MIO; MIO-3D A side-by-side or beam splitter rig with three or more parallel or toed-in cameras, providing a choice of interocular distances for each shot during live events or in post-production. Developed in 2010 by American stereographer Sean Fairburn.

> NOTE: Language purists would hold that the term should be *multiple interaxial* rather than *multiple interocular*, since it involves multiple camera lenses not multiple eyes.

Compare **trifocal stereo.**

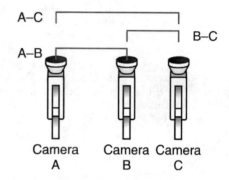

If the inter-camera spacings are unique, then each MIO set-up of *n* cameras can produce $n!/(2*(n-2)!)$ different interocular distances. For three cameras (A, B and C), this results in three different interocular distances to choose from (AB, AC, and BC). Using four cameras yields six different combinations, five cameras yields 10 combinations, and so on.

multiple pixels per point; MPPP The general class of non-glasses-based 3D displays (NG3D) where each display point in an image is represented by more than one pixel, such as lenticular, parallax barrier, and multiple projector displays. *See* **auto-stereoscopic.** *Compare* **single pixel per point.**

multiple points of reference *See* **fixation conflict.**

multiple projector display A system for presenting traditional 2D images or 3D stereograms using two or more projectors. For a high luminosity (very bright) 2D image display, projectors are positioned so their images are superimposed, resulting in a brighter image than can be produced by a single projector. For 3D applications, separate projectors are used to present the left and right components of a stereogram. The projectors are positioned so both images are superimposed, generally with orthogonal polarization filters placed in the individual light beam paths. Synchronizing multiple digital projectors is far easier than maintaining perfect synchronization using film projectors.

multiple viewpoint A 3D presentation system where the original geometry of the recorded scene is preserved and can be correctly observed from more than one vantage point.

Significant research effort is being expended in an attempt to achieve multiple viewpoints from a single 3D recording. So far, all commercial 3D presentation systems are single viewpoint. When a camera rig records a pair of stereogram images, the camera's viewpoint is precisely defined by the geometry of the system. When those stereograms are presented, there is only one viewing position where the perceived images have the same geometry as originally recorded by the camera. All other viewing positions will observe distorted images, depending on the distance and angle from the ideal position.

For example, if a camera records a perfect sphere, it will only appear to be a perfect sphere when viewed from the optimum position. All other locations will experience a distorted sphere. This is not generally a concern in theatrical presentations, since all objects will share some degree of distortion and audiences are used to seeing similar distortions in 2D images. However, it can be a major issue when combining projected objects with real objects in a projected set environment. In a projected environment, the roundness of a physical sphere will contrast with the non-roundness of a projected sphere, causing the projected images to stand out unnaturally. *Compare* **ortho stereo; single viewpoint.**

multiplex; mux To combine multiple signals, images, or programs into a single stream in such a way that they can be separated accurately at the receiving end. For example, combining video with audio into an audiovisual data stream or combining left- and right-eye images into a single stereoscopic presentation.

multiscopic; ~ 3D; M3D Appearing to have 3D depth through the use of three or more stereo images, providing multiple stereo views of the same subject. Most multiscopic systems are auto-multiscopic, allowing the perception of depth without wearing special glasses. *Also* **stereo multiview.** *Compare* **stereoscopic.**

multiscopic image set A collection of three or more images that, taken together, represent a 3D view for a multi-view display. *Compare* **stereoscopic image pair.**

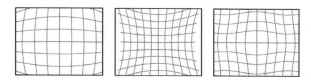

Barrel distortion, pincushion distortion, and mustache distortion (left to right).

mustache distortion; moustache distortion A lens aberration that combines both barrel and pincushion distortion. Over part of the lens, straight lines bow outward, while over other parts of the lens, straight lines bow inward. Moving out from the center of the lens, the focal length first decreases then increases or vice versa. *Also* **complex distortion.**

mux *See* **multiplex.**

mux/demux workflow A process where the left- and right-eye images are multiplexed (combined) into a single video stream for distribution, generally at half-resolution, then de-multiplexed (separated) to recover the separate eye images for presentation to the viewer. *Compare* **2D wrapper.**

MVC; multiview video coding *See* **MPEG-4 MVC.**

MXF file; .mxf The Society of Motion Picture and Television Engineers (SMPTE) standardized digital media container format for video, audio, and associated metadata. MXF is platform-independent and supports a variety of data compression formats. The MXF Web site is www.smpte-mxf.org.

MXF wrapper The container file, independent of the essence streams (audio or video) and metadata found within.

myopia The ability to focus clearly on close objects but not on distant objects. *Also* **near sighted.** *Compare* **hypermetropia.**

narrowband light Light composed of only selected frequencies, such as produced by a laser. Since most projection systems filter broadband, or white, light to produce selected colors, the majority of the energy from the light source is converted to heat and never makes it to the screen. Narrowband light sources, on the other hand, are limited to the desired wavelengths and are theoretically more efficient in operation, though more complex in design. *Compare* **broadband light.**

narrowband spectral eyewear Spectacles used to view sophisticated anaglyphs where the left- and right-eye images are each encoded with specific wavelengths of red, green, and blue light and the corresponding lenses filter all but the designated wavelengths of light. First implemented commercially as the Infitec system. *Compare* **broadband spectral eyewear; spectral eyewear.**

native 3D display format The number and arrangement of pixels in a stereogram.

> NOTE: Confusingly, *native 3D display format* is not the same as *3D native display format*, which refers to the video signal characteristics, rather than the image pixel arrangement.

native 2D display format The number and arrangement of pixels in a display device (television, video projector, computer monitor, etc.).

natural image An image that is recorded from the natural world, generally with a camera, rather than created artificially, as with computer-generated graphics. *Compare* **synthetic image.**

near disparity *See* **negative parallax.**

near plane The 2D surface perpendicular to the camera's lens axis that contains the near point. *Compare* **far plane.**

near point 1. The conjugate points in a stereogram that appear to be closest to the viewer. The near point can change from frame to frame, but should not exceed the maximum allowable distance defined by the depth budget. **2.** The nearest distance that can be seen clearly. *Compare* **far point.**

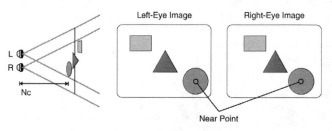

The nearest point from the camera visible in the frame (*Nc*, left) corresponds to the near point depicted in the stereogram (right).

near point distance; NPD The space from the camera to the closest object visible in a stereogram.

near point of accommodation The closest point at which the eyes can focus. Generally taken as the average between the near points of accommodation measured separately for each eye (which often differ). Increases with age as the lens hardens and it becomes more difficult for the eye muscles to reshape the lens to focus at close distances. *Compare* **far point of accommodation.**

near point stress Eyestrain brought about by focusing on close objects for too long or by trying to focus on objects that are uncomfortably close, such as when the near point in a stereogram is too close to the viewer, requiring excessive effort to fuse the image.

> As the capacity to hold close focus, or fusional reserves, is depleted, one may experience difficulty concentrating, blurred or double vision, or headaches, inspiring one to avoid further close viewing. May affect adults, though children are particularly susceptible.

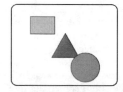 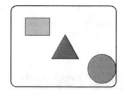

The images are configured for cross-eyed viewing. The circle is depicted with excessive negative parallax, so it should be difficult to fuse the images and see the circle, triangle, and rectangle all at the same time without double images. For example, when the circle is properly fused, either or both of the triangle and rectangle will appear as double images. Prolonged viewing should cause noticeable eyestrain.

near triad; ocular ~ The three physiological actions required to view a close object: accommodation (focus adjustments to the eyes' lenses), vergence (inward turning of the eyes), and miosis (contraction of the pupil to increase the depth of field).

nearsighted *See* **myopia.** *Compare* **hypermetropia.**

negative lens *See* **diverging lens.** *Compare* **converging lens.**

negative parallax When a point in the left-eye image is to the right of the conjugate point in the right-eye image (and vice versa) in a stereogram. Conjugate points with negative parallax will appear to extend out from the screen, occupying the audience space. The viewer's eyes must converge on conjugate points with negative parallax to fuse them into a single image. *Also* **crossed stereoscopic disparity; emergence effect; near disparity; off-the-screen effect.** *Compare* **positive parallax; zero parallax.** *See* diagram at **stereoscopic.**

network artifact A visual anomaly caused by signal corruption or data loss during transmission.

See **capture artifact; coding artifact; compressed depth artifact; decoding artifact; display artifact; production artifact.**

NG3D; non-glasses-based 3D display *See* **auto-stereoscopic.**

Nimslo; ~ format An arrangement for recording quad-image stereograms using a quad-lens camera on standard 35mm film. Nimslo images are generally presented as auto-stereoscopic lenticular prints. Nimslo format cameras were produced under the Nimslo (c. 1980) and Nishika (c. 1990) brand names. Each image is half the width of a standard 35mm still image (4 perforations, rather than the standard 8), allowing the 4-image stereogram to be recorded in the space normally occupied by 2 still images. Named for the developers of the format, American inventors Jerry Nims and Allen Lo. *Compare* **Teco-Nimslo.**

The four exposures of a Nimslo format camera on a strip of 35mm film. The small dot above the left-hand image (created by a red LED inside the camera) marks the beginning of the four-image sequence.

no glasses 3D *See* **auto-stereoscopic.**

nodal points The two points along the optical axis of a lens where the angle of a ray of light upon entry is equal to the angle upon exit with respect to the front and rear nodal points, respectively. If the front and back surfaces of the lens are in contact with the same medium (usually air), then the nodal points will lie upon the principal planes. The principal planes lie perpendicular to the optical axis in a lens. When viewed from the front of a lens, an entering light ray will appear to cross the front principal plane the same distance from the optical axis as it appears to cross the rear principal plane. Depending on the configuration of a compound lens, the principal planes may not lie within the physical lens.

> NOTE: The term *nodal point* is often used to mean *rear focal point*—the point behind a positive, or converging, lens, where all the incoming light rays cross.

Compare **center of perspective; entrance pupil; rear focal point.**

nodal-shift The changes to a varifocal lens' nodal points as the focal length is changed. A natural characteristic of physical lenses that must be simulated for the virtual lenses used in computer graphics.

node The basic component of a scene graph in a virtual reality programming system such as Java 3D or VRML.

noise Any part of a signal that contains unwanted randomness that is not part of the desired signal. In audio, noise results in audible artifacts such as static, hiss, or fuzz. In video, noise can cause visible artifacts such as snow, pixel shimmer, or ghost images. Noise interferes with digital compression, and should be minimized for best results. Each eye image in a stereogram may have different noise patterns, interfering with the 3D effect. *Compare* **crosstalk.**

Nominal Focal Length Lens   Wide Lens   Long Lens

A round ball with negative parallax recorded using the nominal focal length for the given screen size and viewing distance will appear round to the viewer. If the camera focal length is too wide, the ball will appear stretched. If the lens is too long, the ball will appear flat.

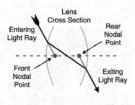 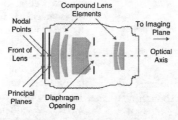

The front and rear nodal points shown in a cross section of a simple lens (left). The incoming light ray is refracted (bent) as it enters and exits the lens, changing its direction of travel. If the incoming angle is extended, it crosses the optical axis at the front nodal point. If the outgoing angle is extended, it crosses the optical axis at the rear nodal point. The principal planes and nodal points of a typical compound lens (right).

nominal focal length The ideal camera lens focal length given the nominal viewer position and anticipated screen size calculated as the ratio of the camera image sensor width to lens focal length compared to the ratio of the screen width to the nominal viewing distance.

Using a wider than optimal lens will result in a stretched perspective, while a longer than optimal lens will foreshorten (flatten) the image perspective.

nominal viewer The physical characteristics of an average viewer assumed when calculating the optimal stereoscopic image recording parameters. For example, the nominal viewer may be presumed to be an adult with an interocular distance of about 65mm (or about 2½"). If a work is targeted at children, a smaller interocular distance may be assumed (something between 40–55mm).

nominal viewer position The position of the theoretically ideal viewer of a stereoscopic work with respect to the screen, used when calculating the optimal stereoscopic image parameters. Generally assumed to be sitting orthogonal to the screen (so that the viewer's gaze strikes the center of the screen at a right angle). The distance between the nominal viewer and the screen (and therefore the angle of view) varies depending on the anticipated viewing environment: traditional theatrical presentation, stadium seating theater, home television viewing, portable media device, etc.

non-depolarizing screen *See* **silver screen.**

non-epipolar Geometric differences between the images recorded by each eye that cannot be explained by horizontal parallax; vertical disparity. *See* **epipolar.**

non-glasses-based 3D display; NG3D *See* **autostereoscopic.** *Compare* **glasses-based 3D display.**

non-parallax-based 3D Three-dimensional vision or display systems that do not rely on the parallax differences between two separate images to create the appearance of depth. This includes monocular depth cues, holography, and volumetric displays. *Compare* **parallax-based 3D.**

non-pictorial depth cue *See* **motion depth cue.** *Compare* **pictorial depth cue.**

notch filter *See* **band-reject filter.**

novelty factor The extent to which popularity is based on freshness of experience. Once something is no longer new, its popularity is more likely to be based on its intrinsic value.

Many early sound films, for example, were billed as "all talking," and that is largely what they were — due to technical limitations with recorded sound and an over-reliance on the novelty factor, the actors did little but stand around and talk. Once the novelty wore off, movies no longer per-

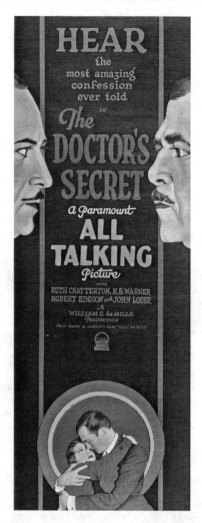

Paramount's *The Doctor's Secret* (1929) took full advantage synchronous sound's novelty factor when it billed itself as "1000% ALL TALKING" (courtesy Heritage Auctions, www.ha.com).

formed well at the box office just because the actors talked. Many of the 3D films produced during the 1950s relied heavily on the novelty factor for their success, and would not have been produced if contemporary standards for story, dialogue, and acting were applied. The technical limitations of the time were not fully addressed until after the novelty of 3D had worn off and 3D movies subsequently diminished in popularity until the digital 3D renaissance initiated in 2005 with *Chicken Little.*

NPD *See* **near point distance.**

NTSC The analog broadcast television and video standard common to North America, Japan, and portions of Latin America. Originally adopted as the U.S. standard by the FCC in April 1941. The Electronic Industry Association's color television standard (RS-170A) was adopted by the FCC in 1953 as the NTSC color standard. The FCC mandated that most, but not all, U.S. television broadcasters switched over to the ATSC digital format by June 2009.

NTSC video features up to 525 interlaced scan lines split between two fields per frame (odd and even numbered scan lines in alternating fields) refreshed at 29.97 frames per second. The original NTSC standard's 30 frames per second was adjusted to 29.97 frames per second as a technical compromise when color was introduced in 1953. The speed change was necessary to avoid audible noise caused by beat-frequency interference between the color subcarrier and the average value of the sound carrier. When NTSC is converted to a digital format, it is generally at 704 × 480 or 720 × 480 pixels.

NTSC is an acronym of *National Television Standards Committee* or *National Television Systems Committee*, though it is also known colloquially as "Never Twice the Same Color" or "Never The Same Color"—a joking reference to its color consistency issues.

Compare **PAL.**

Nyquist frequency The highest signal frequency that can be reproduced accurately when an analog signal is digitally encoded at a given sample rate. Looking at it another way, the Nyquist frequency is the minimum digital sample rate necessary to achieve an accurate approximation of an analog signal, or at least twice the input signal frequency.

For example, the upper range of human hearing tends to be 20 kHz. The Nyquist frequency for digital audio is twice that, or 40 kHz. Audio CDs are generally produced with a sample rate of 44.1 kHz, encoding frequencies as high as 22.05 kHz

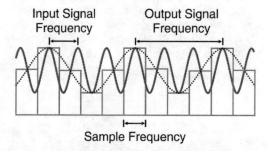

The digital sample frequency is below the Nyquist frequency for the input analog signal, so when the digital samples are converted into an analog output signal, the derived output signal is not an accurate representation of the original input signal.

without distortion. Digitizing sounds with sample rates below the Nyquist frequency may cause audio aliasing, perceived as a buzzing sound. Coined as an eponym, after Swedish-born Bell Laboratories engineer Harry Nyquist.
Also **folding frequency.**

nystagmus A repetitive, involuntary pattern of eye movements that may interfere with stereo depth perception. *See* **saccade; smooth pursuit; vestibulo-ocular reflex; visual fixation.**

object edge plane distortion A type of Z-depth distortion where the edges of an object are perceived to be at a different distance from the viewer than the interior space of the object. Generally a side effect of 2D-to-3D conversion or image keystoning.

object space The area that lies before and is recorded by a camera. *Also* **camera space.** *Compare* **image space.**

objective test A method of measurement that is not influenced by observer bias, based on mathematical analysis or physical examination. *Compare* **subjective test.**

oblique anamorphosis *See* **anamorphosis.**

observer The viewer, or end-consumer, of an audiovisual work.

occluded surface reconstruction; OSR *See* **disocclusion.**

occlusion A blockage or obstruction; when an object that is closer to the observer obscures some portion of an object farther from the observer. Commonly used as a monocular depth cue. If an object that is supposed to be in the audience space is cut off by the edge of the screen, it seems as if the edge of the window surrounding the screen has occluded the nearer object—a situation that cannot occur in the natural world. *Also* **overlap.**

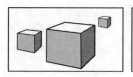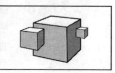

One assumes a different spatial relationship between the cubes with no occlusion (left) than when occlusion is present (right).

occlusion information Stereographic metadata that describes the objects within a scene, indicating whether specific points on each surface are visible or occluded from each viewpoint from which images were recorded. These data allow for adjustments to the binocular disparity for each depicted object, selectively increasing or decreasing the apparent depth in a stereogram.

occlusion resolution The precision with which occlusion information is recorded.

ocular dominance When a particular neuron in the visual system prefers to respond to input from one eye more than the other. Sufficiently strong ocular dominance can result in an overall visual preference for one eye and difficulty perceiving stereoscopic images.

ocular near triad *See* **near triad.**

oculovestibular reflex *See* **vestibulo-ocular reflex.**

OculR The trade name for a 35mm theatrical film projector lens system developed by Oculus3D in 2010 that allowed for the projection of linear polarized, side-by-side, 35mm stereoscopic images. The OculR took the place of a standard projector lens and rotated, polarized, and superimposed the two vertical side-by-side images into a properly aligned polarized stereogram.

Side and front views (left to right) of an OculR projector lens (courtesy Oculus3D, www.oculus3d.com).

oculus dexter; OD The scientific (Latin) term for the right eye.

oculus sinister; OS The scientific (Latin) term for the left eye.

Oculus3D The co-developer (with Look3D) of eco friendly, biodegradable glasses equipped with RealD-certified polarized lenses. The disposable frames are made from plant-based resins and may be recycled or composted. The Oculus3D Web site is www.oculus3d.com.

Prior to developing eyewear, Oculus3D produced OculR, a side-by-side 35mm 3D film format where the stereogram was rotated 90° rather than

having the 50 percent horizontal squeeze typical of digital side-by-side formats. The system worked with a standard 35mm projector (equipped with a special OculR lens) and required the same silver screen as other polarized projection systems. It produced images two to three times brighter than equivalent digital cinema systems, thanks in large part to its use of orthogonal linear polarization (common to theme park applications) rather than circular polarization (found in most theatrical and home entertainment polarized systems).

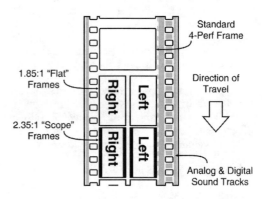

The arrangement of left- and right-eye images on a 35mm film print configured for Oculus3D. (Viewed from the lamp side, looking towards the projector lens.)

OD *See* **oculus dexter.**

off-the-screen effect *See* **negative parallax.**

old eyes *See* **presbyopia.**

1-eye stereoscope A stereoscope design employing two mirrors for one eye and allowing direct view for the other eye. May be hand-held or configured with a head strap to hold the stereoscope in place over one eye. Since two mirrors are used, the stereogram does not need to be altered as it does when using the more traditional single mirror viewing method. May be used to view

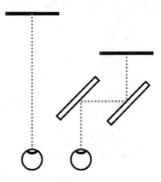

side-by-side or over/under stereograms without an active glasses-based display system.

1-in-30 rule; 1-in-50 rule *See* ⅟₃₀ **rule.**

1-plane mode Stereoscopic content encoding where 2D graphical elements (typically subtitles or interactive graphics) are placed a fixed distance above the 3D video content. *Compare* **2-plane mode.**

¼ wave plate; ¼ wave retarder Specially prepared and oriented optical material that rotates polarized light rays 45°. Used to convert linearly polarized light rays into circularly polarized light rays and vice versa. A ¼ wave plate produces left (counterclockwise) or right (clockwise) circular polarized light, depending on how it is oriented with respect to the incident light rays' polarization direction.

The beam-splitter in a mirror rig acts as a linear

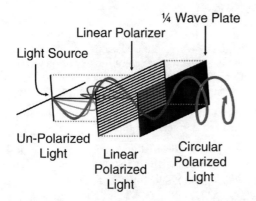

polarizer, delivering polarized light to only one of the two cameras. This creates unwanted visual differences between the two recorded eye images. Adding a ¼ wave retarder to the front of the beam splitter prevents linear polarized light from entering the rig and helps ensure that both cameras record comparable images.

⅟₃₀ rule; ⅟₅₀ rule A rough rule of thumb for stereo camera rigs equipped with normal focal length lenses (neither wide angle nor telephoto) governing the relationship between the interaxial separation and the distance to the nearest object in the frame. According to this rule, shots should be composed with objects no closer than 30 times the interaxial distance for in-home viewing—or 50 times the interaxial distance for theatrical presentation—to avoid exceeding a comfortable depth range. Put another way, the interaxial distance should not be more than ⅟₃₀ (or ⅟₅₀) of the distance to the nearest object in the frame.

NOTE: As a rule of thumb, this only provides a rough starting point and then only applies in specific situations. Over-reliance on this rule could lead to unsatisfactory results.

This rule originated with the Realist 35mm still image stereo film camera. The Realist manual recommended that photographed objects be at least seven feet from the camera, or about 30 times the camera's fixed interaxial separation. This rule of thumb was then extended to other 35mm film formats and eventually stereoscopic image capture in general. However, not all stereo photography situations match those assumed for the Realist camera:

- Parallel lenses;
- 35mm focal length;
- 35mm film;
- Images include both close objects and objects at stereo infinity (clouds, mountains, etc.); and
- The stereograms will be projected onto a (relatively) large screen.

Compare **separation factor.**

OpenEXR *See* **EXR file.**

optical aberration; optical distortion *See* **aberration.**

optical flow Detecting object edges and calculating scene depth information from an image sequence using the frame-by-frame differences caused by relative camera and object motion.

optic axis; optical axis 1. An imaginary line that extends through the physical center of the lens. This represents the optical center of the image created by the lens. 2. The imaginary line that passes through the center of the eye and represents the direction of one's gaze. *Also* **principle axis.**

optic flow The apparent visual movement that results from the observer's own motion through space.

optimal motion *Also* **beta motion.** *See* **apparent motion.** *Compare* **phi phenomenon.**

optimized anaglyph An anaglyph where the colors have been modified according to mathe-

matical rules to achieve a particular goal, such as reduced ghosting, reduced retinal rivalry, improved color reproduction, or
improved depth reproduction.
The first such process, Akumira,
was introduced by Brightland
Corporation in August 2000. *See*
**Akumira anaglyph; Dubois
anaglyph; Wimmer anaglyph.**

0° and 90° Polarization Angles   45° and 135° Polarization Angles

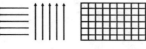 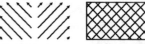

Separate Eye | Superimposed   Separate Eye | Superimposed
Images | on Screen   Images | on Screen

The two most common orientations for orthogonal polarization: horizontal/vertical (left) and cross-angled (right).

orientation The position of an
object relative to a set of reference axes. Object
rotation can be classified as pan or yaw (left/right
movement, rotating on the Y-axis), tilt or pitch
(up/down movement, rotating on the X-axis),
and roll (clockwise/counterclockwise movement,
rotating on the Z-axis).

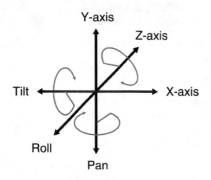

ortho stereo; orthostereoscopic Perfect stereoscopic reproduction; images that appear as did
the original recorded scene without any depth distortions.

> With theoretically ideal stereoscopic viewing con-
> ditions, the interaxial distance used to record the
> stereogram matches the interocular distance of
> the observer; the images are presented using
> lenses of the same focal length as those used when
> the images were recorded, and the stereogram is
> viewed from a distance that ensures the image has
> the same visual angle for the observer as was
> recorded by the camera.

Also **tautomorphic image.** *Compare* **pseudostereo; stereoscopic distortion.**

orthogonal polarization A system of two linear
polarization grids arranged at right angles to each
other. With cross-angled polarization, such as
typically found in theme park applications, the
linear polarization grids are still 90° offset, but instead of being vertical (0°) and horizontal (180°),
they are aligned along 45° diagonals (45° for the
left eye and 135° for the right eye). If viewers tilt
their heads too far to one side, they may lose the
3D effect. *Also* **perpendicular polarization.** *Com-*

pare **cross-angled polarization; crossed polarization elements.**

orthostereoscopic; orthoscopic; ~ image *See*
ortho stereo. *Compare* **pseudostereo.**

OS *See* **oculus sinister.**

OSR; occluded surface reconstruction *See* **disocclusion.**

OU *See* **over/under.**

out of phase Overlapping waves with the same
frequency where the peaks and troughs are not
aligned. When waves combine out of phase, the
effect can be subtractive rather than additive.
Compare and see diagram at **in phase.**

outline aliasing *Also* **jaggies; spatial aliasing;
staircase artifact.** *See* **aliasing.**

overlap *Also* **occlusion; interposition.** *See* **kinetic interposition; static interposition.**
Compare **monocular cue.**

over-slung A stereoscopic camera mirror rig
with the primary camera pointed directly at the
action and the secondary camera set at a right
angle and above the primary (pointing down and
into the beam-splitter). *Also* **high-mode.**
Compare **under-slung.**

over/under; over and under; OU; ~ 3D A technique for recording stereograms where the left-
and right-eye images are recorded one above the
other. The individual eye images may be full size
or compressed vertically so they fit within a standard image frame.

> Over/under-encoded stereograms preserve the
> full horizontal resolution of the original images
> (twice as much as side-by-side stereograms).
> Since all stereoscopic depth information is
> recorded in the horizontal direction, over/under-
> based systems generally deliver superior depth
> representation compared to side-by-side systems,
> which preserve the full vertical resolution at the
> expense of horizontal resolution. In most 35mm
> film applications, each eye image is a half-height
> image two perforations tall, so both fit within a

standard four-perforation film frame. Some 35mm over/under configurations use a narrower gap between the eye images than between frames to provide the projectionist with a visual reference for frame alignment.

Also **TaB; top-and-bottom.**

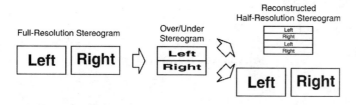

The full-resolution stereogram (left) encoded as an over/under frame-compatible stereogram (center) is reconstructed as a half-resolution stereogram (right).

packaged media Audiovisual content that has been recorded to physical media for use by a consumer, including audio CDs, DVDs, Blu-ray discs, etc. In earlier days, packaged media included vinyl LPs, cassette tapes, VHS tapes, etc.

page flipping Quickly switching between left- and right-eye images in a stereoscopic display system. Viewed using active shutter glasses synchronized to switch in time with the images.

pair comparison method; PC A standardized method for measuring the subjective quality of different changes made to a video signal. Published as part of *ITU-T Recommendation P.910* in September 1999 by the International Telecommunication Union.

This method ranks multiple video manipulation processes in a series of head-to-head comparisons presented to reviewers in a regular pattern: video sequence A followed by a two-second interval then video sequence B. Each test pair is separated by a longer interval (generally ≤ 10 seconds) during which the reviewers indicated their preferred sequence, A or B.

All of the processes under review are compared in all possible pair combinations. For example, if there are three different processes, A, B and C, then the possible pairings are AB, BA, AC, CA, BC, and CB. (For n different processes, there will be $n(n-1)$ pair combinations.) The same video sequence pairs need not be presented more than once during a test session since the test sequence already ensures that each pairing is presented twice, though in a different order each time.

A variation on the PC method allows for the simultaneous presentation of the video sequence pairs side-by-side on the same monitor.

Compare **subjective test.**

PAL The color analog broadcast television and video standard common to Europe and Australia. Originally developed in 1962 as an improvement on both NTSC (the American system) and SECAM (the French system) by Dr. Walter Bruch of Telefunken in West Germany and first broadcast in the UK in 1967.

PAL video features up to 625 interlaced scan lines split between two fields per frame (odd and even numbered scan lines in alternating fields) refreshed 25 frames per second. The key improvement in the PAL system is that it inverts the phase of the reference burst for the color signal on alternate lines. This helps correct inadvertent hue shifts and improves the color fidelity of the signal over that of NTSC.

PAL is an acronym of *Phase Alternation by Line*, *Phase Alternating Line*, or *Phase Alternate Line*. It is also known colloquially as "Perfection At Last"—a joking reference to PAL's improved picture fidelity as compared to NTSC—or "Pay A Lot"—in reference to PAL's relatively high equipment complexity, and therefore increased cost compared to NTSC.

Compare **NTSC.**

pan *Also* **yaw.** *See* **orientation.**

Panavision 3D; ~ system The trade name for a stereogram encoding process where the left- and right-eye images are color-coded using an interference filter and combined into a single image for presentation. Developed jointly by Panavision, Omega Optical, and Deluxe. Similar in concept to the Dolby 3D/Infitec system, but available in both digital cinema and 35mm film-based versions. The Panavision 3D Web site is 3d.panavision.com.

Each image is recorded as a matrix of red, green, and blue (RGB) primary color values, much like a traditional RGB computer image. Different colors are produced by varying the intensity of the individual RGB values of each pixel. To encode the stereogram in a single image, specific wavelengths of each of the primary colors are used for each eye. When viewed through glasses with matching color filters, only the left-eye wavelength of red is visible to the left eye, while only the right-eye wavelength of red is visible to the right eye. Blue and green are similarly filtered. This causes some color distortion in the reconstructed image, but not nearly as much as a more traditional anaglyphic process. Since the projected images are not polarized, they can be presented using traditional white screens rather than the

special silver screens required by polarized 3D systems. The film-based version of Panavision 3D uses a standard 35mm projector equipped with a special lens. The left- and right-eye images are recorded in a single-frame over/under format. The special projector lens aligns the images on screen. As with all interference filter-based 3D systems, the performance of Panavision 3D is very dependent on the color balance of the projector lamp, increasing the importance of proper projector maintenance.
Compare **Dolby 3D; Technicolor 3D.** *See* **interference** filter diagram in color section.

panorama A series of images that form a 360° view, often stitched together from a series of narrower views. *Compare* **discrete view; distributed view; photo bubble; spinography.**

Panum phenomenon; Panum's limiting case A special situation in which correct binocular fusion delivers erroneous depth information because there are confusingly similar points that are not part of a conjugate pair in one of the eye views. For example, when fusing a single vertical line in one eye image with one of two parallel lines in the other eye image, the fused line (with conjugate points in both eye images) will appear to be at a different depth from the un-fused line (with unpaired points). Named after Danish physician Peter Panum who described the phenomenon in *Physiologische Untersuchungen über das Sehen mit zwei Augen* (*Physiological Investigations on Seeing with Two Eyes*, 1858).

Panum's fusion area; Panum's fusional area The region surrounding the horopter where image disparity is small enough that the left- and right-eye images can be fused into a single image. Image details recorded beyond this region contain excessive disparity and can result in double vision, or diplopia. First described by Danish physician Peter Panum.

Within the fovea (at the center of the retina), retinal disparity is limited to about 0.1°— if the conjugate points in the images recorded by the retinas are any farther apart, they cannot be fused. Moving outward from the fovea by 6° increases the acceptable retinal disparity to about 0.33°; at 12° from center, acceptable disparity increases to about 0.66°. Extended viewing times and vergence can extend the

range of fusible disparities to 1.57° for uncrossed disparity and 4.93° for crossed disparity.

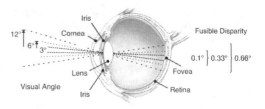

(**National Eye Institute, National Institutes of Health**)

The physical position and size of the fusion area in 3D space depends on the vergence of the observer's gaze. When the eyes are directed at a near object, disparity increases greatly as an object moves away from the horopter, narrowing the fusion area. When the eyes are directed at a distant object, disparity increases slowly as an object moves away from the horopter, extending the fusion area. *Compare* **binocular suppression.**

parabolic real image An upside-down image of an object produced by a parabolic mirror. Two properly constructed parabolic mirrors facing each other will reverse the source image and create a virtual image, allowing for the creation of a reflective hologram that appears to be a solid, 3D object floating in space. *Compare* **reflective hologram.**

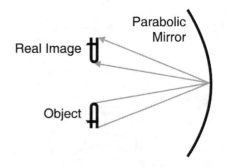

parallax The differences in perspective between two different views of the same subject, interpreted by the brain as representing three-dimensional stereo depth; the distance between conjugate points in the left- and right-eye images of a stereogram.

The parallax in natural vision is normally measured as an angle of so many degrees. Parallax in stereograms may be measured as angular degrees (taking into account both display size and viewing distance), in pixels (image resolution dependent), as a linear distance between conjugate points (taking into account display size), or as a percentage of screen width.

In human binocular vision, each eye records a slightly different image of the same subject because the eyes are on either side of the nose. The brain interprets these differences to infer the distance to the object. Non-reflex cameras suffer from parallax error between the taking and viewing lenses. When the subject is at a significant distance from the camera, this is not enough to notice. As the camera moves closer to its subject, allowances may have to be made for the fact that the two lenses see a slightly different image.

Stereoscopic imaging systems rely on the apparent parallax between left- and right-eye image views to create their 3D images. In such systems, the images present slightly different views to simulate the distance between a pair of human eyes— approximately 50–70mm (the exact distance is adjusted based on the composition of the subject being filmed and its distance from the camera). When these two images are presented one to each eye, the brain interprets the horizontal image parallax to create the impression of 3D depth.

In stereoscopic systems, parallax is characterized with respect to an object's apparent position with respect to the screen:

- **Positive Parallax:** The left-eye image is to the left of the right-eye image (and vice versa) and the object appears to be behind the screen (in the screen space).
- **Negative Parallax:** The left-eye image is to the right of the right-eye image (and vice versa) and the object appears to be in front of the screen (in the audience space).
- **Zero Parallax:** The left-eye image is aligned with the right-eye image and the object appears to be on the surface of the screen (equivalent to a traditional 2D presentation). *Compare* **deviation; disparity.**

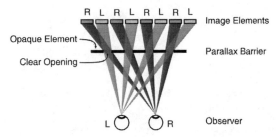

The arrangement of elements in a parallax barrier-based display (viewed from above). If the observer is too far to one side, the right eye could see the left-eye element and vice versa, leading to image ghosting or pseudostereo artifacts.

The conjugate points *AL* and *AR* (from the left- and right-eye images, respectively) are arranged with negative parallax, so point *a* appears in front of the screen. Points *B* have zero parallax and coincide in the two stereogram images, so Point *b* appears on the surface of the screen. Finally, Points *CL* and *CR* have positive parallax, so Point *c* appears behind the screen.

parallax barrier A device placed between an image and the viewer to prevent the off-eye from seeing the wrong image in an auto-stereoscopic display. For example, an array of parallax barriers may be placed on top of an LCD screen and aligned with the pixel columns so that the left eye can only see the pixels that carry the left-eye image and vice versa. Parallax barriers tend to limit the acceptable horizontal viewing angles for the stereogram (too far to one side, and the left eye may accidentally pick up the right-eye image). Multiscopic displays need more than two eye images, or views, per frame to support multiple viewing positions, often up to 16 views per frame. *Compare* **lenticular barrier; simple wall barrier.**

parallax-based 3D Three-dimensional vision or display systems that rely on the parallax differences between two separate images to create the appearance of depth. This includes binocular vision, active displays, lenticular and polarized displays, etc., but does not include monocular depth cues, holography, and volumetric displays. *Compare* **non-parallax-based 3D.**

parallax budget The total range of parallax from largest negative (in front of the screen) to largest positive (behind the screen) that may be comfortably presented by a stereoscopic display system. Essentially the same as the depth budget, but represented by amount of parallax rather than by apparent depth. The total parallax budget is largely dependent on the average viewing distance (increases as with the size of the screen) and the average viewer's interocular distance (larger for adults than children). *Compare* **depth budget; depth range; Percival's zone.**

parallax change *See* **convergence animation; dZ/dt.**

parallax depth cue *See* **binocular cue.**

parallax error An unwanted angular difference between two views of the same subject due to the parallax between the two viewpoints. Vertical parallax is especially problematic as it does not properly occur in natural vision.

parallax panoramagram An auto-stereoscopic image or display technology based on lenticules or parallax barriers. *Also* **parallax stereogram.**

parallax problem The distorted image geometry that is perceived when viewing a single-view stereogram from an angle other than the one from which it was recorded, such as when sitting off to the side in a large theater. *Compare* **multiple viewpoint.**

parallax process Animating a stack of 2D image layers, each with cut-outs or transparent sections through which some portion of the lower layers in the stack can be seen, so that higher layers move faster than lower layers to simulate the effect of motion parallax on distant objects. *Compare* **multi-plane camera.**

parallax resolution The number of individual images used to present a 3D view. The minimum number is two, one for each eye. Certain auto-stereoscopic displays (such as multi-view and volumetric displays) use more than two images to create a 3D representation viewable from multiple angles without special eyewear.

parallax stereogram An auto-stereoscopic image using a simple wall barrier and two independent views. Devised as a photographic process by American inventor Frederick E. Ives and patented in 1903, based on the earlier work of French painter G. A. Bois-Clair, who produced a two-view painting using a parallax barrier in 1692.

> Each eye view is divided into a series of equal vertical strips. The strips are then arranged in left/right pairs with each strip separated by a thin barrier. The barrier prevents the left eye from seeing the right-eye images and vice versa. The vertical barriers are replaced with cylindrical lenses in a lenticular stereogram.

parallel axes *See* **parallel-viewing.**

parallel cameras A stereoscopic camera configuration where the cameras are positioned so the lens axes are parallel, resulting in a fixed interaxial distance to infinity.

> NOTE: Technically, the cameras in a beam-splitter rig are set with their lens axes at a 90° angle, but the beam splitter redirects one of the lenses so the cameras can record parallel views, just as if one were using parallel cameras.

Using parallel cameras avoids the geometric errors common to toed-in cameras and any on-set stereo errors are generally easier to correct in post-production, but parallel images have issues of their own. When recorded, parallel images exhibit only negative parallax. To correct for this, a desired zero parallax plane is selected and the images are re-converged (horizontal image translation) and optionally cropped to restore the original aspect ratio. Still images recorded with parallel cameras are often recorded with a landscape aspect ratio (wider than tall) but presented with a portrait aspect ratio (taller than wide). Post-production horizontal image translation and image cropping can be avoided by using cameras with imaging grids that are off-center from the optical axis (sensor axial offset) since they do not completely overlap.

In a traditional parallel camera setup, the cameras are positioned so that their angles of view are parallel and the zero disparity plane (ZDP) coincides with the region of the scene that will be shown when the images are re-converged and cropped or the imaging grids are adjusted to exclude the portions that do not overlap. In computer graphics, the view frustum of each virtual camera may be made asymmetrical so there is no excess area to be cropped. However, most physical cameras have symmetrical view frustums that will not precisely overlap when the interaxial distance is greater than zero. If the imaging grids cannot be moved horizontally with respect to the lens

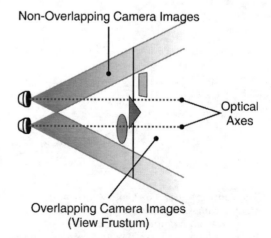

The overlapping (view frustum) and non-overlapping portions of the camera images of parallel cameras.

axes, then the left and right cameras may be record images wider than required so they can be cropped before presentation.

While parallel cameras avoid many of the issues with toed-in in cameras, they may also produce flatter images with a more "cardboard cut-out" feel. Toed-in cameras, on the other hand, tend to record more subjectively natural, "rounded" objects. *Compare* **toed-in cameras.**

parallel rig A mechanical framework designed to support two identical cameras set side-by-side. The optical axes may be set parallel to one another or, if the rig supports convergence adjustments, toed-in by equal amounts. *See* **side-by-side rig.** *Compare* **mirror rig.**

parallel stereo pair A stereogram recorded with parallel cameras.

parallel-viewing; parallel free-viewing; parallel method A stereogram presentation technique where the left-eye image is placed on the left and the right-eye image is placed on the right. The 3D effect becomes apparent when viewers relax their eyes, allowing them to turn outward until they are parallel (as if focusing on a far object behind the images). This works equally well with color or black-and-white images and does not require special glasses. However, many people find it difficult to look through the image and their eyes remain too converged to appreciate the effect. With the exception of Magic Eye and single-image random dot stereograms, parallel-viewing stereograms are generally limited to about 65mm (2½") wide, or the average adult interocular distance. *Also* **divergence viewing; wide-eyed viewing.** *Compare* **cross-eyed viewing; free-viewing; mirror-viewing.**

partial pseudostereo; partial reverse stereo; partial reverse 3D A stereogram with portions of the left- and right-eye images reversed (the left-eye image contains an element intended for the right eye and vice versa), such as when one pair of plates in a composite image is swapped left for right. *Also* **inversion; reverse stereo.** *Compare* **depth mismatch.**

pass-through An electronic device that can receive and re-transmit a signal without altering the content. For example, when sending content from a Blu-ray player through an A/V receiver and on to a display, the audio portion of the signal is manipulated by the A/V receiver, but the video portion is passed-through unaltered to the display for presentation. *Compare* **3D-compatible.**

passive display *See* **passive glasses-based 3D display.** *Compare* **active display.**

passive eyewear; passive glasses Spectacles with fixed lenses that do not physically change during the stereogram presentation process. May be limited to linear or circular polarized lenses, or may be taken also to include spectral glasses, such as traditional anaglyph or Infitec. *Compare* **active eyewear; hybrid eyewear; spectral eyewear.**

passive glasses-based 3D display; PGB3D The general class of glasses-based 3D displays (GB3D) that are viewed with passive eyewear, such as polarized and anaglyph. *Compare* **active glasses-based 3D display.**

passive/passive A passive stereoscopic display technology coupled with passive glasses, as with anaglyphic, polarized, and Pulfrich systems. *Compare* **active/active; active/passive.**

passive retarder *See* **micro-polarizer.**

passive stereo A stereoscopic device that requires the viewer to wear some form of passive eyewear to perceive stereo depth in the image, including anaglyphs, ChromaDepth, and polarized stereograms. *Compare* **active stereo.**

patterned retarder *See* **Dolby 3D; Panavision 3D.**

PC *See* **pair comparison method.**

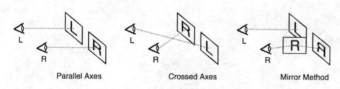

Parallel Axes   Crossed Axes   Mirror Method

In parallel viewing, the optical axes of each eye are parallel, as noted above. When viewing the images below, un-focus your eyes (focus them on a point in the distance beyond the page) until the two images overlap. The circle should appear in front of the triangle with the rectangle in the background

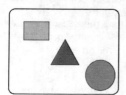 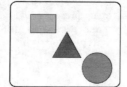

PD; pupillary distance *See* **interocular distance.**

PDP; plasma display panel *See* **plasma.**

peak gain at zero degrees viewing axis Screen gain measured at the brightest point on the screen (generally, in the center of the projection area) from an angle perpendicular to the surface. Screen gain drops moving out from the center of the projection area and as the viewing angle increases. If the gain falls off quickly, a visible hot spot may result. Low-gain screens have wider acceptable viewing angles than high-gain screens but high-gain screens produce brighter images. *Compare* **half-gain viewing angle.**

peak signal to noise ratio; PSNR *See* **signal to noise ratio.**

pellicule; pellicle *See* **beam splitter.**

perceived depth *See* **stereo distance.**

perceived size The apparent size of an object given available visual cues, as opposed to its actual size. *Compare* **relative size; usual size.**

perception The processes of identifying and interpreting sensory stimulation.

perceptual depth cue *See* **depth cue.**

perceptually lossless A lossy compression algo-

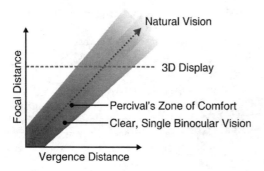

Percival's zone. With natural vision, there is a direct link between vergence (the amount of inward turning of the eyes based on the distance to an object) and accommodation (the focal adjustments to each eye's lens that produce a sharp image given the distance to an object). Objects in stereoscopic images appear to be different distances from the viewer, requiring differing amounts of vergence to align the images of the left and right eyes, but are the same physical distance, requiring that the eyes retain the exact same accommodation regardless of the vergence. (Note that distance is presented in diopters to simplify the diagram.)

rithm that delivers a seemingly lossless result. An exact reproduction of the original cannot be produced because some information has been lost in the compression process, but a standard observer will not be able to tell the difference between the original and compressed versions.

Percival's zone; ~ of comfort The area within the visual field where binocular images can be fused into a single 3D view without particular strain or discomfort; the middle third of the distance between the nearest and farthest fusion points when the eyes are focused at a particular distance. First proposed by British ophthalmologists Archibald Stanley Percival in *The Prescribing of Spectacles* (1920). *Also* **zone of comfort.** *Compare* **accommodation/vergence; Panum's fusion area.**

perpendicular polarization *See* **orthogonal polarization.**

persistence; pixel ~ The amount of time, after deactivation, that a pixel in a display remains visible. Persistence can help avoid discernable flicker by blending one image into the next, but if the delay is too long, it can show up as image smear behind fast-moving objects or result in cross-talk in an active stereoscopic display.

persistence of vision The phenomenon of perceptual psychology that causes a viewer to interpret a series of still images as being in fluid motion, essential to the existence of motion pictures and television. The term was coined in 1826 by British lexicographer Peter Mark Roget.

The brain naturally retains each image seen for a brief interval. If a series of still images with a small visual change from one image to the next is presented so that the next image appears while the prior image is still retained, the brain interprets the separate images as being connected in a continuous series (the beta phenomenon). When viewing at least 16 images per second, persistence of vision causes the brain to retain the images long enough to register fluid motion, although at lower rates, flicker will be perceived. If the images do not come fast enough, the viewer perceives choppy or unsteady motion.

Projected film images are interrupted by intervals of darkness as the film is advanced to the next frame. To help avoid visible flicker, each projected image is flashed on the screen two or three times in quick succession. This increases the effective image presentation rate for a film recorded at 24 frames per second to 48 or 72 images per second.

At particularly high recorded frame rates, near 48 frames per second, moving images begin looking more real than photographed. This phenomenon inspired virtual reality/simulation systems such as Showscan to use very high frame rates as well as large gauge film — 70mm and above — for a heightened sense of reality.

Persistence of vision was first noted by the Roman poet Lucretius in 65 BCE. In 130 CE, the astronomer Ptolemy of Alexandria proved Lucretius' principle. In 1831, Belgian scientist Joseph Antoine Ferdinand Plateau developed the Phenakistiscope, the first documented mechanical device that could produce the illusion of motion from a series of still images.

Compare **critical fusion frequency; phi phenomenon.**

personal media player *See* **PMP.**

personal space *Also* **theater space.** *See* **audience space.**

perspectival anamorphosis *See* **anamorphosis.**

perspective 1. aerial ~; atmospheric ~: The visual phenomenon in which objects appear less distinct, with less contrast, and lighter in color (often taking on a blue tint) as the distance from the observer increases. Caused by atmospheric attenuation (light absorption and scattering). **2. geometric ~; linear ~; visual ~:** The visual phenomenon in which objects appear smaller as the distance from the observer increases. As a consequence, parallel lines (such as railroad tracks) seem to merge in the distance. May be manipulated to create forced perspective. *Compare* **monocular cue; static depth cue.**

perspective frustum The pyramid that results from the intersection of the left- and right-camera view frustums when recording a stereogram.

The two images in a stereogram are slightly offset, so they do not represent identical view frustums. Parallel cameras result in a pyramid-shaped perspective frustum with a rectangular base determined by the image aspect ratio. Converged cameras result in a

Perspective (photographs by Melanie B. Kroon).

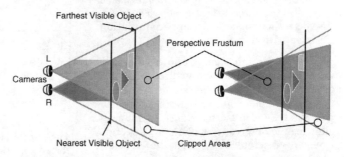

Persective frustum. The two-dimensional geometry of the perspective frustum viewed from above showing the difference between parallel cameras (left) and toed-in cameras (right). Toed-in cameras require less image clipping than parallel cameras, but may introduce image distortions that require post-production correction.

bent pyramid-shaped perspective frustum. The virtual cameras that record synthetic (computer-generated) images may use asymmetrical view frustums to better align the subjective perspectives. When presented for later viewing, only those portions of the original scene included in both view frustums are typically presented. *Compare* **sensor axial offset; view frustum.**

perspective-stereopsis rivalry When there is perceptible conflict between an object's 3D perspective and binocular depth cues, leading to contradictory depth information in the fused image. Common to 2D-to-3D conversions. *Compare* **cue conflict.**

PGB3D *See* **passive glasses-based 3D display.**

Phantaglyph; Phantogram An image that uses perspectival anamorphosis, or the projection of 3D perspective onto a 2D surface so that, when viewed from a particular angle, the 3D image appears to rise from the surface. *Compare* and see diagram at **anamorphosis.**

phi phenomenon; phi effect; phi motion; Ø The mental process that provides the illusion of motion in conjunction with the persistence of vision when one views a series of static images. The phi phenomenon was famously applied to motion pictures by Hugo Münsterberg in *The Photoplay: A Psychological Study* (pub. 1916).

> NOTE: What is commonly called the *phi phenomenon* or *phi motion* is more correctly the *beta phenomenon* or *beta motion*. Both concepts originated with Max Wertheimer's *Experimental Studies on the Seeing of Motion* (1912). Beta motion is the smooth motion perceived from a series of still images. Phi motion is the illusion that an object has moved between two distinct positions in two successive images while still perceived as static in its start and stop states. In beta motion, an object moves smoothly from one position to another without appearing to be static at each interval.

Also **beta phenomenon.** *See* **apparent motion.** *Compare* **critical fusion frequency.**

photo bubble; photo cube; photo sphere An image that presents views in all directions—360° around, above, and below, produced by stitching together multiple images taken from different angles. May be used in a virtual reality environment, allowing the observer to look in any direction. *Compare* **discrete view; distributed view; panorama; spinography.**

photogrammetry The process of calculating physical dimensions from a photograph, traditionally used to produce maps and scale drawings from aerial photographs. *Compare* **analytic photogrammetry; stereophotogrammetry.**

photopic vision Images registered by the cones in the eye's retina. The cones are responsible for color vision and do not operate effectively in low-light situations. Hence, the diminished ability to register color at night. *Compare* **scotopic vision.**

physical barrier *See* **parallax barrier** *Compare* **lenticular barrier; simple wall barrier.**

physical disparity *See* **disparity.**

physical rig; physical camera rig *See* **camera rig.**

picket fence effect A visual aberration appearing as alternating vertical strips of light and dark that may appear when the observer is not positioned correctly when viewing an auto-stereoscopic display.

pictorial depth cue *See* **static depth cue.** *Compare* **non-pictorial depth cue.**

pillow effect *See* **pincushion distortion.**

pinching the presentation Framing a stereogram too tightly, so that an object with negative parallax (seeming to extend out of the screen) is cut off by the edge of the image frame. This leads to a visual/brain conflict that interferes with the 3D effect. *Compare* **edge violation.**

pincushion distortion; pincushion effect A lens aberration where straight lines bow inward toward the center of the image. Results from an increase in focal length moving outward from the center of the lens. Mostly found in long focal length (telephoto) lenses. The effect becomes more pronounced as the image aspect ratio increases. Pincushion distortion is generally expressed as a percentage of the overall picture height. *See* **lens distortion.** *Also* **pillow effect.** *Compare* **barrel distortion; hourglass distortion; mustache distortion.**

 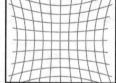

The effects of radial lens distortion: an undistorted grid (left) and that same grid with pincushion distortion (right).

Pinocchio effect The image distortion that results from recording a close object with too wide a lens (too short a focal length) given the nominal screen size and viewing distance. For example, during the production of the stop-motion 3D film *Coraline* (2009), the filmmakers found that during close-ups, the noses of the puppets would extend outward by an exaggerated degree (along with other objects exhibiting non-zero parallax). After the titular character in the Carlo Collodi (née Lorenzini) story *Le Avventure di Pinocchio* (*The Adventures of Pinocchio*, 1881) whose nose would grow unusually long when he was distressed. *See* diagram at **nominal focal length.**

pitch *Also* **tilt.** *See* **orientation.**

pixel Picture element; a single point on a video screen; the smallest distinguishable and address-able area in a video image. Computer image res-olution is measured in pixels, both horizontal and vertical, along with color depth. Television images contain pixels, but are more often measured in horizontal lines of vertical resolution (each line being a row of pixels) and refresh rate (frames/fields per second). *Compare* **voxel.** *See* **raster** di-agram in the color section.

pixel decimation A reduction in image resolu-tion so that both the left- and right-eye images from a stereogram can fit in a single standard image frame. For example, pixels are decimated hori-zontally to fit a stereogram into a side-by-side frame and vertically to fit into an over/under frame.

pixel persistence *See* **persistence.**

pixel shift The traditional process for 2D to 3D conversion where one calculates the depth of se-lected objects in the scene, shifts the pixels that make up each object to create negative or positive parallax in the stereo views, and then paints in any portion of the background exposed when nearer objects were moved.

> With pixel shift, if one then needs to create dif-ferent levels of parallax for different viewing en-vironments (theatrical vs. home viewing, for in-stance), the pixels must be shifted again and new background elements painted in. If one wishes to produce a multi-view version for auto-stereo-scopic use, the process must be repeated for each view. With stereoscopic rendition, an initially more complex process for 2D to 3D conversion, new parallax settings and additional stereo views can be created using the data calculated during the initial processing.

Compare **dimensionalization; stereoscopic ren-dition.**

pixelation; pixellation When the individual pic-ture elements of a video image are perceptible to the viewer. This could mean the image needs anti-aliasing to remove "the jaggies," that its digital compression is breaking down and portions of the image are being presented as blocks of color, or that computer graphics texture maps have too little resolution for their level of magnification. *Also* **mosaic artifact.**

planar Flat; having only two dimensions, width and height but no depth.

planar image A traditional 2D image, such as a photograph. Planar images lack binocular depth cues (disparity and vergence), but may contain static monocular depth cues, such as linear per-spective, shadows and lighting cues, static inter-position, etc. A series of planar images may also present motion depth cues (kinetic interposition and motion parallax). *Also* **2-dimensional image; flat image.**

plane of convergence The virtual depth within a stereoscopic image at which the left- and right-eye images coincide, appearing to be at the depth of the screen. Objects that are closer to the viewer than the plane of convergence will appear to be in front of the screen while objects that are farther from the viewer will appear to be behind the screen. *Also* **stereo window; zero disparity plane.** *Compare* **interaxial convergence.**

plane of polarization The 2D space perpendicu-lar to a light wave's direction of travel that is oc-cupied by the wave's electric field vector, measured at a fixed point in space over one full cycle of the wave. At any single point, the plane of polarization is orthogonal to the plane of vi-bration (perpendicular along two axes).

plane of transmission The plane of polarization occupied by the light that is allowed to pass through a linear polarization filter. For example, the plane of transmission for the left-eye lens used with a linear polarized stereogram only passes light polarized in that same direction. The plane of transmission for the right-eye lens is offset 90° from the left so that only light intended for the right eye passes through.

plane of vibration The 2D space aligned to a light wave's direction of travel within which the wave vibrates. Linear polarized light vibrates within a single plane. Circular and elliptical po-larized light vibrates in two perpendicular direc-tions at once, describing a corkscrew path over time. At any single point in space and time, the plane of vibration is orthogonal to the plane of polarization (perpendicular along two axes).

plane polarizer A filter that only passes linear polarized light — the light waves exiting the filter all vibrate within a single 2D plane. *Compare* **lin-ear polarization.**

plano-stereoscopic A stereogram composed of two planar images.

plasma; ~ display panel; PDP A type of flat-panel display that uses gas plasma technology to create an image.

In a plasma display panel, individual gas cells are arranged in a grid. Each cell is associated with a red, green, or blue phosphor pixel, much like those found behind the face of a cathode ray tube (CRT). An electric charge turns the gas in a cell into plasma (a super-heated state where gas atoms give up their electrons). The free electrons then excite the colored phosphor associated with the gas cell, causing it to glow. The glowing phosphors then create an image on the face of the plasma display.

Plasma is an emissive display technology; when one looks at a plasma screen, one is looking directly at the light source (the colored phosphors of the plasma screen). A plasma monitor has greater contrast, color saturation, color fidelity, and viewing angle than an equivalent LCD monitor (more like a traditional CRT monitor or TV), but plasma monitors are susceptible to both burn-in and burn-out. With burn-in, bright portions of static images are permanently burned into the color phosphors and appear as a ghost image on the screen. Newer techniques such as image orbiting, low-power modes, and inverse modes have significantly reduced the danger of plasma burn-in. With burn-out, the phosphors wear out over time and will be reduced to approximately 50 percent of their original brightness after 10,000 to 15,000 hours of use.

plasticity A relative measure of the natural and subtle depth characteristics associated with a particular object or within a stereogram in general. Poor-quality 2D-to-3D conversions lack plasticity as each object tends to be a flat cut-out, lacking gradations of depth across its surface. *Also* **roundness.**

PMOS *See* **predicted mean opinion score.**

PMP A portable electronic device small enough to fit in the viewer's hand when in use (or a pocket when not) that can play back previously recorded video or audio material, such as the Apple Video iPod.

> **NOTE:** PMP can be interpreted as an initialism of either *Personal Media Player* or *Portable Media Player.*

PNG file; .png Portable network graphics; a graphic file format for still images with lossless compression developed in 1994 as a replacement for the GIF format, which was then subject to patent controversy over its compression algorithm. (That patent expired in 2003.) PNG offers greater color fidelity than GIF by supporting color palettes with 1–8 bits, grayscale with 1–16 bits per pixel, and full RGB color with 24 or 48 bits per pixel. An optional 8- or 16-bit alpha channel for transparency values is supported in certain of the grayscale and RGB color modes. PNG can be used for photographic images, but JPEG produces smaller file sizes for complex images. *Compare* **BMP file.**

point of inversion The rear focal point; the point along the optical axis of a positive, or converging, lens where the converging light rays cross and then begin to diverge. Prior to this point, the image formed by the light rays is oriented in the same direction as the original subject. After this point, it is inverted. *Compare* **rear focal point.**

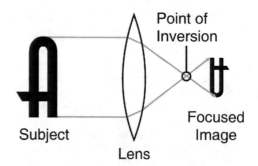

polarization The restriction of light waves in their direction of vibration, defined by the direc-

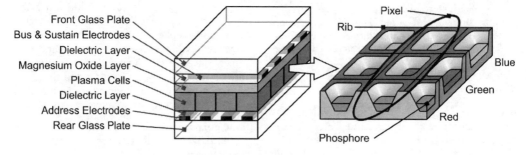

Plasma.

tion of the light wave's electric field (the electric field vector).

Electromagnetic waves (including visible light) have both electrical and magnetic properties. As a light wave travels through space, the wave generates an electric field vector at right angles to its direction of travel. If light is filtered so that only light waves with an electric field vector pointing in a specific direction are allowed to pass, then the light is polarized.

3D display systems based on polarized light filter the left-eye image so that it is only composed of light with an electric field vector pointing in one direction. The right-eye image is filtered so that it is composed only of light with an electric field vector at right angles to the left-eye image (for linear polarization) or that rotates in the opposite direction (for circular polarization). These two images can be projected onto the screen sequentially or at the same time. (Polarized light projection requires a silver screen. A standard white screen would change the direction of polarization in the reflected light, interfering with the 3D effect.) The viewer then wears glasses with polarized lenses so that the left-eye lens only admits light with an electric field vector in the same direction as the left-eye image, while the right-eye lens only admits light from the right-eye image.

The polarization of light was first documented by Danish physician Erasmus Bartholinus in 1669 using Iceland spar crystal. In 1891, John Anderton, a British physician, patented a method for displaying black-and-white or color stereograms using two magic lanterns with 90° offset polarizing filters, matching polarized eyewear, and a silver screen. Anderton's preferred polarizer was a bundle of thin glass plates. The first flexible sheet polarizer was developed by Edwin H. Land in 1929 (patented in 1933).

Compare and *see* diagram at **circular polarization; linear polarization.**

polarization artifact An undesirable difference between the left- and right-eye images in a stereogram recorded with toed-in, or converged, cameras due to the different angles of the surfaces of the lenses with respect to reflective surfaces within the scene. Such differences result in retinal rivalry, interfering with the 3D effect and potentially leading to eyestrain in the viewer.

polarization breakup Unwanted change in reflected or transmitted polarized light — the outgoing rays of light do not all have the same type of polarization as the incoming rays. A common source of ghosting in polarized stereograms. *Compare* **polarization preserving.**

polarization handedness The direction of rotation of circularly polarized light, either right (clockwise) or left (counterclockwise). *See* diagram of **circular polarization.**

polarization maintaining *See* **polarization preserving.**

polarization orientation The direction of polarization for linearly polarized light. Technically, linear polarization could be along any angle, but in most applications, it is generally oriented horizontally, vertically, or diagonally at a 45° angle. *See* diagram at **orthogonal polarization.**

polarization, plane of *See* **plane of polarization.**

polarization preserving A lack of change imposed on reflected or transmitted polarized light — the outgoing rays of light have the same type of polarization as the incoming rays. The di-

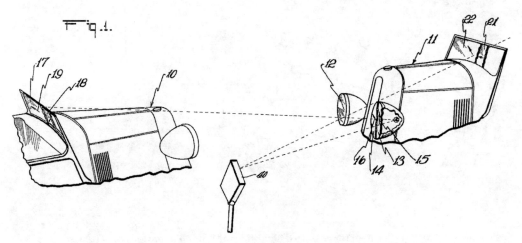

From Edwin H. Land's U.S. patent for polarized film, showing how a polarized windshield could reduce headlight glare (No. 2,099,694, issued November 23, 1937) (U.S. Patent and Trademark Office).

rection of reflected polarized light will be reversed (a mirror image), while transmitted light will remain the same (it simply passes through). *Compare* **polarization breakup.**

polarization switch A filter that can change its direction of polarization. Often used for single-lens polarized 3D projection systems. Images are projected at twice the normal frame rate, first for the left eye then for the right eye in an alternating sequence. The polarization switch sits in front of the projector or monitor and polarizes the left-eye images in one direction then switches and polarizes the right-eye images in a different direction. *Also* **electro-optical liquid crystal modulator.** *Compare* **dual-panel LCD 3D; ZScreen.**

polarized display A stereoscopic display where the left- and right-eye images are polarized in different directions for presentation. This requires passive eyewear with matching polarized lenses.

In theatrical applications, the polarized images are projected on a silver screen so they retain their polarization when reflected back to the viewer. In video applications, there are two different techniques: line-interlaced, where every other line of the display is polarized the opposite direction, requiring the left- and right-eye information to be horizontally interlaced line by line and cutting vertical resolution in half; and passive retarder, where the entire image is polarized in alternating directions.

The polarization can be linear or circular. Linear polarization tends to have the best optical performance, but circular polarization allows viewers more freedom to tilt their heads. Regardless of the type of polarization, horizontally interlaced video displays have a limited vertical viewing angle. If the viewer's angle with respect to some portion of the screen is too great, the polarizing filter on the surface of the screen will no longer align with the correct line of pixels and the 3D effect will either be lost or, in extreme situations, reversed.
Compare **3D display; polarized strip.**

polarized eyewear Spectacles with linear or circular polarizing lenses, each lens orthogonal to the other (for linear, offset by 90°; for circular, rotating in the opposite direction).

polarized images *See* **polarized stereograms.**

polarized stereograms A stereoscopic process developed in the 1930s that improved upon the earlier anaglyphic process by using polarized images and matching polarized lenses to achieve a 3D effect; the image process made popular during the 3D boom of the 1950s.

In the polarized stereogram process, two slightly offset images of the same action are recorded as normal, either using two cameras or a single camera fitted with a stereoscopic lens. Each image — one for each eye — is photographed offset by the approximate distance between a pair of human eyes (between 50–70mm or about 65mm/2½"). Traditionally, polarized projection required two synchronized projectors fit with polarized light filters, one filter oriented vertically and the other horizontally. Newer polarized projection systems use a single projector with either a polarization switch and sequential images or a special split lens

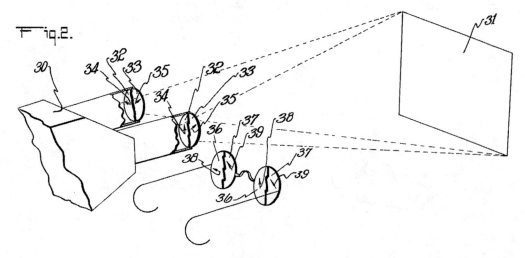

From Edwin H. Land's U.S. patent for polarized film, showing how polarization could be used to present stereoscopic motion pictures (No. 2,099,694, issued November 23, 1937) (U.S. Patent and Trademark Office).

that projects the eye images at the same time. Most polarized video display systems use row-interlaced eye images and an overlay that polarizes alternate rows opposite directions.

Twin projector, single projector/split lens, and row-interlaced video systems run at standard frame rates. Single projector/polarization switch systems run at higher rates to avoid visible flicker (since each eye is only seeing every other image). The RealD 3D system, for example, runs at 144 frames per second.

Regardless of how the polarized images are projected, the viewer wears glasses with matching polarized lenses, ensuring that each eye only sees its intended image. Since each eye sees a slightly different offset image simulating the offset images common to human binocular vision, the viewer perceives the on screen images as having three-dimensional depth. The polarized light process does not use the red and cyan filters common to anaglyphs, so it works equally well with black-and-white and full-color images. *Also* **polarized images.** *Compare* **anaglyph; auto-stereoscopic.**

polarized strip; ~ method A stereogram presentation technique where left- and right-eye images are presented in alternating lines of a raster display with each line polarized a different direction. Viewed using eyewear with polarized lenses that match the polarization type (circular or linear) and direction of the corresponding lines in the display. *Compare* **eclipse method; micro-polarizer; Pulfrich.**

polarizer A device that filters light, passing light that vibrates in a single plane (photons with electric fields oriented a certain direction) and blocking all else. The polarized light may pass through (transmissive) or be reflected (reflective or beam-splitting) and may travel in a single plane (linear) or in a corkscrew pattern (circular — either clock-

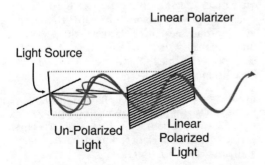

A standard linear polarizer (left). Notice that the polarized wave is at right angles to the polarization grid. Adding a ¼ wave plate to a linear polarizer (right) creates a circularly polarized wave.

wise or counterclockwise). *See* **polarization switch; polarizing filter.**

polarizer blue leak An imperfection common to certain types of linear polarizers that block all unpolarized light, passing only light oriented in the designated direction, with the exception of deep violet/UV light (typically 400nm and below), increasing portions of which may be passed through without polarization. When used with polarized stereograms, this could lead to image crosstalk. Correcting for blue leak often causes red leak at the other end of the visible spectrum.

polarizer red leak An imperfection common to certain types of linear polarizers that block all unpolarized light, passing only light oriented in the designated direction, with the exception of deep red/IR light (typically 650nm and above), increasing portions of which may be passed through without polarization. When used with polarized stereograms, this could lead to image crosstalk. Correcting for red leak often causes blue leak at the other end of the visible spectrum.

polarizing filter; polarizing screen; pola screen; polarizer A filter that transmits light that vibrates in only one direction. Often used to reduce unwanted glare and reflections. Also used with certain 3D theatrical projection systems.

Placing two identical polarizers on top of one another will have little additional effect (since they are both passing light that vibrates in the same direction). With linear polarizers, if one is rotated, progressively more light will be blocked until the filters become opaque when their relative angle reaches 90°. With circular polarizers, simple rotation has no effect, but if the filters are flipped so one is clockwise and one is counterclockwise, then the combination will be opaque.

Polaroid The trade name for a type of iodine-based polarizing film originally patented by Edwin H. Land and Joseph S. Friedman (application filed in 1929, issued in 1933) and later developed and sold by the Polaroid Corporation, founded by Land in 1937. Polaroid film was first used in the manufacture of sunglasses and can now be found in products as diverse as LCD screens and optical microscopes. Polaroid films are now manufactured by 3M under the Vikuiti brand name.

pop-up book *See* **cardboarding.**

portable media *See* **mobile media.**

portable media player *See* **PMP.**

position of primary attention *See* **primary attention.**

positive lens *See* **converging lens.** *Compare* **diverging lens.**

positive parallax When a point in the left-eye image is to the left of the conjugate point in the right-eye image (and vice versa) in a stereogram. Conjugate points with positive parallax will appear to extend into the screen, occupying the screen space. The viewer's eyes must diverge to focus on conjugate points with positive parallax and fuse them into a single image. *Also* **far disparity.** *Compare* **negative parallax; zero parallax.** *See* diagram at **stereoscopic.**

posterization A visual artifact where smooth gradations become bands of color when an image is presented with far fewer tones than were in the original. Often a side effect of color aliasing, recompression artifacts, or the use of too little color depth in a digital image. *Also* **banding; color banding.** *See* **color aliasing.**

predicted mean opinion score; PMOS An estimate of a subjective image quality evaluation score derived by objective measurements and mathematical calculations. *Compare* **mean opinion score.**

premium pricing A higher than normal price charged because of a special characteristic of the item being sold, often due to exclusivity. A 3D viewing experience is considered a premium feature and therefore consumers are charged a premium price. This includes theatrical admission to 3D movies and the cost of 3D-capable Blu-ray players.

pre-render A display element that is generated in advance of presentation. For example, subtitles may be generated on the fly by the display device or produced in advance (pre-rendered) and simply presented by the display device.

presbyopia A stiffening of the eye's lens that occurs with age, generally starting around 40, that reduces the ability to change focus (accommodation) and leaves only far vision. *Compare* **hypermetropia.**

presence The sense of realism and of being physically present at a place created by an immersive virtual environment.

primary attention The area of greatest interest in an image; the area within an image where the viewer is most likely to look.

primary camera An image-recording camera in a multi-camera setup where the additional satellite cameras record depth information. Often used when shooting 2D material for a later 3D conversion or when producing a 3D computer model of a scene.

primary eye The side of a stereogram (either left or right) used as the basis for difference calculation or designated for use in 2D applications. For example, a 2D+delta representation of a stereogram includes one full 2D image (the primary eye) and data describing the differences between that image and the second eye image. The second eye image is then generated dynamically at presentation time. The primary eye image may also be used on its own as a 2D master image. *Also* **hero eye; dominant eye.** *Compare* **second eye.**

primary position When the eyes are level (with the horizon) and parallel (no vergence).

principle axis *See* **optic axis.**

principal plane *See* **nodal points.**

principal point The point where the optical axis of a camera lens intersects the image plane. *Compare* **intrinsic camera parameters.**

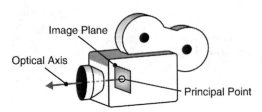

Prisma-chrome 3D The trade name for a type of 3D eyewear designed for viewing side-by-side images in a cross-eyed viewing configuration (left eye to the right of the right eye). Developed by American stereographer Allan Silliphant. Prisms in the glasses move the convergence point necessary to fuse the images to about 12" from the viewer—a common close reading distance. At the same time, integrated blinders block the original images from view. (Normally, with cross-eyed viewing one sees three images—the original image on the left, the original image on the right, and the fused image in the center.) *Compare* **Anachrome.**

production artifact A visual anomaly introduced during image capture, creation, or post-production. *See* **capture artifact; coding artifact; compressed depth artifact; decoding artifact; display artifact; network artifact.**

progression 1. The number of frames by which a stereo film camera advances the film after each exposure. May be the same amount each time or may follow an alternating pattern. **2.** The specialized mechanical film movement that advances the film in a stereo camera.

projected 3D environment *See* CAVE.

projection display A display device where the image is created within the device then focused and cast forward by optical means to create a remote image some surface. In rear-projection (including DLP televisions), the projector sits behind the screen and the audience views a transmissive image through the screen. In front-projection, the projector and audience are both on the same side of the screen and the audience views a reflected image.

projector A device that uses a beam of focused light to cast an enlarged image onto a screen.

Projectors are primarily differentiated based on the source of the image — photographic film (film projector) or electronic signal (video projector). Smaller format film projectors (below 35mm) have already been replaced by video projectors and monitors, while larger format film projectors (35mm and above) are in their final days. The term itself was coined c. 1886 by Louis Aimé Augustin Le Prince and first appeared in print in U.S. Patent No. 376,247, issued January 10, 1888.

projector lamp *See* lamp.

projector stacker A rig designed to hold two projectors, one above the other, when projecting stereoscopic images. Typically used with polarized systems.

propagation direction The primary trajectory of a moving wave. This may be graphed by connecting the peaks (or any series of identified points in the cycle) of a wave with a straight line. *Compare* plane of vibration.

proportionality *See* relative size; *Compare* usual size.

proprioception The sense of the orientation of one's limbs and body. Useful when determining if one's apparent movement through space is the result of one's own actions or an external force. Also necessary when performing any physical action without looking. *Compare* equilibrioception.

pseudoscope A binocular viewing device where the eye images are intentionally re-

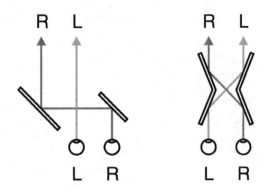

Simple pseudoscopes using two mirrors (left) and four mirrors (right).

versed using prisms or mirrors so that the left eye sees what the right eye would normally see and vice versa. This results in a pseudostereo image. Generally used in the study of stereo vision.

pseudostereo; pseudo stereo; pseudoscopic; pseudo-stereoscopic; pseudo-3D When the left- and right-eye images in a stereoscopic system are reversed (the left eye sees the right-eye image and vice versa). This has the effect of turning things inside out — what should be near appears to be far and what should be far appears to be near. With twin-film 3D systems, such as the polarized process often used during the 1950s, it was possible to invert the film reels and accidentally project in pseudostereo. Pseudostereo also results if one uses the cross-eyed method to free-view a stereogram prepared for parallel-viewing (or vice versa), though turning the image upside down will correct for this. *Also* inversion; reverse stereo. *Compare* ortho stereo; partial pseudostereo.

PSNR; peak signal to noise ratio *See* signal to noise ratio.

psychophysics The scientific study of perception and the relationship between observed stimuli

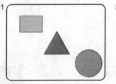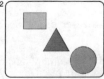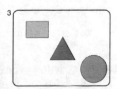

Pseudostereo. Using the parallel-viewing method, images 1 and 2 will produce a proper stereo image with the box behind the page and the circle in front of the page. Images 2 and 3 demonstrate pseudostereo with the positions of the box and circle reversed. (Using cross-eyed viewing, images 2 and 3 produce proper stereo while 1 and 2 demonstrate pseudostereo.)

and the sensations experienced in re-
sponses to those observations. Coined
in 1860 by German experimental psychologist Gustav Fechner as "psy-
chophysik."

Pulfrich; ~ effect; ~ method; ~ stereo
A stereogram presentation technique
where depth is perceived in a moving
2D image by placing a neutral density
(gray) filter over one eye. Named for
German physicist Carl Pulfrich, who
first documented the phenomenon in
1922.

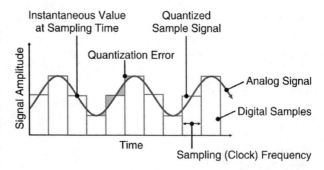

> The darkened image perceived by the covered eye
> takes longer to process and so is matched by the
> brain to a later image coming from the other eye.
> Since the eye images that are fused into a single
> 3D image come from slightly different points in
> time, an object moving horizontally will exhibit
> stereo disparity, which is interpreted as depth.
> The amount of depth will depend on the horizon-
> tal speed of the object (vertical speed has no
> effect). The direction of depth (towards or away
> from the viewer) will depend on the direction of
> travel and which eye is filtered (moving towards
> the filtered eye creates positive parallax, moving
> away from the filtered eye creates negative paral-
> lax). The Pulfrich effect does not apply to static
> images, only those in horizontal motion or
> recorded by a camera in horizontal motion, so it
> has limited application. However, since the images
> require no special processing and are without dis-
> tortion when viewed without special eyewear, the
> process has been used commercially.
>> NOTE: There is a slight Pulfrich effect with active
>> display systems. Since the two eye images are pre-
>> sented sequentially, there is a delay before the cor-
>> responding left- and right-eye images have both
>> reached the brain. This can exaggerate the sense
>> of depth in horizontally moving objects.

Compare eclipse method; polarized strip.

pulling convergence *See* convergence tracking.

pupillary distance; PD *See* interocular distance.

pupillary dynamics *See* miosis.

puppet effect; puppet theater effect *See* Lilliputism.

Q-dos A red/cyan anaglyphic camera lens filter
introduced by Vivitar in 1991 for use with its
Series 1 zoom lens, which could be attached to any
standard 35mm SLR still camera with a Canon-
type lens mount, allowing one to produce
anaglyphs in-camera.

quantization; quantizing; quantisizing Converting the continuous values of an analog signal

into a set of discrete digital values, each sampled
at a regular interval. Once a sample has been
taken, it is converted into a digital number (quan-
tized) that approximates the value of the original
analog sample.

**quantization artifact; quantization distortion;
quantization error; quantization noise** Anomalies introduced when analog material is
converted into a digital form. Since each eye
image will normally have differing noise patterns,
significant quantization artifacts will interfere
with the 3D effect. *Compare* depth quantization
noise; mosquito noise.

quincunx 1. An X-shaped geometric pattern of
five points—four at the corners of a rectangle and
the fifth at the rectangle's center—common to the
five-spot on dice or dominoes. **2.** An anti-aliasing
pattern where the value of each pixel is based on
an average of five different samples taken in the
shape of a quincunx. The pixel itself is aligned
with the center of the quincunx. The corner samples are shared by adjacent pixels, so only twice
as many samples as pixels are required, rather
than five times as many. **3.** The pattern of left-
and right-eye pixels in a checkerboard stereogram, which can be taken to be a series of interlocking X-shaped pixel groups.**R-mount** *See*
Rochwite mount.

**A standard die showing the characteristic quin-
cunx pattern of the five-spot (image by Nino
Satria).**

rack focus The technique of shifting the lens focus from a foreground subject to a background subject, or vice versa, during a shot. This technique is commonly used to draw attention to the second subject in a 2D work, but can cause significant visual confusion and eyestrain in a 3D work due to the conflict between apparent depth and amount of focus in the image.

radial distortion; radial lens distortion *See* **lens distortion.**

rainbow effect The unintended division of a solid color into its red, green, and blue components when presenting an image using a DLP display based on a single DLP chip and a rotating color wheel. *Compare* **screen-door effect.**

Ramsdell rig A type of beam splitter-based camera rig patented by American stereographer Floyd Ramsdell (U.S. Patent No. 2,630,737, issued March 10, 1953).

random dot stereogram A stereogram composed of a seemingly random pattern of dots that, when viewed correctly, displays 3D depth. Within a random dot stereogram, selected dots are shifted to one side to create a 3D shape within the random pattern.

> Computer-generated black-and-white random dot stereograms were developed in 1959 by Dr. Bela Julesz as a test for stereopsis using a pair of images viewed through a stereoscope. Random dot stereograms do not possess normal monocular depth cues, so they allow one to test binocular depth perception in isolation. In 1979, Christopher Tyler and Maureen Clarke collaborated to create computer-generated, single-image random dot stereograms (SIRDS), or random dot autostereograms, that allowed free-viewing using the parallel eye method. In 1991, Tom Baccei, Cheri Smith, and Bob Salitsky collaborated to develop an advanced, full-color image creation technique based on the earlier work of Julesz and Tyler, which they patented as the Magic Eye method.

raster 1. A technique for representing an image by dividing it into a series of regularly spaced rows of picture elements (pixels); a grid of X and Y coordinates in two-dimensional space (or X, Y, and Z coordinates in three-dimensional space) with specific luminance (brightness) or color values at each point that, when taken together, represent an image. Televisions, inkjet printers, and laser printers are all raster-based devices. 2. The active area of a video monitor that contains the picture. *See* **raster** diagram in color seciton.

raster aliasing *See* **aliasing.**

RBT-Raumbildtechnik A German manufacturer of digital and 35mm film-based stereoscopic still image cameras, stereo projectors, and stereo-related equipment. The RBT Web site is www.rbt-3d.de.

RC *See* **right circular polarized light.**

RE The right eye half of a stereogram. *Compare* **Le/Re.**

real image An image of an object composed of light rays that converge together at a single point after passing through a lens with a positive focal length. The light rays will form a sharp, but upside down, image beyond the lens, such as the image formed on the imaging plane by a camera lens or on the retina in the eye. If the object is closer to the lens than the lens' focal length, a virtual image may be formed. *Compare* **virtual image.**

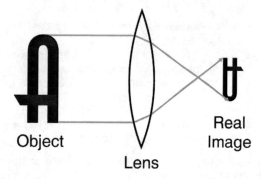

Object   Lens   Real Image

RealD; ~ 3D The trade name for a digital cinema polarized stereoscopic projection system. The RealD Web site is www.reald.com.

> RealD 3D uses an electro-optical liquid crystal modulator (a polarization switch, or ZScreen) placed in the path of the light coming out of the projector. The ZScreen is synced with the projector so the left eye information is circularly polarized counterclockwise, while the right eye information is circularly polarized clockwise. When reflected off a screen, the direction of rotation reverses, so RealD glasses have clockwise left lenses and counterclockwise right lenses.
>
> The projected images flash at 144 Hz to avoid visible flicker. (Standard digital cinema content runs at 24 frames per second. Since each frame requires left- and right-eye images and they are presented in sequence rather than simultaneously, that doubles to 48 images per second. Each image is flashed 3 times to help reduce flicker, resulting in 144 projected images per second.) As with all polarized projection systems, RealD 3D requires a silver screen to maintain the proper polarization in the reflected light.

RealD has also developed the XL "light doubler," which takes the place of the ZScreen in the light beam path and recovers most of the light normally lost during polarization, resulting in a much brighter image.

RealD develops stereoscopic technologies used in digital cinema, manufacturing, marketing, military, scientific research, and theme parks. RealD was established in 2003 and is headquartered in Beverly Hills, California. RealD's first single projector, circular polarized light digital cinema system was installed in 2005. RealD also produces the CrystalEyes line of liquid crystal shutter eyewear for use with active display technologies.

Compare **MasterImage 3D.**

RealD configuration glasses Spectacles with circular polarized lenses that match the handedness and plane of polarization a RealD-formatted stereogram (right eye left circular and left eye right circular with the plane of polarization parallel to the ground).

Realist; ~ format An arrangement for recording still image stereograms on 35mm film where each eye image is five perforations wide rather than the eight traditionally used for still image photography. Originally developed by American stereo hobbyist Seton Rochwite and first produced commercially by the David White Company in 1947. Later adopted as the de facto standard format for U.S. 35mm stereoscopic still cameras.

Realist mount; Stereo ~; R-mount *See* **Rochwite mount.**

rear focal point The point behind a positive, or converging, lens where all of the light rays cross. The focal length of a lens is measured from the optical center to the rear focal point.

When rotating stereoscopic cameras to achieve a particular toe-in, or convergence, angle, the cameras may be rotated about one of two points:

- The camera's integrated tripod mounting point (the easiest method and most common for still image cameras)

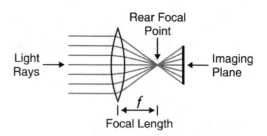

The rear focal point (and focal length) of a simple, converging lens.

- The principal point, or the point where the optical axis of the lens intersects the imaging plane (this point is marked on professional cameras, but the camera rig must be adjusted for each camera model)

Rotating at the imaging plane produces improved results to justify the extra effort, but ideally, the cameras should be rotated at the rear focal point. For compound lenses, this is at the center of the entrance pupil. This is the most difficult method in practice, because rotating about this point means adjusting the rig each time the lens is changed or the focal length is adjusted.

The optical axes of toed-in cameras are not parallel, so the interaxial distance cannot be accurately measured as the horizontal offset between the optical axes as it is for parallel cameras. Instead, it is generally measured at the point of rotation.

Regardless of how the cameras are rotated or the interaxial distance is measured, if the finished work includes a composite of live action and computer-generated images, then the virtual cameras in the computer graphics system must emulate the behavior of the physical cameras or the image geometries and depth characteristics will not align. (This misalignment will increase with increases in the lens focal length or the distance between the camera and each object within the frame.)

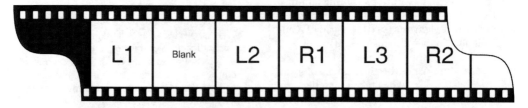

Realist. When recorded by a Realist camera, the corresponding left- and right-eye images were separated by two film frames, positioning each exposed frame behind its corresponding lens and allowing for the use of a simple film advance mechanism. This resulted in an exposure pattern of L1, Blank, L2, R1, L3, R2, L4, R3, and so on.

rear projection An image projection configuration where the projector is behind a translucent screen and the audience views the image from the front of the screen. All else being equal, rear projection is not as bright as front projection.

The principal advantages of rear projection are that objects standing in front of the screen, especially people, do not occlude the light beam path and so do not cast a shadow; it can be used in a well-lit space, rather than a darkened auditorium; and the projector is hidden from view behind the screen. These attributes make rear projection particularly useful for public space, theme park, and virtual reality applications. In consumer applications, rear projection is most often found in DLP televisions, where an internal DLP projector casts an image on the rear surface of the visible screen.

In polarized 3D applications, the rear projection screen surface must not change the polarization state of the transmitted light. Non-uniform optically active, translucent surfaces (such as polycarbonates) transmit the incoming polarized light, but change various properties of its polarization, so they cannot be used for rear projection polarized 3D screens. Front projection screens change the handedness projected circular polarized light while rear projection screens do not. As a result, one must match the polarized lenses in the viewer's eyewear to the polarization of the projection system and the relative position of the screen to ensure each eye views the correct image. Linear polarized light is not affected. *Compare* **front projection.**

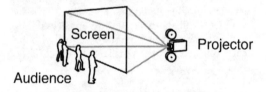

rear silvered mirror A traditional mirror with the reflective material covering its back side so that glass protects the reflective surface. *Compare* **front silvered mirror.**

receiver A device that extracts the data from a transmission and renders it in a useful form, generally part of a larger device. For example, a television includes a receiver that converts the broadcast radio frequency signal into visual and aural signals that can be played back on the screen and through the speakers.

reconstruction filter A filter used to eliminate high-frequency artifacts in an analog signal produced from a digital source.

When a digital signal is converted to an analog equivalent via digital-to-analog conversion, the initial output is a stair-step waveform that contains high-frequency artifacts called *images*. A steep low-pass filter removes the images and produces a smooth analog signal. This filter is similar, or even identical, to the anti-aliasing filter used at the input side of an A/D converter when creating a digital signal from an analog source. *Also* **anti-imaging filter.** *Compare* **decimation.**

re-converge To adjust the apparent depth in a stereoscopic image. *Compare* **convergence animation; horizontal image translation.**

recto The front face of a stereocard. *Compare* **verso.**

red soft focus The tendency for the red side of an anaglyph to exhibit softer image focus than the other half of the stereogram. *Compare* **Anachrome.**

red leak *See* **polarizer red leak.**

reddening The tendency for shorter wavelengths of light (those near the UV band, including shades of blue) to be scattered by dust in the atmosphere and absorbed by molecular oxygen (O_2) and ozone (O_3), leading to a reduction in visible blues and a general red or orange color cast to the light. The thicker the atmosphere, the more visible the reddening, resulting in red clouds at sunrise and sunset, since the sun's light must pass through more atmosphere when it is near the horizon than when it is directly overhead.

reference point conflict *See* **fixation conflict.**

reflection An image of another object viewed in a shiny surface. Very smooth surfaces may also contain specular highlights, or small, bright reflections of a light source. Since visible reflections depend on the relative angle between the subject, reflective surface, and observer, each eye may perceive a different reflected image, or no reflected image at all. When recorded as part of a stereogram, unequal reflections in each eye image can interfere with the 3D effect. *Compare* **sparkle.**

reflection holograms *See* **holographic optical element.**

reflective hologram An image of a 3D object visible without special eyewear, projected into space using two parabolic mirrors. The projected image

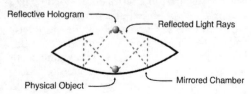

can be viewed from any angle and appears to be the same size as the original object. *Compare* **hologram; parabolic real image.**

reflective-transmissive device *See* **beam splitter.**

refraction The change in direction of an energy wave caused by its change in speed as it passes between two media, such as when light crosses the boundary between air and water.

When passing from a faster medium into a slower one, the wave will bend towards the surface normal line. When passing from slower to faster media, the wave will bend away from the surface normal. Different wavelengths of light travel through the same medium at different speeds due to dispersion, leading to differing amounts of refraction. This phenomenon can be observed when a prism splits white light into a band of colors, since each wavelength is refracted by a slightly different amount on its way through the prism.

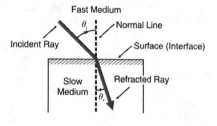

refresh rate The number of times each second that the image on a video screen is updated, expressed in Hertz (Hz). With interlaced video, this is at least equal to the number of fields written to the screen every second. With non-interlaced (progressive) video, it is at least equal to the number of frames (complete pictures) written to the screen every second. Higher frequencies reduce perceptible flicker, so some display systems present the same image more than once. For example, in theatrical 35mm film projection, each image is often presented twice (using a two-blade shutter), while in HD video displays, each image may be presented 4 times (presenting 30 progressive images per second on a 120 Hz display). *Also* **update frequency; vertical scanning frequency.** *Compare* **frame rate.**

registration 1. The image alignment from one frame to the next in a series of recorded images such as those produced by a motion picture or video camera. **2.** The correct alignment of left- and right-eye images in binocular vision. Any differences are then interpreted as providing depth information. **3.** One of the parameters of binocular symmetry. In a stereogram, the left- and

right-eye images differ due to horizontal disparity (parallax), but may share a number of other characteristics, including color, focus, geometry, illumination, and temporal symmetry.

relative height A monocular depth cue used to estimate the depth in a scene by comparing the position of objects with respect to the horizon. The farther an object is from the observer, the closer it is to the horizon. In general, an object on the ground will appear higher the farther away it is while an object in the sky will appear lower the farther away it is. *Compare* **monocular cue.**

relative screen disparity The offset between the conjugate points that comprise a particular object within an image. Successful binocular fusion without double vision can only be achieved for small relative screen disparities (within Panum's fusion area), though these small relative screen disparities may exist within an overall image that has a much larger absolute screen disparity (well outside Panum's fusion area). *Compare* **absolute screen disparity.**

relative size A monocular depth cue used to estimate the depth in a scene by comparing the relative sizes of objects in the scene. The farther an object is from the observer, the smaller it appears. Therefore, two similar objects will appear to be different sizes if they are different distances from the observer, with the nearer object larger than the farther object. If the

Relative height. For the pyramids on the ground (casting shadows), the one higher in the scene is generally taken to be farther away. For the pyramids in the sky (with wings), the one higher in the scene is generally taken to be closer.

observer is familiar with the normal size for a particular type of object, the distance to an instance of that object can be estimated by its apparent size. *Compare* **monocular cue; perceived size; usual size.**

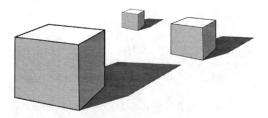

Based on their relative sizes, the left cube is closest and the middle cube is twice the distance as the right cube.

render To produce a visible image from the mathematical formulae and digital data that describe a computer-generated image. The realism of a computer-generated image can be greatly enhanced through the application of sophisticated lighting and shading algorithms—without them,

With a running time of 91 minutes, DreamWork's *Bee Movie* (2007) took an average of 274,725 hours per minute to render (courtesy Heritage Auctions, www.ha.com).

computer-generated images tend to look like everything is made of plastic. The more complex the images, the more computing resources necessary to render them. For example, the computer animated film *Shrek* (2001) required 5,000,000 hours of computer render time while the more visually complex *Bee Movie* (2007) required 25,000,000 render hours.

rendering artifact *See* **decoding artifact.**

repeat-use eyewear; repeat-use glasses Durable stereoscopic spectacles designed to be used multiple times by multiple viewers. When used by commercial exhibitors, such glasses are cleaned between uses, either directly by the exhibitor or through an exchange program with the manufacturer. *Compare* **disposable eyewear.**

resolution 1. The fineness of the segments into which a sensing or encoding system is divided. 2. The ability of a lens or recording medium (film, video, etc.) to register fine details; resolving power. 3. A measure of the sharpness of an imaging system; a subjective measure of the perceived image fineness and details. For television systems, the primary determinants are signal bandwidth, image scan rates, and aspect ratio and may be judged by photographing a test pattern to identify how many horizontal lines per inch can be clearly identified in the resulting image. 4. The number of pixels per unit of area or lines of picture information in a video image; spatial resolution.

When digitizing film, the resolution is often expressed as an approximation of horizontal pixels (in thousands), such as 1K and 2K. Device resolutions, such as computer displays and printers, are often expressed as the maximum number of dots (pixels) in the horizontal and vertical directions or per inch (respectively).

The sharpness of the image on a video display depends on the resolution and the size of the monitor. The same resolution will be sharper on a smaller monitor and gradually lose sharpness on larger monitors because the same number of pixels is being spread out over a larger surface area. Digital video resolution is typically measured in pixels, while analog video resolution is typically measured in lines of picture information. For example, a computer display resolution may be expressed as 1920 × 1080 while a VHS image is said to have 240 lines.

5. The number of complete images captured per unit of time; temporal (time-based) resolution. Common temporal resolutions include:

- 24 frames per second for film;
- 29.97 or 25 frames per second for standard-definition video (NTSC or PAL, respectively); and

• 24, 25, 29.97, 30, 50, 59.94, and 60 for high-definition video.

6. The number of bits per pixel in a digital image; color resolution. Eight bits per pixel, allowing 256 possible colors or shades of gray, is the minimum number necessary to produce an acceptable video image.

retinal disparity The physical distance between conjugate points in the left- and right-eye images recorded on the retinas of an animal with binocular vision. *See* **binocular disparity; disparity.**

retinal fovea *See* **fovea.**

retinal image size The size of an object as projected onto the retina of the eye. The retinal image size is a function of the actual size of an object and its distance from the observer, so retinal image size can be used as a monocular depth cue. *Also* **size depth cue.** *Compare* **monocular cue; usual size; visual angle.**

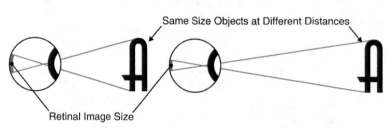

All else being equal, the farther away an object is, the smaller its retinal image size. As a consequence, image detail also diminishes with distance.

retinal rivalry The reception of images by the eyes that contain differences between the left- and right-eye image that are not due to horizontal disparity and interfere with stereoscopic fusion. This can lead to distraction, eyestrain, headache, or nausea. Often caused by vertical parallax, color rivalry (different colors perceived by each eye), and luminance rivalry (different levels of brightness perceived by each eye). Some rivalries occur naturally and are not stereoscopic defects, such as iridescence, sparkle, and occlusion. *Also* **dichoptic error.** *Compare* **color bombardment; cue conflict; discrete rivalry.**

retroreflector; retroflector A surface or device that reflects light back in the same direction as its source, along a parallel but slightly offset path. This creates a highly efficient (high-gain) reflective surface, useful in safety reflectors and front projection screens. *Also* **cataphote.** *Compare* **Scotchlite.**

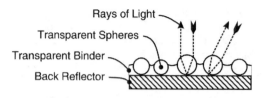

Retroreflectors on a Scotchlite screen. Normally, light is reflected off a surface at an equal but opposite angle. Retroreflectors reflect light at the incoming angle, sending it back in the direction of its original source.

reverse stereo; reverse 3D; reversed parallax *Also* **inversion.** *See* **pseudostereo.**

RGB 1. Red, green, and blue; the additive primary colors of light. Mixing all three together in equal amounts produces white. The absence of light produces black. **2.** The color model (color space) most often used with digital computers. The color of each pixel is described by the strength of its red (R), green (G), and blue (B) components from 0 to 100 percent of full intensity (or from 0–1). This color space directly translates to the red, green, and blue phosphors used in computer monitors. The RGB color space has a very large gamut, meaning it can reproduce a very wide range of colors.

rig *See* **camera rig.**

right circular polarized light; RC Polarized light that travels through space in a clockwise corkscrew pattern with the electric vector completing a full rotation around the axis of propagation in the time it takes the light ray to move forward exactly one wavelength.

The electric vector of circular polarized light is not constrained to a single plane of vibration. The wave can be broken down into the sum of two linear polarized waves, where each wave has the same amplitude, is 90° out of phase from its companion, and travels along right angle planes (rotated 90° from each other). When these planar waves combine, they create a 3D wave that follows a helix, or corkscrew, path through space. When measured at a specific point, the tip of the passing RC wave's electric field vector travels in a clockwise circle, completing one full rotation around the axis of propagation in the time it takes the wave to move forward one wavelength.

NOTE: In optics (and therefore most stereoscopic

applications), the direction of circular polarized light spin is measured from the perspective of the viewer, while in electrical engineering, it is measured from the perspective of the source.

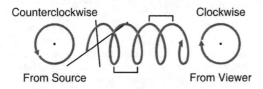

right eye; RE The right half of a stereo image pair; the image intended to be viewed by the right eye.

right eye dominance Using the right as the starting eye for a sequential 3D application.

right field Information from a stereogram intended for the right eye only. *See* **image field.**

right homologue A point in a right-eye image that corresponds to a point in the matching left-eye image. *Compare* **conjugate points.**

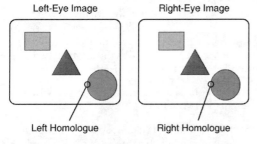

ringing; ~ artifacts A digital compression artifact affecting the edges between areas of contrasting color or luminance levels, causing a loss of image fidelity along the borders. Visible as unexpected oscillations in chrominance, luminance, or depth information surrounding the affected areas. JPEG (with discrete cosine transfer, or DCT, compression) and JPEG 2000 (with wavelet compression) are both susceptible to ringing artifacts. *Compare* **color ringing; depth ringing; Gibbs phenomenon.**

rivalry *See* **discrete rivalry; retinal rivalry.**

RMSE *See* **root mean squared error.**

Rochwite mount; R-mount The de facto standard format for 35mm still slide stereogram presentation, measuring 4" × 1⅝" (about 102mm × 41mm) with 2½" (about 64mm) image centers. Generally available in cardboard and plastic versions. Named for American stereo hobbyist Seton Rochwite, developer of the Realist 3D camera format.

rod A receptor cell in the retina responsible for peripheral and night (scotopic) vision. The rods only register image brightness, not color. *Compare* **cone.**

roll *See* **orientation.**

rolling shutter An electronic image acquisition scheme where each scan line is recorded in sequence rather than all at once. Typical of CMOS-based image sensors. Rolling shutters can cause image distortions with fast-moving subjects or cameras and when the amount of illumination changes significantly during the exposure. This can lead to retinal rivalry when used in mirror rigs if the reflected camera is not mounted in reverse, since one eye image will be scanned from top-to-bottom while the other is scanned bottom-to-top. The scan direction of some image sensors can be reversed to correct for this issue. *Compare* **global shutter.**

root mean squared error; RMSE An objective measure of system accuracy or signal fidelity calculated by taking the square root of the mean square error (MSE). The data sets compared by an RMSE could be the differences between predicted and actual values, between signal-to-noise ratios for input and output signals, between original and compressed images, etc. For video signals, this is typically applied to a pixel-by-pixel comparison of a single attribute, such as the pixel's hue, saturation, or value. This can be calculated using the equation at right, where n is the number of samples in the data set, X is the value of a sample from

$$\sqrt{\frac{\sum_{i=1}^{n}(X_i - X_i')^2}{n}}$$

one set and X' is the corresponding value from the other set. (Since the difference between the sets is squared, it does not matter which one is subtracted from the other.) The greater the difference between the two sets, the greater the RMSE. If the two sets are equal (there is no error to measure), then the RMSE = 0. *Compare* **mean square error.**

rotating wheel 3D A stereoscopic image presentation system where the alternate eye images are encoded by projecting them through a rotating filter synchronized to the projection of the left- and right-eye images. A similar technique is used with single-chip DLP projectors where color is introduced into each image by a rotating color wheel.

rotation *See* **6DoF; orientation.**

rotation artifact *See* **tilt.** *Compare* **twist.**

roundness *See* **plasticity.**

row A horizontal array of pixels in a raster image. The 2D grid of pixels that make up a raster image (computer, television, laser printer, etc.) is arranged into a set of vertical columns and horizontal rows. *Compare* **column.** *See* **raster** diagram in color section.

row-interleaved; ~ 3D A 3D raster image format where left- and right-eye image information is presented in alternating rows within the image. By convention, one starts with the left eye in the top row of the image and moves down. May be used with an interlaced or progressive scan system. Generally viewed on a polarized display. *Also* **IL; interleaved; line-by-line.** *Compare* **column-interleaved; time-sequential.**

Full-Resolution Stereogram

Row-Interleaved Stereogram

Reconstructed Half-Resolution Stereogram

Left / Right

RT *See* **real-time.**

saccade The rapid, involuntary eye movement used to take in a large or complex image. The human eye only senses image detail at the center of the visual field. Therefore, it is necessary to move the eye over a large object in order to take it in. On average, the eye moves once every $\frac{1}{20}$ of a second — approximately the time span of persistence of vision. This is a subconscious action, but these eye movements are not random and tend to follow general visual patterns. Still, different people will scan the same image differently, and therefore have a different subjective experience. Sounds, unlike images, are taken in all at once. There is no aural saccadic equivalent. *Compare* **nystagmus; smooth pursuit; visual fixation.**

saccadic suppression The natural inability to perceive the image blurring that would otherwise be caused by saccades.

satellite camera A secondary camera (or pair of cameras) used to record depth information while the primary camera records visual information. Often used when shooting 2D material for a later 3D conversion or when producing a 3D computer model of a scene.

saturation; color ~ The purity, brilliance, or vividness of a color's hue; in the Munsell color system, the degree of difference between a color and a shade of gray with the same level of lightness or brightness.

Three-strip Technicolor films, such as *Gone with the Wind* (1939), have very rich, saturated colors. *The Three Amigos* (1986) spoofed the highly saturated look of three-strip Technicolor during its desert campfire musical number. At the opposite end of the spectrum are films such as *Saving Private Ryan* (1998) that have intentionally desaturated colors, verging on the monochromatic at times. The color control on a television adjusts the display's color saturation, though apparent color saturation can also be affected by the signal's luminance level.

Compare **hue; value.** *See* **color** diagram in color section.

SbS *See* **side-by-side.**

scalable video coding; SVC *See* **MPEG-4 SVC.**

scene/camera space *See* **camera/scene space.**

scene depth factor; SDF A mathematical ratio used to summarize the total amount of depth depicted in a stereogram. Calculated as the far point distance divided by the total scene depth.

scene graph The ordered collection of nodes represented in Java 3D or VRML.

Scotchlite The trade name for a type of reflective cloth manufactured by 3M that is used to produce very light-efficient (high-gain) front projection screens. The surface of the screen is covered by small glass or plastic spheres that act as retroreflectors to reflect incoming light back along a parallel path. *See* diagram at **retroreflector.**

scotopic vision Images registered by the rods in the eye's retina. The rods are responsible for peripheral and night vision and only register image brightness, not color. *Compare* **photopic vision.**

screen The physical surface upon which an image is presented, such as a television screen or theatrical projection screen.

In 2D presentations, the images appear to be on the surface of the screen, though monocular depth cues may provide a sense of depth within the image. In 3D presentations, the left- and right-eye images are multiplexed onto the same surface and then separated by a special selection device — usually a pair of spectacles. Different portions of the stereoscopic image may appear to be in front of (negative parallax), on (zero parallax), or behind (positive parallax) the screen. *Also* **display surface.** *Compare* **stereoscope.**

screen disparity *See* **absolute screen disparity; relative screen disparity.** *Compare* **disparity.**

screen-door effect A fixed-pattern noise artifact where the black spaces between pixels become visible, as if the image is being viewed through a fine wire mesh. Common to certain LCD and DLP projectors. May be corrected by micro-lenses—individual lenses that slightly enlarge each pixel, causing it to overlap its neighbor and fill in the black gap — or by presenting the image slightly out of focus. *Compare* **rainbow effect.**

screen gain The amount of projected light reflected from a screen as compared to the amount of light reflected from a standard reference white surface coated with magnesium oxide. A white screen with a gain of 1.0 reflects the same amount of light as the reference surface. A gray screen with a gain of 0.8 reflects 20 percent less light than the reference, while a silver screen with a gain of 2.4 reflects 140 percent more light.

Screen gain is generally measured from a vantage point perpendicular to the surface at the center of the screen where the reflected image is at its brightest (or, *peak gain at zero degrees viewing axis*). Screen gain drops moving out from the center of the projected area (luminance drop off). In higher gain screens (generally above 1.3), this drop off may be sharp enough to create a visible hot spot in the center of the screen. Screen gain also drops as the viewing angle increases. The rate of drop is greater with higher gain screens. This is measured as the viewing angle where the illumination is half its perpendicular peak value (or, *half-gain viewing angle*). Wider half gain viewing angles allow for larger viewing areas, so lower gain screens allow for larger audiences, all else being equal. *Compare* **flatness of field; high-gain screen; low-gain screen.**

screen parallax 1. The physical distance between conjugate points when a stereogram is presented on a particular size screen. 2. The plane of zero parallax aligned with the surface of a display screen. *Compare* **disparity.** *See* **screen parallax** diagram in color section.

screen plane *See* **display plane.**

screen space The perceived area behind the plane of the screen in display/viewer space. When objects in a stereogram appear behind the screen, they are said to occupy the screen space. *Compare* **audience space; display plane; positive parallax.** *See* diagram at **display plane.**

screen width The horizontal dimension of a display screen. An important factor in stereoscopic calculations.

SDF *See* **scene depth factor.**

SDSCE *See* **simultaneous double stimulus continuous evaluation.**

second eye The dependent side of a stereogram, regenerated at display time based on the primary eye image and data describing either the differences between the eye images (2D+delta) or the depth within the scene (2D+depth). *Compare* **primary eye.**

secret sauce Special knowledge, expertise, tools, etc. that are not made public so they remain a competitive advantage for their owner.

segmentation The separation of overlapping objects at different depths in a scene when extracting Z-depth data or converting 2D to 3D. Outside edges, where one object overlaps another, are most common, but inside edges, where an object overlaps itself, can be particularly challenging. For example, when an actor's arm extends towards the camera, it should be closer to the camera than the torso, but it can be difficult to segment the arm from the torso when they are both the color of the actor's costume.

selection device The physical component that separates and directs the left- and right-eye images of a stereogram to the corresponding eye. Autostereoscopic devices include an integrated selection device (generally lenticular or parallax barrier). Other technologies use some form of eyewear, either passive (anaglyph or polarized) or active (mechanical or liquid crystal shutters). ChromaDepth and the Pulfrich effect use special types of selection device eyewear to create a 3D effect from a single flat image. *Also* **analyzer.**

semi-transparency The property of an object through which slightly distorted views of more distant objects can be seen. Semi-transparent objects provide a particular challenge for 2D-to-3D conversion since the object itself is at one distance from the viewer while more distant objects with different depth-characteristics are partially visible through the near object.

Sensio The trade name for a 3D video encoding technique developed by Sensio Technologies Inc. Sensio-encoded video requires a special decoder to view, but fits both left- and right-eye views into a standard MPEG-2 video stream, so it can be processed, recorded, and broadcast using standard digital television equipment. The Sensio Web site is www.sensio.tv.

sensor axial offset The extent to which the center of a digital camera's imaging grid is shifted horizontally from the lens' optical axis. An important factor in stereoscopic calculations.

Most cameras have a fixed imaging grid aligned with the optical axis. When using a pair of parallel cameras to record a stereogram, the two camera views will not exactly overlap unless the imaging grids are adjusted outward horizontally. Without this adjustment, the non-overlapping edges may have to be cropped from the final images in post-production.
Compare **monocular area; perspective frustum.**

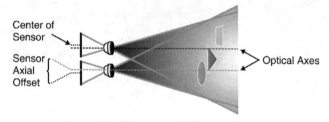

Illustration by the author; based on materials from Andrew Woods, www.andrewwoods3d.com.

sensoric fusion The neural process within binocular fusion where the brain combines the separate but overlapping 2D left- and right-eye images recorded by the fovea at the center of each retina into a single 3D representation. To fuse objects that do not lie within the fovea requires motoric fusion to re-align the eyes. *Compare* **motoric fusion; Panum's fusion area.**

separation 1. The degree of isolation between signals flowing in two paths; a lack of crosstalk. **2. interaxial ~:** The distance that separates the left and right cameras in a stereoscopic process, measured along the optical axes of the cameras' lenses; interaxial distance. **3.** The distance between the conjugate points in a stereogram.

separation factor; SF The mathematical ratio between the interaxial distance (or stereo base) and the near point distance, often expressed as the $\frac{1}{30}$ (or $\frac{1}{50}$) rule.

septum A physical divider between left- and right-eye images that prevents one from bleeding into the other, such as the gap between frames on 35mm film, the gap between images on a stereocard, the physical barrier in a single-lens camera or projector, etc.

sequential; ~ 3D *Also* field-sequential 3D; frame-sequential 3D *See* **time-sequential.**

sequential stereogram A stereoscopic image where the left- and right-eye images are recorded one at a time by the same camera, shifting the camera horizontally by the desired interaxial distance between exposures. If a toed-in configuration is desired, then the camera must also be rotated the correct amount between exposures. This works best when the subject is not in motion (since the two images are not recorded at the same instant in time) and when camera movement can be carefully controlled.

Stop-motion stereography often employs a motion-control camera rig to achieve precise horizontal separation of the left- and right-eye views, such as for the movie *Coraline* (2009). For handheld photography, the horizontal offset may be achieved by simply shifting one's weight from one foot to the other (the *shifty* or *cha-cha method*). This latter technique is not generally employed by professional stereographers.
Compare **twin camera stereo photography.**

setback The apparent distance from the viewer to the nearest object in a stereogram.

SF *See* **separation factor.**

shading Slight variations in an object's color or brightness that offer visual clues to the object's shape and size. *Compare* **monocular cue.**

shadow cue *See* **lighting cue.** *Compare* **monocular cue.**

shear distortion A stereoscopic malformation that occurs when the viewer's gaze is not perpendicular to a stereoscopic display. As the viewer moves progressively off-axis horizontally, objects nearer than the screen (with negative parallax) will shift in the viewer's direction while objects farther than the screen (with positive parallax) will shift away from the viewer. In addition to geometric shear, any movement in the stereogram along the Z-axis will take on unintended movement along the X-axis.

After a short time, most viewers who are significantly off-axis get used to the shear distortion. In presentations where the viewer is free to move about, shear distortion may be used as a creative effect, causing still images to appear to move as the viewer changes position. Anamorphosis can be used to correct for shear distortion by recording the natural perspective of the depicted

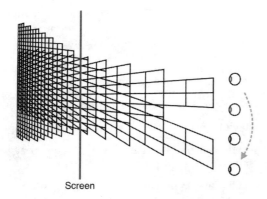

Screen

Illustration by the author; based on materials from Andrew Woods, www.andrewwoods3d. com.

scene from the viewer's off-axis position. However, this only works from the one defined off-axis viewing position and exhibits shear distortion from all others.
Also **3D skew.**

shifty method A technique for recording a sequential stereogram by recording one image, moving to the left or right by the desired interaxial distance (perhaps by shifting one's weight from one foot to the other), and recording a second image with the same camera. This works best when the subject is not in motion (since the two images are not recorded at the same instant in time) and when camera movement can be carefully controlled (with a camera rig). Not generally employed by professional stereographers. *Also* **cha-cha.** *Compare* **sequential stereogram; slide bar.**

shimmer *See* **sparkle.**

Showscan The trade name for a widescreen process that uses 65mm negatives (70mm prints) shot at 60 frames per second. Because the film moves through the projector so fast, one can also use more powerful lamps without running the risk of melting the film. The large format, high speed, and bright illumination combine to create a visual image that approaches reality in clarity and fluidity of motion. Showscan was developed in 1984 by Douglas Trumbull and is mostly used for special venue presentations such as 3D and simulation rides. The Showscan Entertainment Web site is www.showscan.com.

shutter glasses *See* **active eyewear.**

siamese To create a twin-lens stereoscopic camera using parts from two identical donor cameras. A siamesed camera generally has a fixed interaxial distance. Coined in reference to conjoined "siamese" twins, after brothers Chang and Eng Bunker, conjoined twins of Chinese ancestry who were born in Thailand (then Siam) and gained international fame c. 1830 appearing in curiosity shows.

side-by-side; SbS; ~ 3D A technique for recording stereograms where the left- and right-eye images are compressed horizontally and recorded next to each other in the same frame.

In video applications side-by-side 3D is used more often than over/under 3D. Since side-by-side configurations preserve the vertical resolution but reduce the horizontal resolution by half (and all stereoscopic depth information is recorded in the horizontal direction), they generally do not deliver the same depth representation as over/under configurations, which preserve the horizontal resolution but reduce the vertical resolution by half. For line-interlaced displays, every other line is discarded when the images are expanded to their full width to fill one frame, resulting in individual eye images that are ¼ the resolution of the original.

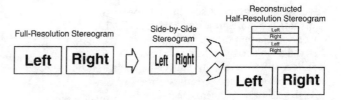

A full-resolution stereogram (left) encoded as a side-by-side frame-compatible stereogram (center) is reconstructed as a half-resolution stereogram (right).

side-by-side rig A mechanical framework designed to support two identical cameras set next to each other. The two cameras may be fixed in a single position or the rig may allow them to be moved horizontally to adjust the interaxial distance or turned symmetrically inward from parallel (toed-in) to converge at the desired plane of zero parallax. When toed-in, the recorded images may contain geometric distortions that have to be corrected in post-production to ensure proper registration when presented as part of a stereogram.

The characteristics to consider when selecting a side-by-side rig include:
  • The ability to align the cameras (to ensure equal angles on the subject)
  • The ability to toe-in the cameras (for converged, rather than parallel, stereograms)

- Rigidity of the rig (so the cameras remain properly aligned)
- Physical size (side-by-side rigs are smaller and lighter than comparable mirror rigs)

See **parallel rig.** *Compare* **mirror rig.**

The Stereotec Side-by-Side MAXI (left), holds two digital cinema cameras, such as the Silicon Imaging SI-2K or RED ONE, and supports inter-axial distances up to 350mm (≈14") and up to 8° of convergence. The Side-by-Side MINI (right) is designed for smaller cameras and Steadicam or handheld applications (courtesy Stereoscopic Technologies GmbH, www.stereotec.com).

signal-to-noise ratio; S/N ratio; SNR A comparison of desired content (signal) to unwanted noise, often measured in decibels and applied to signals such as found in a television broadcast, sound recording, video playback system, etc. The higher the S/N ratio, the better.

silver screen; silvered screen A high-gain motion picture projection screen that does not affect the polarization of the projected light reflecting off its surface. The screen coating is typically a silver-based compound, giving the screen its name.

In the early days of cinema, highly reflective silver screens helped compensate for relatively dim projectors, but limited the viewing angle. When brighter projectors became available, theaters switched to white screens, which produce a suitable image across a wide viewing angle. Polarized stereograms cannot be viewed on a white screen because the screen depolarizes the image, so both film-based and digital cinema polarized 3D projection systems require a silver screen. *Also* **non-depolarizing screen.**

simple wall barrier An opaque sheet with regularly spaced slits through which the image beyond may be perceived, creating a parallax barrier. *Compare* **lenticular barrier.** *See* diagram at **parallax barrier.**

simultaneous double stimulus continuous evaluation; SDSCE A standardized method for measuring the subjective quality of a change made to a video signal using a continuous scale. Short (10 second) video sequences are presented to re-viewers two at a time. The reviewers are asked to judge the test (modified) sequence in relation to the reference (original) sequence using a sliding scale ranging from "bad" to "excellent." Published as part of *Recommendation ITU-R BT.500–12* in 2009. *Compare* **subjective test.**

simulator sickness *See* **cybersickness.**

single binocular vision *See* **Panum's fusion area.**

single-camera stereography *See* **sequential stereogram.**

single-image random dot stereograms; SIRDS *See* **random dot stereograms.**

single-lens camera A camera that records two or more views of the same scene through a single lens from sufficiently different vantage points that they can be used to construct a stereogram. Single-lens 3D cameras avoid the bulk and inconvenience of multiple cameras and the image fusion problems that can result from multiple camera misalignment, zoom or focus mismatch, etc., though they are generally limited to a fixed interaxial distance. *Compare* **common objective rig.** *Compare* **fixed interaxial.**

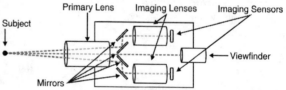

A simplified view of a single-lens 3D camera showing the paths of light rays originating from a single subject as they are redirected by mirrors into left- and right-eye imaging devices and the camera's viewfinder.

single pixel per point; SPPP The general class of non-glasses-based 3D displays (NG3D) where each display point in an image is represented by a single pixel, such as volumetric displays. In such systems, the pixels are generally time-multiplexed and actively steered to create separate eye images that are blended together into a single stereoscopic image by persistence of vision. *See* **autostereoscopic.** *Compare* **multiple pixels per point.**

single-projector; ~ 3D; ~ system A stereogram presentation system where the left- and right-eye images are presented using a single film or video projector. This generally avoids stereogram misalignment and pseudostereo, which tend to plague dual-projector systems, and is less complex to install and operate. All common 3D presentation systems are supported, including both passive (anaglyph and polarized) and active (eclipse method). *Compare* **dual-projector system.**

single stimulus continuous quality evaluation; SSCQE A standardized method for measuring subjective video quality using a continuous scale. Long (≥5 minute) video sequences are presented to reviewers who are asked to judge the image quality using a sliding scale ranging from "bad" to "excellent." Published as part of *Recommendation ITU-R BT.500–12* in 2009. *Compare* **subjective test.**

single stimulus method *See* **absolute category rating.**

single-use eyewear; single-use glasses *See* **disposable eyewear.** *Compare* **repeat-use eyewear.**

single viewpoint A 3D presentation system where the original geometry of the recorded scene is preserved and can be observed correctly from only one vantage point, such as with a basic autostereoscopic display. *Compare* **multiple viewpoint; ortho stereo.**

SIP *See* **Stereo Image Processor.**

SIRDS; single-image random dot stereograms *See* **random dot stereograms.**

Sirius 3-D *See* **ColorCode 3-D.**

6DoF Six degrees of freedom; the ability to move through 3D space without restriction, including translation (forward/backward, left/right, or up/down movement) and rotation (left/right, up/down, or clockwise/counterclockwise).

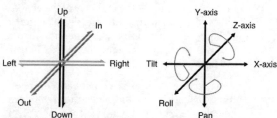

size depth cue *See* **perceived size; relative size; retinal image size; usual size.**

size/depth distortion *See* **depth/size distortion.**

slide bar A simple camera rig for recording sequential stereograms with a single camera by providing a means for controlled horizontal movement between exposures. The camera is mounted to the slide bar, the first image is recorded, the camera is slid to the left or right by a controlled

distance, and the second image is recorded. This provides more accurate interaxial distances and greater control over vertical parallax and rotation than similar hand-held methods. *Compare* **sequential stereogram; shifty method.**

smearing A video image artifact where objects appear to extend horizontally beyond their normal boundaries, creating a blurred image. Typically seen trailing behind moving objects due to compression or display artifacts. *Also* **streaking.**

smooth pursuit; ~ eye movement Voluntary adjustments to the orientation of the eyes, mostly used to track moving objects. *Compare* **nystagmus; saccade; visual fixation.**

SNR *See* **signal to noise ratio.**

Society of Motion Picture and Television Engineers *See* **SMPTE.**

soft video player Software that runs on a general-purpose computer and performs the functions of a dedicated video player. The video content may be read directly from commercial packaged media (DVD, Blu-ray disc, etc.), a local hard drive, Internet data stream, etc.

soft window violation An edge violation involving a largely featureless object (such as a field of grass or pavement) with negative parallax intersecting the stereo window edge. *Compare* **hard window violation; legal window violation.**

SoliDDD A manufacturer of a 3D theatrical projection lenses compatible with both over/under and side-by-side 35mm film and digital formats. SoliDDD introduced its first product, a 35mm over/under lens, at ShoWest 2010. The SoliDDD Web site is www.soliddd movies.com.

spaceball A pointing device used to indicate a movement along a full six degrees of freedom (6DoF). Often used in virtual reality systems.

Space-Vision 3-D An over/under 35mm film-based 3D projection format where two 2.35:1 widescreen images are presented within a single standard 4-perf frame. A special dual lens both polarized and aligned the images on the screen. First used by Arch Oboler for *The Bubble* (1966). Oboler was a long-time advocate for the 3D format and is famous for producing *Bwana Devil* (1952), which kicked off the 1950's 3D boom. *Compare* **Panavision 3D; Technicolor 3D.**

sparkle Bright, localized highlights on a surface that vary in a random pattern; glitter.

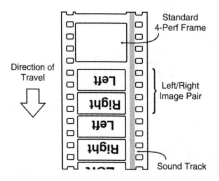

Space-Vision 3-D. The arrangement of left- and right-eye images on a 35mm film print configured for Space-Vision 3-D. (Viewed from the lamp side, looking towards the projector lens.)

Sparkle originating at the same point source tends to affect each eye to a different degree and therefore is recorded differently in each view of a stereogram. This is very difficult to recreate accurately by artificial means, and so does not appear as it should in most 2D to 3D conversions. Similar issues affect iridescent surfaces (where colors change with a change in the angle of view — therefore each eye sees a different color) and surfaces with shimmer, such as brushed metal (a softer sparkle), or specular highlights, such as polished metal (a very bright highlight).
Compare **reflection.**

spatial aliasing *Also* **jaggies; outline aliasing; staircase artifact.** *See* aliasing.

spatial binocular disparity The difference between the left- and right-eye images recorded by the eyes in binocular vision. Only disparity parallel to the viewer's eyes contributes to depth perception. *Compare* **disparity.**

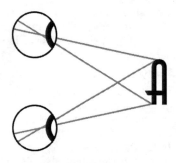

spatial capture Recording scene depth information (each object's size, shape, position, etc.). This may be combined with visual images of the same scene to provide Z-depth for stereoscopic representation or used to create a 3D computer model of the recorded space. Spatial capture is also used in virtual reality and gaming systems to capture the user's body position and hand gestures. *Also* **depth acquisition; depth-sensing.** *Compare* **3D flash LIDAR.**

spatial decimation An image compression technique that removes redundant information from within a single image. *Compare* **decimation; temporal decimation.**

spatial display A stereoscopic presentation device where the left- and right-eye images are physically separate and presented independently to each eye rather than being multiplexed onto the same screen and separated at the eyes by a selection device. This method has been used by stereoscopes since they were first developed by Charles Wheatstone in 1832. Contemporary head-mounted displays use a variation on this technique where each eye has its own video monitor. *Compare* **3D display.**

spatial multiplexing Recording the individual views from a stereogram or multi-view 3D image in a single image frame, as with an over/under film process or row-interleaved video process, so that later they can be separated and directed to the correct eyes for viewing. *Compare* **temporal multiplexing.**

spatial-temporal multiplexing Recording the individual views from a stereogram in a single image frame so that later they can be presented in sequence and directed to the correct eyes for viewing, as with checkerboard systems. *Compare* **temporal multiplexing.**

spatially immersive display An image presentation system that fills the majority of the viewer's field of view, creating an immersive experience. A feeling of immersion arises when the field of view is greater than roughly 60°–90°. *Compare* **CAVE; IMAX.**

special venue A theater with enhanced presentation capabilities, including extra-large screens and enhanced sound systems (such as IMAX), 4D presentations, motion simulation, etc. *Compare* **location-based entertainment.**

spectral eyewear; spectral glasses Spectacles with fixed lenses that do not change during the stereogram presentation process and filter the incoming images based on the wavelengths of light. The most basic type are broadband anaglyph glasses that use two different colored lenses, such as red/cyan, to filter the left- and right-eye images. More complex are narrowband glasses, such as Infitec, where the images are encoded in specific wavelengths of red, green, and blue for each eye. *Compare* **active eyewear; hybrid eyewear; passive eyewear.**

spectral filtration *See* **interference filter.**

specular highlight *See* **reflection, sparkle.**

spectral sensitivity The differential sensitivity of a visual system to different wavelengths of light. Different visual recording systems, such as human eyes, digital video, and photographic film, have different levels of sensitivity to different wavelengths of light, resulting in different spectral sensitivity curves.

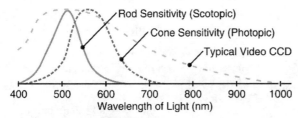

The relative spectral sensitivity of human vision (rods peak at around 507nm, while cones peak at around 555nm) and a typical video CCD imaging grid. Notice that the CCD's spectral sensitivity extends far into the infrared spectrum, well beyond the range of human vision.

spectral shift A change in the observed frequency of light compared to its source.

spherical A lens whose surface is a section of a sphere — either concave (thinner in the middle than at the edge) or convex (thicker in the middle than at the edge). Unintended distortions aside, a spherical lens magnifies or reduces images in the same proportion in all directions. *Compare* **anamorphic.**

spinning mirror display A type of volumetric 3D display that makes use of a high-speed rotating mirror to present multiple 2D views of the same subject taken from different angles. The images are presented on a 2D display above the rotating mirror, which is angled at 45° to reflect the image outward. As the mirror rotates, the display image changes to match the view from that angle. An observer could then walk around the spinning mirror and see the subject from all angles. *Compare* **3D display.**

spinography A method of recording and presenting 360° panoramic views by stitching together a series of individual images taken 10°–20° apart. The recording camera can either face inwards, recording a subject from all sides, or outwards, recording a scene from all angles. With an electronic display, the viewer can spin left or right

to view the full panorama. *Compare* **discrete view; distributed view; panorama; photo bubble.**

split-lens 3D projection; over/under ~ *See* **Panavision 3D; Technicolor 3D.**

split-resolution; ~ **3D;** ~ **encoding** *See* **half-resolution.** *Compare* **2D wrapper; mux/demux workflow.**

SPPP *See* **single pixel per point.**

squeeze An undesired reduction in the apparent depth in a stereogram, usually caused by viewing the image from less than the optimal viewing distance. *Compare* **stretch.**

SSCQE *See* **single stimulus continuous quality evaluation.**

stacked display A display composed of two or more LCD screens layered on top of each other. A two display stack may be used to modulate the polarization of the light passing through the stack, creating a stereogram that can be viewed with passive polarized glasses. A stack of two or more displays may be used to create a volumetric display, where each LCD screen presents a different depth slice of the stereogram. *Compare* **dual-panel LCD 3D.**

staircase artifact *Also* **jaggies; outline aliasing; spatial aliasing.** *See* **aliasing.**

standard aspect ratio The most common image aspect ratio of the day.

The definition of "standard" has evolved over the years. During the Silent Era (c. 1886–1930), 1.33 (1.33 times as wide as tall) was the standard. Following the introduction of Movietone sound-on-film, the Academy proposed a new standard of 1.37:1 (the Academy aperture standard). With the introduction of Cinerama and CinemaScope, the standard aspect ratio was changed again to better compete against "widescreen" aspect ratio films, eventually settling on 1.85:1 in the U.S. and 1.66:1 in Continental Europe. Television adopted a stan-

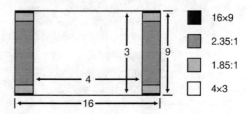

The 16 × 9 widescreen TV aspect ratio is wider than the standard 4 × 3 TV aspect ratio, but not quite as wide as the standard 1.85:1 U.S. theatrical aspect ratio.

dard aspect ratio of 4 × 3 — the original silent film aspect ratio of 1.33:1— which it retained until the popularity of high-definition, flat-screen televisions pushed that up to 16 × 9 (1.78:1).

static depth cue A monocular cue that can be represented in a still image. For example, if two similar objects appear to be different sizes, the smaller one is assumed farther away; a near object may block part of a far object, etc. Static depth cues include: aerial perspective, linear perspective, relative height, relative size, retinal image size, shadows and lighting cues, static interposition, and texture gradient. *Also* **pictorial depth cue.** *Compare* **motion depth cue.**

static interposition A monocular depth cue where a nearer object partially obscures or casts a shadow upon a farther object, allowing the observer to interpret the relative depths of the objects. *Compare* **kinetic interposition; monocular cue.** *See* **diagram at lighting cue** and **occlusion.**

static 3D An image that has 3D depth, but no motion, such as the still images depicted on stereocards.

static-volume display *See* **volumetric 3D.**

steerable Able to be aimed in different directions. For example, a steerable display may track head or eye movement to optimize 3D viewing.

ste-fra LANC The trade name for a wired LANC stereoscopic camera controller developed by German stereographer Werner Bloos and produced by digi-dat. The ste-fra LANC provides remote synchronization and operation of a pair of matching camcorders, including power on/off, camera start/stop, zoom, focus, and interval exposure for time-lapse photography. In addition, the ste-fra LANC can control all menu functions for Sony camcorders made since 2009, including white balance and exposure. The digi-dat Web site is www.digi-dat.de. *Compare* **LANC Shepherd.**

stereo Solid or three-dimensional. Generally used as a prefix as in stereographic (literally, writing with solids) or stereophonic (literally, three-dimensional sound).

stereo acuity 1. The ability to perceive depth or distance based on stereoscopic visual cues. 2. The accuracy with which depth or distance can be perceived. Measured as the smallest angle of parallax that can be resolved through binocular vision.

stereo base; stereobase *See* **baseline; interaxial distance.**

stereo blind; stereoblind Unable to perform stereopsis and fuse separate left- and right-eye images into a single, 3D image. One who is stereo blind may still be able to perceive depth to a certain degree using vergence and monocular depth cues, but will not be able to appreciate the 3D effect in a stereogram. Approximately 5–10 percent of the population is stereo blind to a measurable degree. *See* **binocular vision disability.** *Compare* **accommodative insufficiency; amblyopia; diplopia; convergence insufficiency; strabismus.**

stereo+depth; stereo+Z A left- and right-eye image pair with depth data that describe the 3D nature of the objects depicted. *Compare* **2D+depth.**

stereo disparity *See* **disparity.**

stereo distance The perceived distance from the viewer to an object in a stereogram, measured as a percentage of the distance from the viewer to the display surface.

In stereograms, objects do not extend out from or into the screen by a fixed amount. Instead, the apparent distance varies with the screen size. All else being equal, the larger the screen, the greater the apparent distance separating an object with non-zero parallax from the surface of the screen.

- Objects with zero parallax (appearing on the surface of the screen) have a stereo distance of 100 percent — the apparent distance from the observer is equal to the distance to the screen.
- Objects with negative parallax (appearing closer to the viewer than the screen) have a stereo distance < 100 percent. Generally, objects should not have a stereo distance less than 50 percent, or half the distance from the viewer to the screen (hyper-convergent).
- Objects with positive parallax (appearing farther than the screen) have a stereo distance > 100 percent. Generally, objects should not have a stereo distance more than 200 percent,

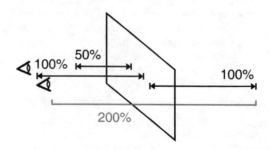

The point of hyper-divergence is 100 percent beyond the screen, or a total of 200 percent of the distance from the viewer to the screen.

or twice the distance from the viewer to the screen (hyper-divergent).
Also **perceived depth.**

stereo extinction ratio The degree to which the left- and right-eye images in a stereoscopic display can be seen by the opposite eye; a measure of crosstalk, perceived as ghosting.

stereo field *See* **Panum's fusion area.**

Stereo Image Processor; SIP The trade name for an electronic device produced by 3ality Digital, designed to perform a number of stereoscopic adjustments in real time, including image synchronization, geometric and color correction, image alignment, and output to anaglyph, frame-compatible, and frame-sequential display formats.

stereo images *See* **image pair; stereogram; stereoscopic image pair.**

stereo imaging device A complete apparatus used to record a stereogram, such as a single-lens 3D camera or a side-by-side rig with cameras attached.

stereo infinity The maximum distance at which binocular vergence (the inward turning of the eyes) can be used to judge depth. Beyond this point, generally 200 meters, the eyes are parallel and do not continue to diverge when viewing more distant objects.

stereo latency The time it takes, after cutting to a completely new image in a stereoscopic work, for the viewer to fully perceive the depth characteristics of the new image. The period of stereo latency increases if the amount of convergence in the new shot differs measurably from the prior one.

stereo multiview *See* **multiscopic.**

stereo pair *See* **image pair; stereogram; stereoscopic image pair.**

Stereo Realist mount *See* **Rochwite mount.**

stereo-restitution *See* **stereophotogrammetry.**

stereo script A shot-by-shot description of the planned depth in a stereoscopic work.

stereo to multi-view conversion The process of producing two or more stereograms for use with an auto-stereoscopic display from a single set of left- and right-eye images, generally those originally produced for a standard glasses-based stereoscopic display.

stereo vision; stereovision *See* **stereopsis.** *Compare* **depth perception.**

stereo window 1. The plane of convergence; the point within a stereogram where the left- and right-eye images meet, coinciding with the surface of the display screen. **2.** The frame through which a stereogram is viewed. Regardless of whether an object is perceived as being in front of, on, or behind the screen, it cannot extend outside the stereo window bounded by the flat-sided pyramid that extends from the center of the viewer's gaze through the edges of the screen. *Compare* **edge violation.**

A one-sheet poster for Warner Bros.' *House of Wax* (1953), breaking the stereo window to present a sense of three-dimensionality in a two-dimensional image (courtesy Heritage Auctions, www.ha.com).

stereoangle *Also* **angulation.** *See* **toe-in; vergence.**

stereocard The images from a stereogram mounted side-by-side on a piece of cardboard (traditionally 7" × 3½") for 3D viewing with a stereoscope.

stereocomparator A device that can analyze two stereo views and calculate the disparities between the conjugate points, producing a disparity map from which image parallax can be derived.

A traditional stereogram mounted on a stereocard, intended for home viewing with a stereoscope: "Gen. Custer at his Headquarters" by Mathew Brady, c. 1864. The original measures 7" × 3½" (courtesy Heritage Auctions, www.ha.com).

stereogram; stereograph A pair of left- and right-eye images that, when properly viewed, create the appearance of depth. Stereograms may be presented in a variety of ways (anaglyph, checkerboard, over/under, side-by-side, etc.) so long as they are matched to the proper viewing mechanism. The term "stereograph" was coined in 1859 by American physician Oliver Wendell Holmes, Sr. from Greek roots meaning, "to write with solids."

> NOTE: A distinction may be made between *stereogram*, a recorded stereoscopic image pair, and *stereograph*, the 3D image perceived when viewing a stereogram.

Also **stereo pair.**

stereographer One who specializes in the technical and aesthetic aspects of recording stereoscopic images.

The roles of stereographer and cinematographer may be combined or the stereographer may act as a technical advisor (stereoscopic supervisor) working with the cinematographer. According to American stereoscopic supervisor Phil McNally, "One can teach the whole theory of stereoscopy in two hours. You can learn all about 3D moviemaking in two months. That will never give you the 10 years of experience needed to master it. Good movies are made with experience, not with knowledge."

The mathematical calculations necessary to establish the optimal interaxial distance, toe-in angle, focal length, etc. may be performed using a spreadsheet or a special purpose stereoscopic calculator.

stereographic photography *See* **3D.**

stereographoscope A type of stereoscope that also includes a monocular magnifying glass for viewing 2D images in greater detail. Available in

A stereographoscope produced between 1889 and 1905 by the H.C. White Co. of North Bennington, Vermont. The large central lens magnified 2D images, such as CDVs (cartes de visite), a popular photographic print format first developed in France c. 1854 that featured a 2⅛" × 3½" image mounted on a 2½" × 4" card, and cabinet cards, a larger version of the CDV mounted on a 4¼" × 6½" card that gained popularity in the early 1870s. Beneath the 2D lens is a pair of stereoscope lenses for viewing traditional stereocards (courtesy Del Phillips).

hand held and table-top models, popular from c. 1870–1910.

stereography The art and technique of recording 3D images, which requires expertise in cameras, film stock or video characteristics, lighting, aesthetic image composition, and the mathematics of stereo image recording. *Also* **stereoscopy.**

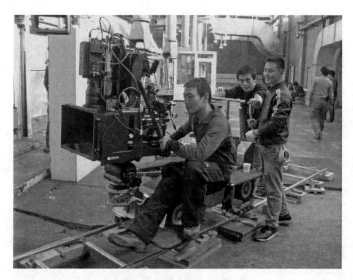

Stereography on location in China, shooting with a mirror rig and two RED ONE digital cinema cameras (courtesy Stereoscopic Technologies GmbH, www.stereotec.com).

StereoJet The trade name for a process for printing polarized, still-image stereograms. Separate left- and right-eye images are printed onto sheets of stereoscopically aligned polyvinyl alcohol plastic using a high-resolution inkjet printer. The sheets are laminated together along with a ¼ wave retarder on the front surface to create a circularly polarized stereogram viewable in 3D with standard circularly polarized glasses. The StereoJet Web site is www.stereojetinc.com.

stereomacroscopy Recording highly magnified stereoscopic images of very small objects using a smaller than normal interaxial distance, often less than 1cm (about ⅓") depending on the size of the subject, focal length, and depth effect desired. The recorded image is generally the same size or larger than the original object. *Also* **macro stereo.** *Compare* **gigantism; hypostereo.**

stereophotogrammetry The process of extracting the 3D coordinates that describe an object's geometry from a stereogram. Technically, any set of two or more images of the same subject taken from different perspectives can be used in stereophotogrammetry, but using properly prepared stereo images simplifies the process considerably. *Also* **stereo-restitution.** *Compare* analytic photogrammetry; stereoscopic rendition.

stereoplexing *See* **stereoscopic multiplexing.**

stereoplotter A device that extracts elevation contours from a pair of stereo images. Used to produce topographic maps from aerial stereograms. *Compare* **analytical stereoplotter.**

stereoprojection The presentation of a stereoscopic image using one or more 2D image projectors to present the individual stereo views.

stereopsis The ability to register depth in a 3D image or judge distance between objects based on the disparity (parallax) between left- and right-eye images. Depth perception involves both binocular depth cues (stereopsis and vergence) and monocular depth cues (relative size, occlusion, geometric perspective, motion parallax, etc.).

The function of stereopsis can be demonstrated by observing a Necker Cube (named for Swiss scientist Louis Albert Necker, who first published this optical illusion in 1832 based on his observations of line drawings of crystals.). Is the dot at the top right or the bottom left of the front face of the cube? With only 2D (monocular) depth cues, the brain will alternate between the two states since there is insufficient information to be sure. If the cube existed in 3D space, then stereopsis (binocular depth cues) would come into play and resolve the controversy.

Also **stereo vision.** *See* **depth perception.**

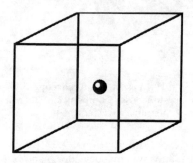

stereopsis-perspective rivalry *See* **perspective-stereopsis rivalry.**

stereopticon A twin-lens magic lantern (an early type of slide projector) that can dissolve from one flat (2D) image to another, but does not display moving or 3D (stereoscopic) images. Generally with one lens above the other rather than side-by-side. The device was developed in Philadelphia c. 1850 by brothers William and Frederick Langenheim, but the term was not coined until c. 1863.

> NOTE: Because of the twin lenses, *stereopticons* are often confused with stereoscopic projectors. The term is also often (incorrectly) used as a synonym for *stereoscope*.

stereoscope A stereoscopic presentation device where separate left- and right-eye images are viewed through independent optical paths. The term "stereoscope," which derives from Greek roots and literally means "a device for seeing solids," first appeared in 1838 and is generally attributed to English inventor Charles Wheatstone.

Unlike screen-based displays, which have many presentation variables, the depth effect of a stereoscope is principally a function of the focal length of the eyepiece lenses or mirrors. First developed by Charles Wheatstone in 1832 for use with hand-drawn images. The development of photographic printing c. 1841 and the Holmes stereoscope c. 1860 helped drive the widespread popularity of the stereoscope and stereoscopic imagery. Perhaps the best known contemporary stereoscope is the View-Master with its characteristic round image discs.

Compare **Taxiphote.**

A wooden Holmes/Bates stereoscope produced by the Keystone View Company c. 1921 (courtesy Heritage Auctions, www.ha.com).

StereoScope International A stereoscopic process and systems developer and service provider founded in 1972 by American stereographer John A. Rupkalvis. StereoScope has devel-

oped over/under 35mm and 70mm 3D film systems, such as the one used for *Metalstorm: The Destruction of Jared-Syn* (1982), 3D virtual reality systems, and a variety of HD, 2K, and 4K 3D digital video systems.

stereoscopic; ~ 3D; S3D Appearing to have 3D depth, often applied to the perception of 3D depth from a pair of 2D images.

Stereoscopic systems often present separate, 2D images for the left and right eyes and then rely on the brain to fuse them into a single 3D image. The two images are typically separated by the average distance between a pair of human eyes— between 50mm–70mm, or about 65mm (2½"). This simulates the distance between the two images normally recorded by the left and right eyes, leading the brain to interpret the composite image as having depth in addition to height and width. The actual distance between the images can be adjusted to enhance the 3D effect, with greater separation for distant subjects, though care must be taken when a single image includes both near and far objects lest the depth appear distorted.

> NOTE: The term *stereoscopic 3D* is slightly redundant. It was coined as a retronym to distinguish 3D visual display systems, which have been around for over 180 years, from 3D computer

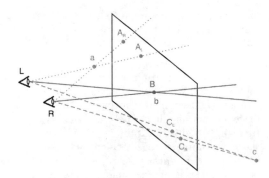

When the left and right eyes are presented with slightly offset images, the brain identifies the conjugate points in the two images and fuses them together, resulting in the perception of three-dimensional depth. If the conjugate points in the two views from a stereogram coincide in each eye's image (as with Point *B*), then that point appears to be on the surface of the screen. If the point in the left-eye image is to the left of the point in the right-eye image (as with Points *CL* and *CR*, respectively), the fused image appears to be behind the screen (Point *c*). If the point in the left-eye image is to the right of the point in the right-eye image (as with Points *AL* and *AR*), the fused image appears to be in front of the screen (point *a*). Points *c* and *a* demonstrate positive and negative parallax, respectively.

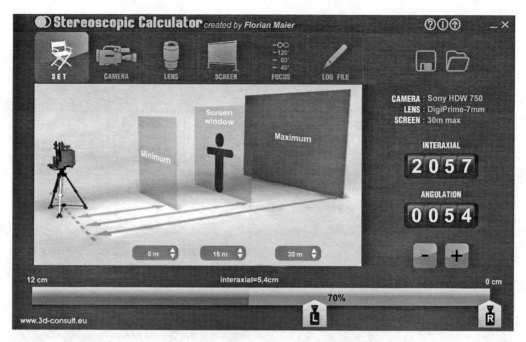

A stereoscopic calculator created by Florian Maier (courtesy Stereoscopic Technologies GmbH, www.stereotec.com).

graphic systems, which simulate a virtual 3D space but cannot present visual depth without a stereoscopic display.
See **3D**. *Compare* **auto-stereoscopic; multiscopic.**

stereoscopic calculator An electronic tool that helps calculate the optimal interaxial distance and convergence given a variety of factors including the type of lenses used, the lenses' focal length, and the target viewing angle (a function of screen size and viewing distance). Such tools range from basic spreadsheets to special purpose programs.

stereoscopic camera *See* **multi-rig camera, parallel cameras, toed-in cameras; twin-lens camera.**

stereoscopic content *See* **image pair; stereoscopic image pair.**

Stereoscopic Digital Cinema Addendum *See* **DCI.**

stereoscopic display A 3D imaging system that uses special eyewear to present two separate views of the same subject to the left and right eyes. The two images are encoded by the display so that the eyewear can filter the light arriving at the eye to ensure that each eye sees only the correct image. There are four main types of stereoscopic displays: temporal, polarization, wavelength, and spatial. *Compare* **auto-stereoscopic display.**

stereoscopic distortion A visual difference between an original scene and a stereoscopic representation. *See* **depth non-linearity, depth plane curvature, depth/size distortion, keystone distortion, shear distortion.** *Compare* **ortho stereo.**

stereoscopic image channel The electronic carrier for either the left- or right-eye information for a stereogram.

stereoscopic image pair The left- and right-eye images that together comprise a stereogram and present a 3D view using a stereoscopic display. *Compare* **multiscopic image set.**

stereoscopic JPEG *See* **JPS file.**

stereoscopic latency The time delay between the presentation of a stereogram and the viewer's perception of depth. *Also* **hunting time.**

stereoscopic multiplexing Combining the data necessary to reconstitute left- and right-eye stereoscopic images into a single data stream no larger than for a standard 2D image, including half-resolution video formats and anaglyphs. *Also* **stereoplexing.**

stereoscopic photography; stereoscopy *See* **3D.**

stereoscopic rendition A high-quality, analytical process for 2D to 3D conversion that first generates a 3D mathematical representation of a 2D scene and then uses virtual cameras to produce computer-generated stereo views of the scene.

The traditional technique for 2D to 3D conversion calls for first calculating the depth of selected objects in the scene, shifting the pixels that make up each object to create negative or positive parallax in the stereo views, and then painting in any portion of the background exposed when nearer objects were moved. If one then needs to create different levels of parallax for different viewing environments (theatrical vs. home viewing, for instance), the pixels must be shifted again and new background elements painted in. If one wishes to produce a multi-view version for autostereoscopic use, the process must be repeated for each view. With stereoscopic rendition, new parallax settings can be generated by moving the virtual cameras and re-rendering the scene. Additional stereo views can be added simply by adding additional virtual cameras. *Compare* **dimensionalization; pixel shift.**

stereoscopic supervisor; stereo supervisor *See* **stereographer.**

stereoscopic vision *See* **stereopsis.**

stereoscopist One who specializes in the design or construction of stereoscopes. *Compare* **stereographer.**

stereoscopy *See* **stereography.**

stereotaking The process of recording a stereogram.

stereo+2Z The images and depth data obtained from two separate cameras recording the same scene.

stereoview *See* **stereocard.**

Stereovision 3-D A side-by-side 35mm filmbased 3D projection format where two 1.37:1 images are squeezed anamorphically and presented within a standard 4-perf frame. During projection, the images are un-squeezed, polarized, and aligned on the screen. Later variants of the system included an over/under arrangement and a 70mm release format. Famously used for *The Stewardesses* (1969), an adult 3D film that remains one of the world's most profitable motion pictures on a percentage basis, earning more than $25 million at the box office on an initial investment of just over $100,000. *Compare* **Panavision 3D; Technicolor 3D.**

S3D; S-3D *See* **stereoscopic.**

sticky motion *See* **dirty window.**

still stereo view *See* **chip.**

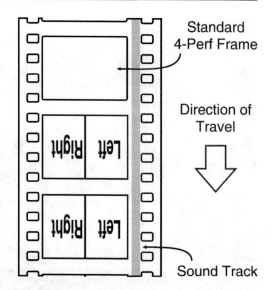

Stereovision 3-D. The arrangement of left- and right-eye images on a 35mm film print configured for the original Stereovision 3-D configuration. (Viewed from the lamp side, looking towards the projector lens.)

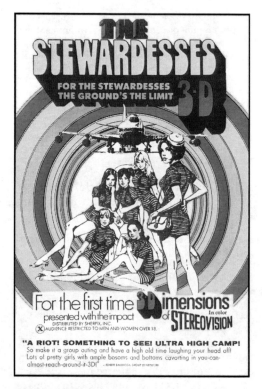

Stereovision 3-D. Hollywood Films' *The Stewardesses* (1969), presented in Stereovision 3-D (courtesy Heritage Auctions. www.ha.com).

strabismus An inability to align the eyes on a fixed point, due to a lack of coordination among the muscles controlling the eyes. Caused by a disorder of either the muscles or the brain. Often confused with amblyopia. May be corrected with some combination of glasses, surgery, or visual therapy, depending on the cause and severity of the disorder.

Strabismus interferes with binocular vision and may affect depth perception and one's ability to perceive 3D objects in a stereoscopic display. Adult onset strabismus can cause double vision (diplopia).

With strabismus, when one eye is fixed on an object, the other eye may angle in, out, up, or down. If the optical axis of the second eye over-converges and the eye turns inward, this may be called "cross-eyed." If the second eye under-converges and turns outward, this may be called "wall-eyed."

Also **esotropia; exotropia; hyperphoria; lazy eye; wandering eye.** *Compare* **accommodative insufficiency; amblyopia; convergence insufficiency; diplopia.**

straddle To split the depth in a stereoscopic scene between audience and screen space; to mix some amount of both negative and positive parallax in the same image.

streaking *See* **smearing.**

stretch An undesired exaggeration in the apparent depth in a stereogram, usually caused by viewing the image from beyond the optimal viewing distance. *Compare* **squeeze.**

stutter Uneven, interrupted motion. Often the result of a video processing delay that prevents smooth and even playback.

sub-pixel An addressable component of a pixel. Color pixels are often composed of separate red, green, and blue elements. The individual sub-pixel intensities are varied to create different colors in the pixel. *See* **sub-pixel** diagram in color section.

subjective test A method of measurement that is based on an observer's impressions or perceptions, such as an absolute category rating or the pair comparison method. The impact of observer bias can be reduced by using multiple observations by multiple observers and averaging the results.

Common subjective tests used to measure video quality include:
- Absolute Category Rating (ACR)
- Degradation Category Rating (DCR)
- Double-Stimulus Continuous-Quality Scale (DSCQS)
- Double-Stimulus Impairment Scale
- Pair Comparison Method (PC)
- Simultaneous Double Stimulus Continuous Evaluation (SDSCE)
- Single Stimulus Method

Compare **objective test.**

subtitle Text, other than credits, that appears overlaid atop the main action, occasionally beneath a letterboxed image on television.

Typically, subtitles are used to translate dialogue into another language or to convey information to the audience that is not readily apparent, such as a particular time or place where the action is set.

Graphic overlays (text or images, including subtitles and film credits) are a particular problem with stereoscopic works, since they can easily cause edge violations, exceed Percival's zone of comfort, or conflict with the apparent depth of the occluded screen objects. If overlays are placed on the surface of the screen (at zero parallax), any object that extends beyond the screen into the audience space could be occluded by the overlay, causing a visual conflict that cannot exist in the natural world, interfering with the 3D effect, and making the overlays hard to see. On the other hand, if the overlays are brought forward into the audience space so they never conflict with any objects coming off the screen, then in most scenes there will be too much separation between the overlays and the deep background, interfering with the viewer's ability to fuse the images and leading to double vision and eyestrain.

The optimal solution is to move each overlay in and out so it stays just above the closest object it naturally occludes (ranging from zero to negative parallax) without ever retreating significantly behind the screen (avoiding positive parallax). The overlays can either move dynamically to stay just on top of the occluded images or each could be placed at a static depth just above the background objects.

super multi-view; super-multiview; ~ display An auto-stereoscopic multi-view display that provides more than two simultaneous views for each eye. *Compare* **2-view display; multi-view.**

suppression *See* **binocular suppression.**

surround The black border on a theatrical motion picture screen. The border can be adjusted within certain limits (sides in/out, top and bottom up/down) to accommodate movies with different aspect ratios, making the screen fit the image. *Compare* **bezel.**

SVC; scalable video coding *See* **MPEG-4 SVC.**

sweet spot 1. The area within an image frame where the audience is most often looking (or can most conveniently look); the central portion of the frame. For the most part, action is concentrated within the sweet spot so audience members do not have to turn or tilt their heads to take in important details. **2.** The area(s) within the field of view of a camera lens that delivers the greatest image clarity and color fidelity. **3.** The volume of space within which a viewer's head must be placed in order to perceive a full stereoscopic effect; the head box. A particular display technology may have one or more sweet spots. **4.** The area within a listening environment that delivers the optimal sonic image, taking into account the number, type, and placement of the speakers; the shape of the listening environment; the materials covering the walls, floor, and ceiling; the other objects within the space; etc.

swept-volume display *See* **volumetric 3D.**

switchable parallax barrier A parallax barrier produced using an LCD panel, allowing it to be turned on or off depending on whether the associated display is presenting 2D or 3D images.

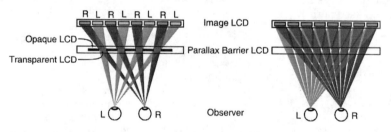

With select pixels turned on in the parallax barrier LCD (left), the left eye is limited to the pixels in the image LCD that represent the left-eye image while the right eye is limited to the pixels of the right-eye image, producing a half-resolution stereogram. With the parallax barrier LCD turned off (right), all pixels in the image LCD become visible to both eyes, allowing for the presentation of a full-resolution 2D image.

symmetric compression *See* **compression.**

sync error; synchronization error A timing mismatch between the left and right images in a motion stereogram where the left and right eyes are one or more frames out of registration. Generally introduced during post-production or playback. *Also* **temporal mismatch.** *Compare* **genlock error.**

synchronous 3D A stereoscopic display system where the left- and right-eye images are presented at the same time. Most anaglyphic and polarized 3D systems are synchronous. *Compare* **asynchronous 3D**

synthesis *See* **2D to 3D conversion.**

synthetic image An image that is created, rather than recorded, such as computer-generated graphics. *Compare* **natural image.**

TaB; top-and-bottom *See* **over/under.**

tactile feedback A simulation of the sense of touch applied to the skin of the user of a virtual reality system. *Compare* **force feedback; haptic.**

Targa file; .tga A raster graphic file format for digital still images with lossless compression, originally developed in 1984, with version 2.0 (the current version) following in 1989.

When rendering a motion picture using Targa, each individual frame is a separate file. This works out to about 130,000 Targa files for an average 90-minute feature film plus a separate file for audio (since the Targa format does not support synchronous sound recording). For convenience, longer works are often broken up into individual reels, or roughly 20-minute segments.

Targa is a relatively simple, patent-free format that supports 8-, 16-, 24-, and 32-bit color images (32-bit color is implemented as 24-bit color with an 8-bit alpha channel for transparency values). The Targa and TIFF file formats were developed at about the same time, but Targa was better suited to high-resolution, full-color image storage and remains popular in animation, gaming, and video applications. TARGA was originally an acronym of Truevision Advanced Raster Graphics Adapter while TGA was an initialism of Truevision Graphics Adapter, both developed by Truevision, Inc., a spin-off of AT&T now owned by Avid Technology, Inc. The terms Targa and TGA are now both used to reference the characteristic file format. *Compare* **DPX file; EXR file; TIFF file.**

tautomorphic image *See* **ortho stereo.**

Taxiphote The trade name for a type of mechanical stereoscope that could present up to 25 Verascope stereocards from an internal tray, developed c. 1883 (patented 1899) by the Jules Richard Company of Paris and available into the 1930s. Originally sold as the Stereo-Classeur, or stereo sorter. *Compare* **Verascope.**

TDVision A developer of 3D acquisition, encoding, decoding, and visualization technologies based on the 2D+delta encoding method. The TDVision Web site is www.tdvision.com.

Technicolor Certifi3D The trade name for a 3D certification service created by Technicolor in 2010 to establish minimum visual quality standards for 3D content to ensure viewer comfort and satisfaction. Certifi3D evaluates a 3D work based on 15 different criteria including hyper-convergence, vertical parallax, and pseudostereo.

How to Train Your Dragon (2010), the first Technicolor 3D commercial release (© 2010 DreamWorks Animation).

Technicolor 3D; Tech3D The trade name for the 35mm theatrical film projection system developed by Technicolor in 2010 that supports frame-compatible, over/under, circular polarized, stereoscopic images. With the Technicolor 3D lens replacing the standard projection lens, the two over/under images in each full 35mm frame are polarized and aligned on screen.

Final Destination (2009) was used for the first theatrical test of Technicolor 3D; the first commercial releases using the system were *How to Train Your Dragon* (2010) and *Clash of the Titans* (2010)

Vignetting and jitter are two notable issues that affect film-based polarized 3D systems. If the viewer is to perceive the full 3D effect, the images must be properly aligned vertically as well as horizontally, and the illumination across each image must be consistent for both the left and right eyes.

Vignetting causes uneven illumination across the image frame. With Technicolor 3D, the bottom of the left image is brighter than the top, and the top of the right image is brighter than the bottom, interfering with the 3D effect. To prevent this, the exposure of each frame is adjusted to deliver consistent illumination in both the left- and right-eye images.

Jitter results from unsteady image registration in the projector's gate. Because the Technicolor 3D images are half the usual height, jump (vertical motion) is doubled, while weave (horizontal motion) is unaffected. Since both images are aligned in the same direction, they always move in unison on screen, thereby eliminating jitter as a particular 3D concern, though not all images will remain steady on screen (most obvious with white text against a black background).

The design, style, and age of the lamp, and frequency and proficiency of maintenance of individual projectors significantly contribute to the type and degree of vignetting and jitter. If the projector is properly adjusted and maintained, these effects can be nearly eliminated.
Compare **Panavision 3D.**

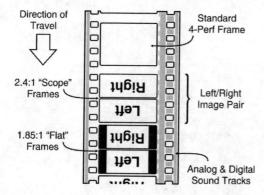

The arrangement of left- and right-eye images on a 35mm film print configured for Technicolor 3D. (Viewed from the lamp side, looking towards the projector lens.)

Teco-Nimslo A Nimslo 4-exposure auto-stereoscopic camera modified by California-based Technical Enterprises in the 1980s to expose only 2 images at a time (lenses 1 and 4 remained active, while lenses 2 and 3 were disabled) so the camera could produce standard stereo image pairs. *See* **Nimslo.**

telepresence; tele-presence A technology or system that provides a remote observer with the sensation of being physically present at a distant place, including sight and sound and possibly also including smell or touch.

temporal aliasing *Also* **motion aliasing.** *See* **aliasing.**

temporal decimation An image compression technique that removes redundant information over time from within a sequence of images. *Compare* **decimation; spatial decimation.**

temporal display A stereoscopic display where the left- and right-eye images are transmitted by the display one at a time in a repeating sequence. This requires active eyewear with shutters that switch on and off in time with the transmission sequence so that light is transmitted to an eye only when the display is showing the appropriate image. Early temporal displays used eyewear with mechanical shutters, while contemporary displays use eyewear with liquid crystal shutters that are activated electronically. To avoid perceptible flicker, such systems run at two or more times the standard frame rate — 48 frames-per-second (fps) for film-based systems (24 fps for each eye) or 120 Hz and 240 Hz for video-based systems (a nominal 60 Hz or 120 Hz for each eye). *Compare* **3D display.**

temporal mismatch *See* **sync error.**

temporal multiplexing; temporal separation Separating the individual views in a stereogram or multi-view 3D image in time and presenting them in sequence. *See* **time-sequential.** *Compare* **spatial multiplexing.**

temporal symmetry 1. The expectation in binocular vision that a single object will exhibit the same motion characteristics through each eye. If the eyes perceive motion differently, the disparity may be interpreted as arising from parallax and cause a false sense of image depth due to the Pulfrich effect. 2. One of the parameters of binocular symmetry. In a stereogram, the left- and right-eye images differ due to horizontal disparity (parallax), but may share a number of other characteristics, including color, focus, geometry, illumination, and registration.

texture gradient A monocular depth cue where the surface details of an object become less noticeable and the surface appears smoother the farther it is from the observer. Technically, a special case of linear perspective. *Compare* **monocular cue.**

theater space *Also* **personal space.** *See* **audience space.**

theme park configuration glasses Lightweight, reusable, rigid frame eyewear (the earpieces are not hinged) equipped with linear polarized lenses (generally oriented at 45° and 135°).

themed entertainment *See* **location-based entertainment.**

therapeutic 3D The use of stereoscopic images to improve visual skills including binocular coordination, depth perception, and eye teaming. Originally developed in the 1850s and now used in behavioral optometry, developmental optometry, orthoptic therapy, and vision training.

3D; 3-D Having, or seeming to have, three dimensions: height, width, and depth. All physical objects in the natural world are 3D, while most images—from simple line drawings to photographs to computer-generated imagery — are 2D depictions of the 3D world. Stereoscopic audiovisual works simulate a full, 3D view using 2D images.

With most stereoscopic images, the viewer must wear special glasses to appreciate the effect (autostereoscopic and holographic systems excepted). The glasses, which are either passive or active, ensure that each eye only sees the appropriate image for that eye. Passive eyewear uses either colored or polarized lenses. Active eyewear switches the left and right lenses on and off in time with the presented images. When the eye images are presented in sequence rather than simultaneously, the left-eye image is generally presented first, followed by the right-eye image.

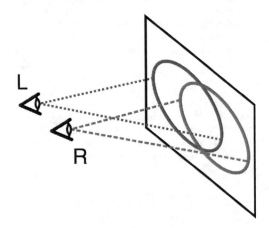

3D projection systems were first developed near the end of the nineteenth century. Several processes were developed over the years, but none caught on until the 1950s. This boom in 3D popularity waned in the years that followed. Then, in 2005, the development of digital 3D breathed new life into the format, sparking a 3D renaissance.

Most early 3D projection systems relied on the anaglyph method where black-and-white images for the left and right eyes are tinted two different colors (originally orange and blue, but typically red and cyan) and viewed through glasses with corresponding colored lenses. In the 1920s, several competing 3D projection systems were developed. The Fairall Process was used for the first 3D feature film, *The Power of Love* (1922), which premiered on September 27 at the Ambassador Hotel Theater in Los Angeles, but 3D failed to catch on with the public before the novelty wore off.

In the 1930s, the anaglyph process was replaced with polarized-light stereograms as the most popular 3D format. As with most 3D processes, anaglyphs require a camera with two lenses, but the two eye images can be combined into a single recorded image and presented using a standard projector or television. Polarized-light stereograms use polarized filters in place of colored filters. This still requires a two-lens camera to produce the paired images and projector or television filters to present the polarized images. However, the polarized process can be used to produce full-color images and a closer luminance match between images (which causes less eyestrain) compared to the earlier, color-based anaglyph process.

Various 3D movies were produced during the 1930s and '40s, including *Robinzon Kruzo* (1946),

the first color 3D feature film with sync sound, produced by the Soviet Union's Aleksandr Andriyevsky using an auto-stereoscopic process, so audiences did not have to wear special glasses. Still, 3D technology did not gain wide success until the 1950s when competition from television inspired filmmakers to experiment further with 3D movies.

In 1951, the Festival of Britain commissioned and screened several polarized stereoscopic short films to demonstrate the latest improvements in the technology. 3D filmmaking then enjoyed a brief run of popularity, beginning with the November 30, 1952 release of Arch Oboler's *Bwana Devil*. Numerous 3D films were produced over the next several years such as the first 3D musical, Paramount's *Those Redheads from Seattle* (1953)—which narrowly beat out MGM's *Kiss Me Kate* (1953) for this distinction. The most enduring 3D films of the 1950s were horror films: Universal's *Creature from the Black Lagoon* (1954) and Warner Bros.' *House of Wax* (1953).

Creature from the Black Lagoon was the first commercial single-strip/single-projector polarized film, produced using over/under image frames. (Previous polarized films used two strips of film

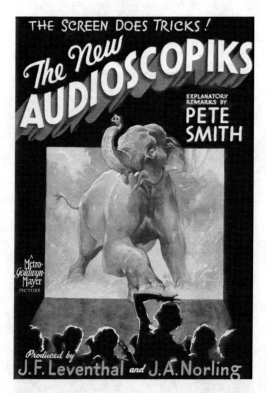

MGM's second 3D production, *The New Audioscopiks* (1938), was a sequel to the popular Academy Award–nominated 3D documentary short *Audioscopiks* (1935). The earlier *Audioscopiks* opened with an overview of human depth perception and instructions on how to use 3D glasses (courtesy Heritage Auctions, www.ha.com).

The prototypical 1950s 3D motion picture, Arch Oboler's production of *Bwana Devil* (1951) (courtesy Heritage Auctions, www.ha.com).

and synchronized projectors.) 3D filmmaking hit its peak in 1953 when Hollywood studios released a total of 23 3D feature films. In 1954, 13 new 3D features were released, including Alfred Hitchcock's *Dial M for Murder.*

In 1954, Polaroid and Technicolor announced a full-color form of the Vectograph 3D process originally developed by Polaroid in 1939. Vectographs create images through varying degrees of polarization directly on the film and so do not require polarized filters on the projector. Both left- and right-eye images occupy the same film frame, cutting the length of polarized release prints in half. (The dual strip polarized processes uses twice as much film as a standard 2D image or an anaglyph stereogram.) Vectographs would have reduced the limit imposed on the theatrical 3D market by the scarcity of 3D-equipped theaters, since they would have worked in a standard 35mm film projector, but they arrived just as the 1950's 3D boom ended.

The popularity of 3D diminished after the 1950s due in large part to increasing competition from the newly developed widescreen processes. The competition between 3D and CinemaScope is evidenced by the CinemaScope marketing slogan, "The modern miracle you see without glasses!"

3D films continued to be made and the technology continued to advance, despite the waning interest in the technological novelty. 3D adult films were popular for a time. (The X-rated 3D film *The Stewardesses* (1969) remains one of the world's most profitable films on a percentage basis, earning more than $25 million at the box office on an initial investment of just over $100,000.) 3D television broadcasting (using the traditional anaglyphic process) began in Melbourne, Australia in 1979. In the U.S., the first 3D presentation on cable TV (1953's *Miss Sadie Thompson*) took place in Los Angeles on December 19, 1980. This was followed by the first U.S. 3D broadcast (1955's *Revenge of the Creature*) on WGNO in New Orleans on February 9, 1982. Several new 3D films were also released theatrically during the early 1980s including *Metalstorm: The Destruction of Jared-Syn* (1982), *Parasite* (1982), *Friday the 13th Part 3* (1982), and *Amityville 3-D* (1983). These new works demonstrated technical improvements, but did not revive the theatrical format.

Over the following years, new 3D works were released, such as *Spy Kids 3-D: Game Over* (2003) and the "Still Life" television episode of *Medium* (2005–2011), but perhaps the most financially suc-

Columbia Pictures' *Miss Sadie Thompson* (1953) (courtesy Heritage Auctions, www.ha.com).

Twentieth Century–Fox's *Avatar* (2009), the highest grossing 3D film of all time (© 2009, 20th Century–Fox & Dune Entertainment).

cessful — and certainly the longest-running — 3D film was the Francis Ford Coppola short subject *Captain EO* (1986), produced for the Disney theme parks. Even so, 3D remained mostly a special venue medium until the availability of digital stereogram projection systems, which has inspired a contemporary 3D renaissance beginning with *Chicken Little* (2005), the first all digital 3D feature film.

Initially, broadcast television and home entertainment 3D systems were limited to anaglyphs, since they can be transmitted and presented using standard 2D technologies. The original active eyewear-based "3D Ready" TVs supported a variety of frame-compatible stereogram formats, all running at half the standard image resolution so that twice the number of images (separate left and right eyes) could be delivered via traditional means, including broadcast, DVD, and Blu-ray.

In 2010, the Blu-ray 3D format was released, supporting full-resolution 1080p images for each eye. *Monsters vs Aliens* (2009) was the first 3D feature film delivered using this format. Since Blu-ray 3D uses dual MPEG-4 MVC image streams recorded on a single disc, a properly encoded Blu-ray 3D disc can be used in a compatible 2D Blu-ray player to present a 2D version of the 3D content. *Also* **stereovision.** *See* **stereoscopic.** *Compare* **2D; 4D; anaglyph; auto-stereoscopic; hologram; polarized stereograms.**

3D adjustment; ~ setting A change in the depicted depth in a stereogram at the point of presentation. *Also* **user-adjustable depth.** *Compare* **interocular adjustment.**

3D@Home Consortium A trade association formed in 2008 to accelerate the development and adoption of stereoscopic technologies for home viewing. The 3D@Home Web site is www.3dathome.org.

3D Blu-ray; 3D BD *See* **Blu-ray 3D.**

3D cinema Theatrical presentation of a stereoscopic work.

3D-compatible An electronic device that can detect and pass stereoscopic content on to another device without altering or acting upon the stereoscopic content in any way.

3D-compliant An electronic device that can detect and correctly process (decode, scale, etc.) stereoscopic content before presenting it or passing it on to another device. *Compare* **3D-enabled; 3D-ready.**

3D content Visual material consisting of two (or more) views of the same subject that, when presented together, produce the appearance of 3D depth.

3D depth *See* **Z-depth.**

3D display An image delivery system that presents separate views to the left and right eyes, creating a 3D representation. Commercially available 3D displays can be categorized generally as stereoscopic (requiring special eyewear) and auto-stereoscopic (viewable directly without eyewear).

3D distribution data Stereoscopic content produced from a 3D home master (itself produced from a 3D source master) that is compressed and encrypted as necessary prior to distribution to consumers.

3D distribution format The medium used to deliver a stereogram to a consumer. Historically, the most common 3D distribution format was motion picture film or analog broadcast television. Digital distribution formats now dominate the market and include digital cinema, terrestrial broadcast, cable or satellite broadcast, Internet delivery, and home entertainment packages such as Blu-ray discs. *Also* **3D transport format.**

3D DVD A DVD that contains stereoscopic content encoded as an MPEG-2 stream. Due to storage limitations, 3D DVDs generally contain anaglyphs or half-resolution stereograms. *Compare* **Blu-ray 3D.**

3D edge feathering Adjustments made to the depicted depth of an object near its borders to smooth the visual transition between overlapping objects or an object and the background. Helps avoid sudden changes in image depth that may otherwise lead to a cardboard cutout-type effect.

3D-enabled An electronic device (or coordinated collection of devices) that is fully capable of decoding a stereoscopic data stream and rendering it properly on a stereoscopic display. For example, a 3D-enabled system may be a single, self-contained unit or a set of linked devices that work together to display stereoscopic content, such as a 3D-compliant set-top box that accepts and decodes 3D data for presentation on a connected 3D-ready display. *Compare* **3D-compliant; 3D-ready.**

3D-exclusive content Audiovisual material intended by its creator for 3D viewing only. It may be technically possible to extract a 2D image from 3D-exclusive content, but the material was not prepared with this use in mind. *Compare* **compatible 3D content.**

3D eyewear; 3D glasses *See* **active eyewear; hybrid eyewear; passive eyewear; spectral eyewear.**

3D flash LIDAR A means of recording detailed depth information in a scene by illuminating the scene with a series of brief light pulses, often in the invisible infrared spectrum, and analyzing the reflections to calculate object size and position. *LIDAR* is an acronym of *LIght Detection And Ranging. Compare* **spatial capture.**

3D format A standard for recording, distributing, or displaying stereoscopic content, such as frame-sequential, side-by-side, IMAX, etc. *Compare* **3D in-home format.**

3D from 2D *See* **2D to 3D conversion.**

3D home master Content produced from a 3D source master that is ready for use in the creation of 3D distribution data. The 3D home master is presented in an uncompressed and unencrypted format and is not intended for use by a consumer.

3D in-home format A recorded stereogram format suitable for home viewing, usually with lower resolution and higher compression than formats used in production, post-production, and theatrical exhibition.

3D content may be encoded in a compound in-home format where the 3D stereograms are enveloped in a standard video format, requiring two layers of decoding before presentation. The highest quality 3D in-home format presents 1080p HD images in full resolution, recorded on a Blu-ray disc for viewing on a digital display.

3D jump cut *See* **depth jump cut.**

3D metadata Additional information recorded along with stereograms to assist in their decoding or presentation.

3D monitor *See* **3D display.**

3D native display format The stereoscopic video format unique to a particular type of display. This may differ from the format of the original stereoscopic signal, requiring pre-processing before presentation (either by the display or by an external device), but once in the 3D native display format, no further 3D processing is required (though further 2D video processing may still be necessary).

NOTE: Confusingly, *3D native display format* is not the same as *native 3D display format*, which refers to the number and arrangement of the image pixels, rather than the video signal format.

3D previz A simulation of what a 3D set, shot, or sequence will look like when it is complete, either computer-generated or recorded with low-resolution cameras. A 3D pre-visualization is much quicker and less expensive to produce than the final shot itself, and allows the filmmakers the freedom to experiment in pre-production when a project is still in the planning and budgeting stages. One could think of them as highly-accurate, fully-animated, 3D storyboards.

Pre-visualization may also be used during production and post-production to help judge the effect of a shot before it has been produced. During production, this helps the director, DP, or stereographer adjust to last-minute changes or visualize how a post-production composite will look with the material being shot on set. During post-production, this helps the creative team visualize what composites or other visual effects shots will look like before they are finished. Pre-visualization may also be used at any stage in the process to judge how a particular stereoscopic composition will look given different viewing conditions, such as IMAX, theatrical, home entertainment, or portable media.

NOTE: Some choose to use the terms *previz*, *durviz*, and *postviz* to differentiate between pre-visualization used during pre-production, production, and post-production, respectively. Others use the term previz to cover all three situations.

3D projection system Stereoscopic presentation using a digital image or film projector set some distance from the screen, allowing for an enlarged image and a large audience. May use active (eclipse method) or passive (anaglyph, polarized, etc.) eyewear. (In 1946, the Soviet Union developed an auto-stereoscopic projection system, but the process did not catch on.)

3D-ready; 3D Ready Able to accommodate a standard stereoscopic data stream when equipped with a separate pre-processor, decoder, or similar adaptive device. For example, a 3D-ready display can present stereoscopic content with the addition of a compatible 3D decoder.

Technology "ready" devices arrive in advance of the wide adoption of the related technology with the promise of being compatible with the new technology when it is later released. For example, the first "3D Ready" HDTV was released in 2007, while the first 3D Blu-ray player was not available until 2010.

Compare **3D-compliant; 3D-enabled.**

3D rendering 1. Generating stereoscopic images from supplied data rather than pre-recorded images. **2.** The final step in 3D signal processing before display.

3D signage An auto-stereoscopic presentation in a public place with an informational or promotional message.

3D signal processing The analysis and manipulation of electronic data unique to stereoscopic images. Processing equipment must be aware of the type of signal it is processing (2D or 3D) so that it can take appropriate steps to produce the desired result. *Compare* **2D signal processing.**

3D skew *See* **shear distortion.**

3D source master The original material from which a stereoscopic program is produced. Before being released for digital cinema, the 3D source master is first assembled into a collection of uncompressed picture, sound, and data elements (the digital cinema distribution master, or DCDM) and then compressed and encrypted to form the digital cinema package (DCP) for delivery to the theater. Alternatively, before being released to the home entertainment market, the 3D source master is first assembled into an uncompressed and unencrypted 3D home master and then compressed and possibly encrypted into 3D distribution data.

3D tile format A frame-compatible stereogram format combining two 720p images (for left and right eyes) for transmission in a single 1080p frame using standard H.264 video compression. Developed by the Sisvel Group in conjunction with Quartarete TV, a digital terrestrial TV broadcaster, and first offered by Quartarete in northwest Italy in December 2010.

3D transport format *See* **3D distribution format.**

3D viewing *See* **binocular vision; depth perception.**

3 R's rule A mnemonic for remembering the effect of changing parallax on apparent image depth: Right, Right, Recede. If one moves an object in the right-eye image to the right, it will appear to recede from the viewer in the fused stereogram. (Moving an object in the left-eye image to the left will also cause it to recede, but "2 L's and an R" is not as easy to remember.)

threshold A sensory limit: stimulus below a threshold cannot be perceived, while stimulus above a threshold can be perceived. *Compare* **discrimination threshold**

through-the-window effect A stereogram with negative parallax so that an object seems to extend through the stereo window and out into the audience space.

TIFF file; .tif A graphic file format for digital still images. Supports lossy and lossless compression, black-and-white, color, and multi-page documents.

When rendering a motion picture using TIFF, each individual frame is a separate file. This works out to about 130,000 TIFF files for an average 90-minute feature film plus a separate file for audio (since TIFF does not support synchronous sound recording). For convenience, longer works are often broken up into individual reels, or roughly 20-minute segments.

TIFF is an acronym of *Tagged Image File Format*. The TIFF format was developed in 1986 by an industry committee chaired by the Aldus Corporation (now part of Adobe Software). Microsoft and Hewlett-Packard were among the contributors to the format. As one of the most common graphic image formats, TIFF files are used in desktop publishing, faxing, 3D applications, and medical imaging applications. TIFF files can be in any of several classes, including black-and-white, gray scale, color palette, or full-color RGB, and can include files with JPEG, LZW, or CCITT Group 4 standard run-length image compression. *Compare* **DPX file; EXR file; Targa file.**

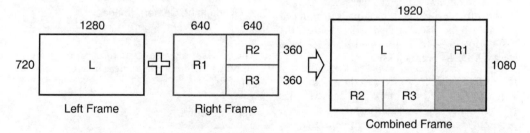

3D tile format. When encoding a 720p stereogram using the 3D tile format, the left-eye frame remains intact while the right-eye frame is cut into three pieces — one 640 × 720 pixels and two 640 × 360 pixels each. The stereogram frames are then placed inside a standard 1080p video frame (1920 × 1080 pixels) as shown. The left-eye frame can be extracted and viewed as a 2D image. Reconstructing the full stereogram also requires extracting and re-assembling the three pieces of the right-eye frame.

tilt 1. A misalignment between left- and right-eye images where both images are rotated out of proper alignment, generally because the cameras were not horizontal. *See* **tilt & twist** diagram in color section. **2.** Up/down rotation; rotation along the X-axis; pitch. *Compare* **orientation; twist.** *See* diagram at **orientation.**

time-sequential; ~ 3D A stereoscopic display system where left- and right-eye images are presented one at a time in a high-speed alternating pattern. Only one eye is receiving an image at any given time, but the switching is so fast that this is imperceptible to the viewer. Active or passive eyewear ensures that each eye sees only the correct images. Polarized time sequential systems alternate the polarization direction as each image is presented, while active systems turn the lenses in the eyewear on and off in time with the left/right image sequence. By convention, one presents the left-eye image first, followed by the right-eye image.
  • For interlaced video display systems, the eye images are in alternate fields of the same frame (field-sequential).
  • For checkerboard systems, the eye images are combined into a single frame, alternating the presented eye with each pixel.
  • For all other time-sequential display systems, the eye images alternate with each frame (frame-sequential).
Also **dual stream; eye-sequential; frame-sequential.** *Compare* **column-interleaved; row-interleaved.**

tint *See* **hue.**

tissue stereocard A stereogram printed on thin photographic paper, hand tinted on the reverse side, and mounted to a card with cut-outs so the images could be illuminated from behind. When light was shown through the stereocard, colors "magically" appeared on the otherwise black-and-white stereogram. Pinpricks were occasionally used to provide highlights. Originally introduced in France in the 1850s. The name derives from the tissue paper used to protect the back side of the stereocard. *Also* **French tissue.**

title; ~ file A data file stored by a theatrical digital video projector to retain various lens settings (amount of zoom, left/right position, up/down position, etc.) developed through experimentation and observation during the initial show set-up, for use when presenting that particular program in the future. *See* **lens memory.**

toe-in The degree to which the lens axes of a pair of stereoscopic cameras are turned inwards from parallel so that they converge at a distant point. *Also* **angulation; stereoangle.** *See* **convergence.**

toed-in cameras A stereoscopic camera configuration where the cameras are rotated so the lens axes converge at a point. This also causes the right and left edges of the recorded images to align at that point. Objects at the same depth as this point will appear to be on the screen in the final stereoscopic presentation, while other objects will appear to be in front of or behind the screen corresponding to their relationship to the point of convergence.

The amount of image disparity (perceived 3D depth) primarily depends on the interaxial distance (the distance between the camera lens axes), but is also directly affected by the lens focal length, the vergence distance (the distance from the film plane to the point where the lens axes converge), the size of each object, and how far each object is from the point of convergence.

Since the cameras are set at an angle with respect to each other, the film planes are not parallel. This causes keystone distortions in the left- and right-eye images. These may appear as object height distortions that introduce artificial vertical disparities that can become uncomfortable to view if not corrected. *Also* **verging cameras.** *Compare* **parallel cameras.**

Non-Overlapping Camera Images

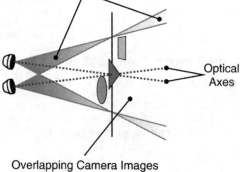

Optical Axes

Overlapping Camera Images
(View Frustum)

The overlapping (view frustum) and non-overlapping portions of the camera images of toed-in cameras.

tone *See* **value.**

top-and-bottom; TaB *See* **over/under.**

total scene depth The distance between the near and far points when recording a stereogram. May be calculated as the far point distance less the near point distance. *Compare* **depth range.**

tracking Monitoring the position and orientation of some object in 2D or 3D space, such as a 3D system viewer's head or eyes or the full body of a virtual reality participant. *Compare* **eye tracking; head tracking.**

tracking convergence *See* **convergence tracking.**

transcoding To convert from one file or signal format to another or from one media type to another. *Compare* **decoding; encoding.**

translation *See* **6DoF.**

transmission artifact *See* **network artifact.**

transmission hologram *See* **holographic optical element.**

transmission, plane of *See* **plane of transmission.**

transmissive display An electronic display where the image cannot be seen unless a separate light source is shown through it, such as an LCD-based flat panel display. *Compare* **emissive display.**

trapezoidal magnification disparity *See* **keystone distortion.**

TriDef *See* **DDD.**

trifocal stereo The use of three interlinked cameras to capture image and depth information simultaneously. *Compare* **multiple interocular.**

TrioScopics 3D The trade name for a stereogram viewing system composed of a proprietary digital encoding process and an anaglyphic glasses design that uses special green and magenta filtered lenses, originally introduced in 2008 and since used for a number of feature film home entertainment releases. The TrioScopics Web site is www.trioscopics.com.

    TrioScopics 3D uses sophisticated digital image processing to combine the original left- and right-eye image streams into a single image sequence with improved depth reproduction and significantly reduced ghosting compared to traditional anaglyphic processes. TrioScopics 3D also delivers a wider range of colors (particularly orange, red, and blues), and better left/right eye luminance balance than red/cyan processes. Unlike polarized and active glasses-based systems, anaglyph-based systems do not require special 3D-enabled delivery or presentation equipment, so TrioScopics 3D works can be viewed in the home on a standard color television with very good picture quality and little eyestrain, even after prolonged viewing.

See **TrioScopes 3D** in color section.

TriOviz The trade name for a stereogram viewing system where the left- and right-eye images are encoded using complex magenta and green filters, respectively. There are three different versions of TriOviz available, balancing the traditional anaglyphic tradeoffs between color and depth fidelity: Force 1, for best color reproduction with subtle 3D effects; Force 2, balances color and depth reproduction; and Force 3, for muted colors with superior 3D effects. The magenta/green filters provide better left/right eye luminance balance than a standard red/cyan anaglyphic process, resulting in reduced eyestrain, even after prolonged viewing. The TriOviz Web site is www.trioviz.com.

Tru-Vue The trade name for a type of stereoscope designed to use card-mounted filmstrips, first introduced in 1931. In 1951, the company was purchased by Sawyer's Photo Services, the manufacturer of the View-Master line of film disc-based stereo viewers, largely to gain access to Tru-Vue's exclusive stereoscopic contract with Disney. The Tru-Vue line was discontinued in the 1960s.

Turing test A benchmark for measuring the sophistication of machine-based intelligence by comparing a computer to a human being. May also be used as a quality measure for artificial recreations of natural experiences. (Is a recorded sound indistinguishable from a natural sound? Is a computer-generated image indistinguishable

Alan Mathison Turing FRS OBE (1912–1954).

from a photograph? Is a stereoscopic image indistinguishable from a view of the natural world?)

Named for British computer scientist Alan Turing and generally used in reference to his Imitation Game, first proposed in "Computing Machinery and Intelligence" (1950). In this classic test of machine intelligence, an isolated interrogator attempts to tell a human from a computer by asking each a series of typed questions. If the interrogator is not able to identify the computer, then the machine is assumed to possess an independent intelligence comparable to a human.

twin camera stereo photography Recording both left- and right-eye stereogram images at the same time using two identical cameras. *Compare* **sequential stereogram.**

twin-cams A two-camera stereo photography rig, generally with the cameras mounted side-by-side rather than shooting through a beam splitter.

twin-lens camera A stereoscopic camera with two separate lenses and an integrated imaging system that allows for the capture of two images at the same time. *Compare* **fixed interaxial.**

The Panasonic 3DA1 3D twin-lens camcorder records two 1920 × 1080 image streams to dual internal SD cards or to external recorders via dual HD-SDI or HDMI 1.4 connectors. The lenses have a fixed interaxial distance, but the camera supports optical convergence adjustments (courtesy Panasonic, www.panasonic.com).

twist A misalignment between left- and right-eye images in a stereogram where one of the images is rotated out of proper alignment with respect to the other. *Compare* **tilt.** *See* **tilt & twist** diagram in color section.

twister An image with a rotational misalignment along the Z-axis.

2D; 2-D Having only two dimensions: height and width, but no depth.

A physical film or television image on a screen is two-dimensional, though it may depict a 3D scene. (Such images contain monocular depth cues, and so provide a 3D representation, even though they lack the binocular depth cues of natural vision and stereoscopic 3D.) The individual views in a stereogram or multi-view display are still two-dimensional, though when viewed properly they provide both monocular and binocular depth cues for more natural 3D perception. Volumetric images physically occupy 3D space so both the image and scene depicted are three-dimensional.
Compare **3D.**

2D compatibility The extent to which stereoscopic content can be processed by standard 2D equipment without a negative impact on the content.

2D-compatible 3D content *See* **compatible 3D content.**

2D for 3D; ~ capture Applying stereoscopic best practices when shooting and editing a 2D work to support a possible later 2D to 3D conversion. Otherwise, the finished work may be difficult to convert to 3D or may deliver disappointing 3D results.

2D from 3D The process of producing a 2D image from a 3D source. This may be as simple as presenting just one of the 3D eye views (the primary eye in the stereogram, typically the left).

2D+D *See* **2D+delta; 2D+depth; 2D+DOT.**

2D+delta A stereogram recorded as a 2D image and a set of difference (delta) data that describes how the second-eye image differs from the supplied image. This requires more processing power during playback than providing separate left- and right-eye images, but consumes far less bandwidth for storage and delivery. Implemented in the MPEG-4 MVC standard as base/dependent view encoding. *Compare* **B-D view; difference map; asymmetric coding.**

2D+depth A stereogram derived from a single 2D image and depth data that describe the 3D nature of the objects depicted. This requires more processing power during playback, but consumes far less bandwidth than providing separate left- and right-eye images. *Also* **2D+Z.** *Compare* **depth map; stereo+depth.**

2-dimensional image *Also* **flat image.** *See* **planar image.**

2D+DOT A stereogram derived from a single 2D image and additional data that describe the depth (D), occlusion (O), and transparency (T) of the objects depicted. This requires more processing power that 2D+depth encoding, but generates a far more naturalistic result.

2D+Z *See* **2D+depth**

2D signal processing The analysis and manipulation of electronic data without regard to whether the signal represents 2D or 3D imagery. A 3D signal may take longer to process if it contains more information than an equivalent 2D signal, but all of the processing steps and transformations remain essentially the same. *Compare* **3D signal processing.**

2D to 3D conversion The process of producing a 3D image from a 2D source. This is a computationally complex process. Low-quality, inexpensive conversions have a cardboard cutout feel, with a series of flat objects set at different distances within the scene. Often used in consumer electronics to deliver 3D content from 2D masters in real time. Higher quality and considerably more expensive conversions can equal the appearance of works originally recorded with full stereoscopic views, but this process is only semi-automated and cannot be performed in real time. *Compare* **cloning; dimensionalization; pixel shift; stereoscopic rendition.**

2D wrapper A 3D video encoding scheme that encodes the stereoscopic data in a standard 2D video data stream, including anaglyph, side-by-side, over/under, and checkerboard. *Compare* **half-resolution; mux/demux workflow.**

2D/3D compatible A system that is capable of simultaneously recording 2D and 3D images; 3D images formatted so that one of the eye views can be used for 2D display.

2K Digital video with a maximum resolution of 2,048 horizontal pixels and 1,556 vertical pixels (when scanned from 35mm film), or 2048 × 1080 for digital cinema; the standard acceptable digital video resolution for a film finish or for digital theatrical projection. *Compare* **4K.**

2-perf; two-perf Thirty-five millimeter film with a widescreen image and two perforations, or sprocket holes, per image frame rather than the standard four. For example, used in film-based over/under formats to fit both the left- and right-eye images in the same space as a standard 35mm film frame, allowing the use of an unmodified

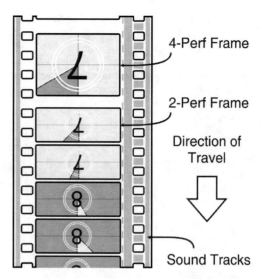

The standard arrangement for 2-perf 35mm film frames compared to a 4-perf Academy aperture frame.

film projector equipped with a special lens that superimposes the two images during projection. *Compare* **4-perf.**

2-plane mode Stereoscopic content encoding where graphical elements (typically subtitles or interactive graphics) can be placed in one of two independent planes set different distances above the 3D video content. For example, a menu item could move from one plane to another so that it moves closer to the viewer when it is selected. *Compare* **1-plane mode.**

2-view display An auto-stereoscopic display where separate left- and right-eye images are directed to the corresponding eyes. Two-view displays typically have a limited viewing position, though some can track the viewer's head movements to adjust the display to follow the eyes and provide a wider viewing range. The two most common technologies in a two-view display are lenticular, where special lenses direct the images to the left and right eyes, or parallax slit barriers, where the barrier blocks the left image from the right eye and vice versa. Somewhat contrary to expectation, a two-view display is generally used by only one viewer at a time. *Compare* **3D display; multi-view; super multi-view.**

2 × 1080p A stereoscopic video system where both eyes receive progressively scanned images with 1,080 lines of resolution. *See* **full HD.**

ultraviolet; UV; ~ light Invisible energy in the ultraviolet band of the electromagnetic spectrum (wavelengths ranging from 10 to 400 nanometers), located just above the violet end of the visible spectrum; black light. Ultraviolet light is invisible to the human eye but strongly affects photographic materials. White and specially-coated surfaces visibly glow under ultraviolet light. *Compare* **infrared; visible light.** *See* **ultraviolet** image in color section.

un-crossed axes *See* **parallel-viewing.**

un-crossed parallax *See* **negative parallax.**

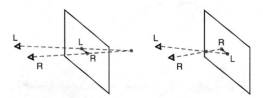

With un-crossed stereoscopic disparity (left), the left-eye image is to the left of the right-eye image, the eyes' views do not cross, and the represented object appears behind the screen. With crossed stereoscopic disparity (right), the left-eye image is to the right of the right-eye image, the eyes' views cross before reaching the screen, and the represented object appears in front of the screen at the point where the views cross.

un-crossed stereoscopic disparity; un-crossed disparity The horizontal image displacement that is characteristic of objects farther than the horopter; the relationship between conjugate points in an image pair where the left point is to the left of the right point and vice versa. This gives the impression that the point lies in screen space, beyond the plane of the screen. *Compare* **crossed stereoscopic disparity; positive parallax.**

under-slung A stereoscopic camera mirror rig with the primary camera pointed directly at the action and the secondary camera set at a right angle and below the primary (pointing up and into the beam-splitter). *Also* **low-mode.** *Compare* **over-slung.**

unfusable images Left- and right-eye images in a stereoscopic pair that contain conjugate points with

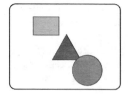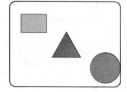

The images are configured for cross-eyed viewing. The rectangle is depicted with excessive positive parallax, while the circle has excessive negative parallax. It is not possible to fuse all three shapes into single images at the same time. For example, when the circle is properly fused, the triangle and rectangle will appear as double images. Prolonged viewing will cause noticeable eyestrain.

excessive parallax, either positive or negative, such that the individual images cannot be fused into a 3D view.

update frequency *See* **refresh rate.**

upper The image with the greatest amount of upwards vertical shift in a stereogram that exhibits vertical parallax. Generally only used in reference to still stereo images.

upper/lower *See* **over/under.**

upstream device One device that precedes another in a data distribution chain. For example, in a cable TV system, the decoder in a subscriber's home is an upstream device with respect to the connected television. *Compare* **downstream device.**

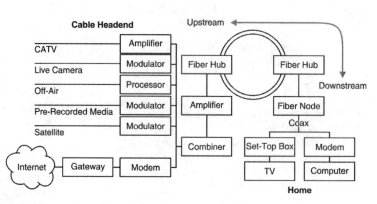

Upstream device. A simplified view of a cable TV system from the headend to an in-home television and computer. All of the headend devices are upstream from the home, while the headend combiner is downstream of the modulators. The in-home computer is upstream from the gateway at the headend when it is sending data to the Internet, but when it receives data from to the Internet, the home computer becomes the downstream device and the modems and gateway are upstream.

user-adjustable depth *See* **3D adjustment.**

usual size The size one expects a familiar object to be based on past experience. One can compare this size to the size an object appears to be and use any discrepancy as a monocular depth cue to estimate the distance to the object. *Also* **expected size.** *Compare* **monocular cue; perceived size; relative size; retinal image size.**

UV *See* **ultraviolet.**

v number; v value *See* **dispersion.**

value The relative lightness or darkness of an area; a shade of gray, ranging anywhere from pure white to pure black; brightness or lightness in the Munsell color system. Low values are dark; high values are light.

> NOTE: Shades of gray have no color (hue) and are properly called *values*, not *colors.*

Also **tone.** *Compare* **hue; saturation.** *See* **color** diagram in color section.

valve *Also* **liquid crystal shutter.** *See* **active eyewear; LCD shutter eyewear.**

variable-polarization-angle display *See* **dual-panel LCD 3D; ZScreen.**

varifocal lens display *See* **volumetric 3D.**

VC-1; VC1; SMPTE ~ Video Codec-1; the Society of Motion Picture and Television Engineers (SMPTE) standardized version of Microsoft's Windows Media 9 (WMV9) video encoding format. Used in HD-DVD, IPTV, and digital HD terrestrial and satellite broadcast. *Compare* **MPEG-4 AVC.**

VE *See* **virtual environment.**

vection The illusion that one is in motion while remaining stationary, caused by viewing an immersive moving image. The sense of physical motion is generally in the opposite direction of the observed motion. For example, when sitting in a stationary train watching another train pass by through the window, the observer may experience the sensation that the passing train is stationary and that the observer is moving in the opposite direction. Immersive virtual reality and 3D display systems may also induce vection in the observer. *Also* **visuo-vestibular conflict.** *Compare* **cybersickness.**

Vectograph A theatrical 3D process developed by the Polaroid Corporation in 1939 that encoded polarized left- and right-eye images on the same strip of film, allowing the projection of polarized stereograms using an un-modified 35mm projector.

The initial process was black-and-white, with the shades of gray represented by differing amounts of polarization rather than the more traditional crystals of metallic silver. In 1954, Polaroid and Technicolor announced a full-color version of the Vectograph process. Color Vectographs would have reduced the limit imposed on the theatrical 3D market in the 1950s by the scarcity of 3D-equipped theaters, but they arrived just as the 3D boom came to an end.

Compare **Technicolor 3D.**

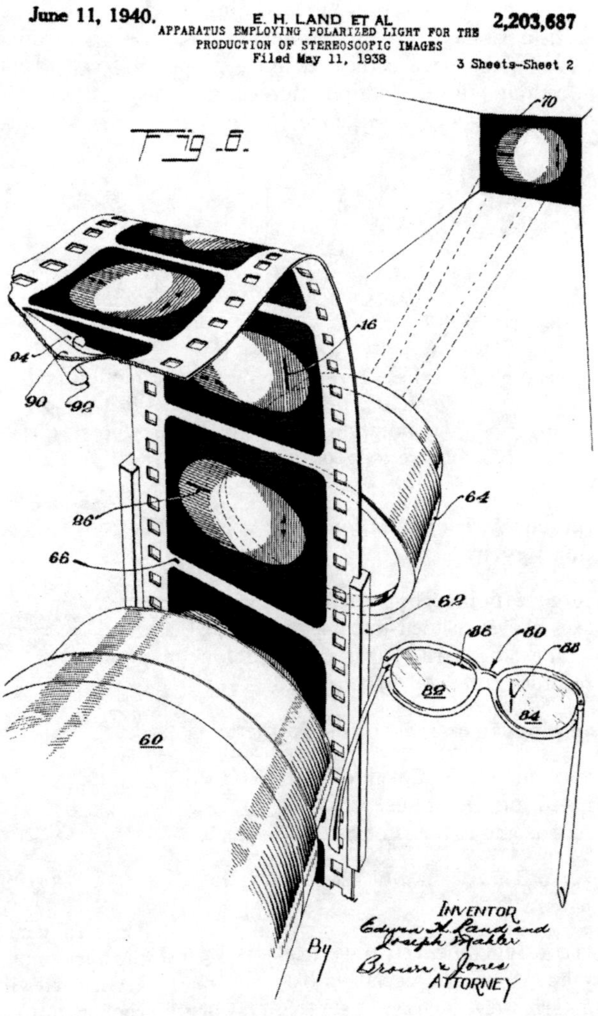

U.S. Patent No. 2,203,687 issued June 11, 1940 (U.S. Patent and Trademark Office).

vector quantization; VQ *See* **compression.**

Verascope The trade name for a type of hand-held stereo camera, patented in 1891 by the Jules Richard Company of Paris. Originally designed to record 12 stereo images on photographic glass plates. The last model of the series, introduced c. 1946, recorded 21 stereo images on a standard roll of 35mm film. *Compare* **Taxiphote.**

vergence; ~ eye movement The coordinated inward (convergence) or outward (divergence) turning of the eyes when focusing on an object or when adjusting one's gaze from one point to another point at a different distance. This has the effect of projecting the object of interest onto the fovea at the center of the retina where clear, full-color vision is possible. Vergence is only effective for objects up to about 200 meters away (stereo infinity). When viewing objects beyond this point, the eyes are held parallel. Unlike other types of eye movements, with vergence, the eyes move in opposite directions. *Also* **angulation; stereoangle.** *Compare* **convergence; divergence; toe-in.**

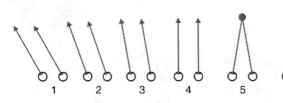

In Examples 1–3, the eyes rotate in the same direction as they pan from left to right until they are parallel in Example 4. Examples 5 and 6 show how the eyes rotate in opposite directions to turn inward to focus on near objects.

vergence/accommodation... *See* **accommodation/vergence...**

vergence point The point in space where the lens axes of eyes or toed-in cameras cross. This also defines the zero disparity plane for images recorded with toed-in cameras.

verging cameras *See* **toed-in cameras.**

version; ~ eye movement The coordinated turning of the eyes in the same direction and to the same extent.

verso The back face of a stereocard. *Compare* **recto.**

vertical alignment error; vertical misalignment A vertical deviation between left- and right-eye images in a stereogram where one of the images is higher than it should be so that horizontal points do not align.

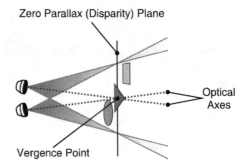

Vergence point

vertical disparity; vertical error; vertical offset; vertical parallax The vertical distance between conjugate points in the left- and right-eye image pair that makes up a stereogram. Only disparity in the same plane as the viewer's eyes (generally assumed to be horizontal) contributes to depth perception, so vertical disparity should be avoided. Small amounts can be ignored, but too much vertical disparity will interfere with 3D image fusion, leading to viewer discomfort and double vision. *Also* **height error.** *See* **parallax.** *See* **vertical disparity** image in color section.

vertical scale factor The distance between pixel rows in an imaging grid; the height of a pixel. *Compare* **intrinsic camera parameters.**

vertical scanning frequency *See* **refresh rate.**

vertical viewing angle The figure formed by extending a line from the center of the viewer's gaze to the surface of the screen, measured in relation to its vertical offset from a line perpendicular to the surface of the screen.

For simplicity, the viewing angle is generally meas-

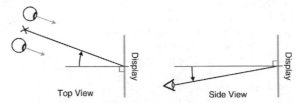

The arrangement of viewer and display when measuring the horizontal viewing angle (left, seen from above) and vertical viewing angle (right, seen from the side). The viewing angle decreases as the distance between viewer and display increases, so the impact of certain image distortions can be reduced if viewing distance is increased.

ured from the center of the viewer's gaze to the center of the screen. Certain 3D display technologies, such as line-interlaced polarized displays, have a limited vertical viewing angle, while others, such as lenticular displays, have a limited horizontal viewing angle.

vertigo *See* **cybersickness; vection.**

vestibular system The structures within the inner ear that register physical motion (both rotation and linear acceleration), contributing to balance and spatial orientation. Disruptions in the vestibular system can cause vertigo and nausea. Conflicts between physical motion recorded by the vestibular system and apparent motion recorded by the eyes can lead to motion sickness. *Compare* **cybersickness; equilibrioception; vection.**

vestibulo-ocular reflex; VOR; oculovestibular reflex Automatic eye movements based on motion data recorded by the vestibular system that help stabilize images on the retina and allow for clear vision when the viewer's head moves. VOR is reflexive, and still operates in complete darkness or when the eyes are closed.

vibration direction *See* **plane of vibration.**

video essence The collection of data that represent a video stream. Often used within the parlance of Society of Motion Picture and Television Engineers (SMPTE) standards, especially MXF.

Vieth-Müller circle A theoretically perfect horopter (the area within the field of vision that results in zero parallax between the eye images) measured in a horizontal plane and set so that the circle passes through the point behind the pupil of each eye where all light rays cross and the point in space where the visual axes converge (assuming the eyes are turned inward from parallel). *See* **horopter.**

view An image presented for observation. Traditional flat images present one view per image. Stereoscopic images present two (or more) views per image.

view discrepancy A difference between the left- and right-eye views in a stereogram that is not explained by horizontal parallax and interferes with the 3D effect, such as may be caused by dust on one of the camera lenses, reflections, sparkle, etc. *Compare* **cue conflict; retinal rivalry.**

view frustum; viewing frustum The flat-top pyramid that encompasses the volume of space recorded by a camera, particularly a synthetic camera recording a computer-generated image.

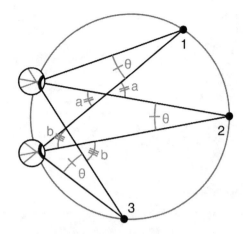

Vieth-Müller circle. The rays of light entering the eyes from any point on the Vieth-Müller circle (such as 1, 2, or 3) have the same interior angle, θ. In addition, the alternate angles formed by the crossing rays from two points are equal — the crossing rays from points 1 and 2 create equal alternate angles a, while the crossing rays from points 2 and 3 create equal alternate angles b.

The view frustum through a lens is conical, but photographic images are recorded with a rectangular aspect ratio, so a camera's view frustum is shaped like a pyramid. The front plane of the view frustum is defined by the closest object visible to the camera. In computer graphics, near objects are excluded from view by a clipping plane so the computer does not have to perform unnecessary calculations. Similarly, the back plane of the view frustum is defined by the farthest object visible to the camera or the back clipping plane in a computer-generated image. *Compare* **perspective frustum.**

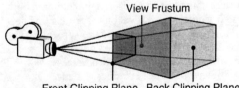

The shape of the view frustum is determined by the focal length of the lens and the aspect ratio of the exposed area of the imaging device.

view interspersing *See* **crosstalk; ghosting.**

View Magic The trade name for a type of stereoscope that uses mirrors to align over/under stereo pairs. Common models support images up to 4" or 12" tall (about 4cm–30cm).

View-Master The trade name for a type of stereoscope designed to display seven image pairs mounted on a disc. The View-Master was originally developed by William B. Gruber and manufactured by Sawyer's Photo Services starting in 1939 (U.S. Patent No. 2,189,285, issued February 6, 1940). During the 1950s, a number of 3D motion pictures were promoted using View-Master discs, ranging from *House of Wax* to *Those Redheads from Seattle*. View-Master viewers and picture discs are now made by Fisher-Price. *Compare* **Tru-Vue.**

viewer discomfort; viewer fatigue *See* **asthenopia.**

viewer/display space *See* **display/viewer space.**

viewer's gaze The observer's visual focus; the line extending from the mid-point between the optical center of the observer's eyes to the object at the center of the observer's visual field, which is generally the focus of the observer's interest.

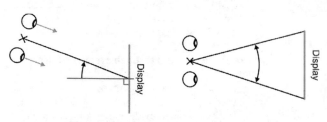

The two uses of viewing angle: measuring the relative position of the viewer with respect to the screen (left) and measuring the apparent size of the screen within the observer's field of view. Both can be measured horizontally (as shown) or vertically, though for stereoscopic purposes, the horizontal viewing angles tend to be more important.

viewing angle 1. The figure formed by extending a line from the center of the viewer's gaze to the surface of the screen, measured in relation to both its horizontal and vertical offsets from a line perpendicular to the surface of the screen. 2. The horizontal angle of view when observing a display screen. An important factor in stereoscopic calculations. Calculated as a function of the screen width and viewing distance and measured in degrees. *Compare* **angle of view; horizontal viewing angle; vertical viewing angle.**

viewing distance The space from the observer to the display surface. An important factor in stereoscopic calculations. Generally measured from the center of the viewer's gaze to the center of the screen.

viewing zone The volume of space within which a viewer's head must be placed in order to perceive the full stereoscopic effect. A particular display technology may have one or more viewing zones, often a central zone and side zones. *Also* **head box; sweet spot.**

viewing zone angle The extent of the viewing zone measured as an angle from the center of the display, either horizontally or vertically.

vignetting The tendency for illumination in an image to drop off as one moves out from the center, resulting in sides that are darker than the middle. Caused by a combination of optical vignetting (a lens defect that causes a loss of illumination along the physical edges of a lens) and uneven illumination (projected light is brightest at the center of the beam). Digital cameras may employ a lens shading feature to correct for vignetting. The silver screens used with polarized 3D systems tend to exaggerate this effect more so than the flat white screens more commonly used in theatrical exhibition.

virtual environment; VE The space that appears to exist within a virtual reality system. *Compare* **virtual world.**

virtual image An image of an object composed of light rays that diverge after passing through a lens. Such an image cannot be projected onto a screen, but when viewed directly, the image is larger than, and oriented the same direction as, the original object when viewed directly. Virtual images are produced by magnifying glasses and the micro-displays typically found in head-mounted display systems. *Compare* **real image.**

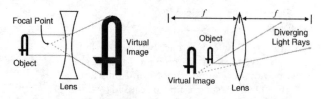

The most common way to form a virtual image is with a negative, or diverging, lens (left), as with a traditional magnifying glass. However, if the distance between an object and a positive, or converging, lens (right) is less than the lens' focal length (f), then the light rays passing through the lens diverge and a virtual image is formed.

virtual print fee; VPF A payment made by a theatrical distributor to an exhibitor when the exhibitor accepts a digital copy of a motion picture in place of a film print. Intended to help compensate the exhibitor for the cost of installing a digital cinema projection system by sharing the cost savings associated with digital distribution.

virtual reality; VR A computer-generated simulation of a seemingly real environment that combines a visual display system (often a head-mounted 3D display) with a means for the user to interact with the virtual world (such as a motion capture device). The term is generally attributed to American computer scientist Jaron Z. Lanier c. 1980. *Compare* **artificial reality; augmented reality.**

Virtual Reality Modeling Language *See* VRML.

virtual retinal display; VRD A display system that scans an image directly on the retina of the viewer's eye. By varying the image offset for each eye, stereograms can be formed. Developed at the HIT (Human Interface Technology) Lab at the University of Washington in 1991.

virtual rig; virtual camera rig *See* **camera rig.**

virtual world A complete, self-contained virtual environment, or universe, within a virtual reality system. *Compare* **virtual environment.**

visible light The portion of the electromagnetic spectrum that is registered by the human eye and interpreted by the brain as light. Visible light ranges in color from violet to red with shades of blue, green, yellow, and orange in between. Electromagnetic energy outside the visible spectrum includes radio waves, microwaves, gamma rays, ultraviolet (black light), and infrared (heat). *Compare* **infrared light; ultraviolet light.** *See* **visible light** diagram in color section.

vision The process by which the brain translates optical information received through the eyes into the perception of sight.

visual angle A measure of the size of an image on the retina based on the angle formed by the object at the surface of the eye. *Compare* **retinal image size.**

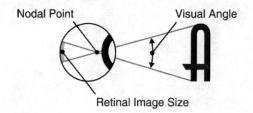

Nodal Point   Visual Angle

Retinal Image Size

visual/brain conflict; visual confusion A contradiction between a visual image and what the brain has come to expect from the natural world. For example, if left- and right-eye stereo images are reversed, then objects will appear inside out (portions that should be near will seem to be far and vice versa). Alternatively, if an object with negative parallax (seeming to extend out of the screen and into the audience space) is cut off by the edge of the screen, the brain will not know how to interpret this. Far objects cut off by the edge of the screen are natural (this is how a window behaves), but objects closer than the window should not be cut off by the edge of the window, leading to a visual/brain conflict. *Compare* **edge violation; pseudostereo; retinal rivalry.**

visual convergence *See* **convergence.**

visual cortex The region of the brain primarily responsible for vision. Located in the posterior pole of the occipital lobes where the left lobe of the brain processes visual information from the right eye and vice versa. *Compare* **anterior intraparietal cortex.**

visual cues *See* **binocular cue; monocular cue.**

visual discomfort A subjective measure of physical or mental distress caused by visual fatigue, including headache, sore eye muscles, burning, tearing, and dryness; eyestrain.

visual fatigue An objectively measurable decrease in the performance of the human vision system due to overexertion including prolonged exposure to conflicting visual cues. *Compare* **asthenopia.**

visual field The area that can be seen with one eye without moving the head or eye.

visual fixation The maintenance of a relatively steady gaze between periods of saccade or smooth pursuit. The majority of visual processing occurs during periods of visual fixation.

visual mismatch When an object appears in only one half of a stereogram or when there are significant differences between the same object in the left- and right-eye views that cannot be explained by visual parallax (the offset between the left and right eye). Generally introduced during post-production by compositing errors (as with depth mismatch and partial pseudostereo) or by rendering errors in computer-generated images. *Compare* **contamination; cue conflict; retinal rivalry.**

visual occlusion *See* **occlusion.**

visual parallax *See* **parallax.**

visual perspective *See* **perspective.**

visual processing unit; VPU *See* **graphics processing unit.**

visuo-vestibular The combined interpretation of information received from the eyes and the labyrinth of the inner ear that result in a sense of balance and spatial orientation. Disruptions can lead to motion sickness. *Compare* **cybersickness.**

visuo-vestibular conflict *See* **vection.**

voltage gain *See* **gain.**

volume reshaping *See* **depth warping.**

volumetric space Three-dimensional space, either in the natural, physical world or a computer-generated, virtual world.

volumetric 3D; volumetric display An autostereoscopic presentation system that physically creates an image in three dimensions, generally one that can be viewed from any angle. These include holographic displays, swept-volume displays (where a display element moves through space at a high speed — often by rotating on a central axis— to present a different view in each position so that persistence of vision blends the individual views into a single, 3D view); static-volume or layered displays (where a block of transparent voxels— often created by stacking 2–20 flat image displays— are selectively activated to create an image in three dimensions); and varifocal lens displays (where lenses position multiple image slices at different optical depths from the viewer). *Compare* **3D display.**

voxel Volume element; a 3D pixel; the smallest addressable space in a three-dimensional display, having height, width, and depth (where a pixel has only height and width). *Compare* **pixel.**

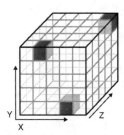 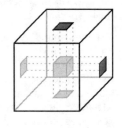

VPF *See* **virtual print fee.**

VPU; visual processing unit *See* **graphics processing unit.**

VQ; vector quantization *See* **compression.**

VR *See* **virtual reality.**

VRD *See* **virtual retinal display.**

VRML Virtual Reality Modeling Language; a standard text file format for describing 3D geometry often used in the construction of virtual worlds. Originally developed in 1994. VRML has since been superseded by X3D. *Compare* **Java 3D.**

WALL-E camera A twin-lens stereo camera, such as the Panasonic 3DA1 3D camcorder, after the similarity of its lenses to the eyes of the titular character from the movie *WALL-E* (2008).

Courtesy Panasonic, www.panasonic.com.

wall-eye When the eyes are angled outward beyond parallel, as when trying to view a stereogram with excessive positive parallax that requires greater than 1° of parallel divergence. *See* **strabismus.** *Compare* **cross-eye.**

wandering eye *See* **strabismus.**

wavelength display A stereoscopic display where the left- and right-eye images are color-coded and then superimposed upon one another. This requires passive eyewear with matching color-coded lenses, as with the traditional anaglyph (red/cyan) process or the more complex interference filter process.

wavelength interference; wavelength multiplex visualization *See* **interference filter.**

weave *See* **jitter.**

Wheatstone stereoscope The original stereoscope design; a two-mirror stereoscope developed by English scientist Charles Wheatstone in 1832 and later described in a paper presented to the Royal Society of London on June 21, 1838. The Wheatstone stereoscope pre-dated photography (not introduced until 1839), so Wheatstone produced perspective drawings by hand. *See* **mirror stereoscope.** *Compare* **spatial display.**

The original Wheatstone stereoscope design. The stereo images are mounted to each side with the mirror viewer in the center. Since the mirrors show a mirror-image, the original images must be reversed (as shown). The handle on the lower right adjusts the worm screw to bring the side supports in or out depending on the size of the stereo images.

wide-eyed viewing *See* **parallel-viewing.**

wiggle stereo *See* **wobble stereo.**

Wimmer anaglyph A full-color red/cyan anaglyphic image where the colors in each eye view have been mathematically optimized to reduce ghosting and retinal rivalry. The process replaces the reds in a stereogram with a mixture of blue and green, sacrificing some color fidelity for improved viewing characteristics. Created by Austrian stereoscopic software developer Peter Wimmer. *See* **optimized anaglyph.** *See* **Wimmer anaglyph** diagram in color section.

window *See* **stereo window.**

window effect The appearance of a stereoscopic work with no negative parallax. Since none of the objects seem to extend out from the screen, the viewing experience is equivalent to looking through a window to the outside world.

window, floating *See* **floating window.**

window violation; WV *See* **edge violation.**

wireless shutter eyewear *See* **active eyewear.**

wobble stereo An auto-stereoscopic display technique based on observed motion parallax. Two (or more) stereo views are presented in quick succession, with each one held long enough to be perceived as an individual image — not fused into a single image by persistence of vision, but fast enough so that the brain interprets the

visual differences as being caused by motion. (Generally, about ½ second each.) This results in an illusion of stereo depth that even the stereo-blind can perceive. *Also* **wiggle stereo.**

wobulation A technique developed at Hewlett-Packard c. 2005 for increasing the apparent resolution of a projected digital video image, originally applied to digital micro-mirror display (DMD) devices and later used as the basis of the checkerboard 3D display system, first introduced commercially by Samsung in April 2007.

With wobulation, a single image frame is divided into two (or more) sub-frames and the sub-frames are projected with a diagonal offset. The overlap of the two sub-frames creates the impression of greater resolution than actually exists in the original image. For example, if 2 3 × 3 pixel sub-frames (with a total of 18 large pixels between them) are superimposed with a ½ pixel diagonal offset, they overlap to give the visual impression of a 7 × 7 pixel grid composed of 47 smaller active pixels. (After the diagonal shift, two of the opposite corners do not contain image data, so instead of 49 simulated pixels, the technique achieves only 47.)
Compare **checkerboard 3D.**

world coordinate system A neutral, three-axis (X, Y, and Z) system of Cartesian coordinates (oriented so X, Y, and Z represent width, height, and depth, respectively and grow in a positive direction to the right, up, and away, respectively) commonly used in computer graphics applications. *Compare* **camera coordinate system.**

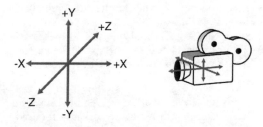

The axes of the world coordinate system (left) and camera coordinate system (right).

WV; window violation *See* **edge violation.**

X-axis The horizontal axis in a two- or three-dimensional coordinate system, perpendicular to the Y- and Z-axes. *Compare* **Y-axis; Z-axis.**

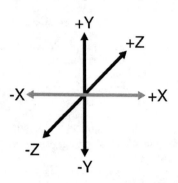

X-cube A mirrored prism that combines three separate incoming beams of light into a single outgoing beam. Often used in LCD projectors to merge separate red, green, and blue images into a single projected image.

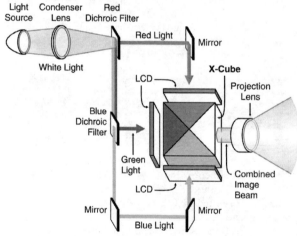

XpanD The trade name for a line of active liquid crystal shutter glasses and 3D arcade gaming systems produced by X6D Limited of Ljubljana, Slovenia. In March 2008, a division of X6D acquired NuVision Technologies and now sells NuVision's product line under the XpanD brand. The XpanD Web site is www.xpandcinema.com.

Xpol The trade name for a variation on the micro-polarizer (μPol), developed by Arisawa Manufacturing, where a black mask is introduced between each row of polarized pixels to reduce 3D image ghosting and improve the vertical viewing angle for polarized 3D video displays. *Also* **passive retarder.** *Compare* **micro-polarizer.**

X3D A standard file format and run-time architecture for the representation of 3D scenes and objects, often used in the construction of virtual worlds. Developed in 2005 as an extension of VRML (Virtual Reality Modeling Language) based on XML (eXtensible Markup Language) syntax. The X3D Web site is www.web3d.org. *Compare* **Java 3D.**

Y-axis The vertical axis in a two- or three-dimensional coordinate system, perpendicular to the X- and Z-axes. *Compare* X-axis; Z-axis.

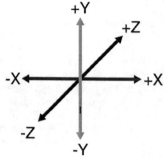

yaw *Also* **pan.** *See* **orientation.**

Z-axis The depth axis in a three-dimensional coordinate system, perpendicular to the X- and Y-axes. When presented in two-dimensions, the Z-axis extends into and out of the surface. *Compare* X-axis; Y-axis.

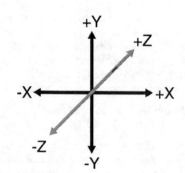

Z-buffer Computer memory used to store image depth information and calculate object occlusion so only visible pixels are displayed.

Z-depth The horizontal offset between conjugate points in the left and right images in a stereogram. Larger Z-depth values result in an increased 3D effect. Positive values provide depth away from the viewer while negative values provide depth towards the viewer. *Also* **3D depth.**

Z-depth plot; Z-depth script; Z-depth storyboard *See* **depth plot.**

Z distortion Unintended deviations in the Z-depth of a stereogram causing visible image depth distortions. Most noticeable along horizontal edges.

ZDP *See* **zero disparity plane.**

zero binocular retinal disparity When the images recorded by the left and right retinas are perfectly aligned, resulting in zero parallax between the conjugate points. *See* **binocular disparity; disparity.**

zero disparity plane; ZDP The distance in a scene at which objects will appear to be on the screen in a stereogram. The ZDP divides a scene into objects that appear in audience space (in front of the screen) and in screen space (behind the screen surface). *Also* **HIT point; plane of convergence; zero parallax depth.** *See* **vergence point.**

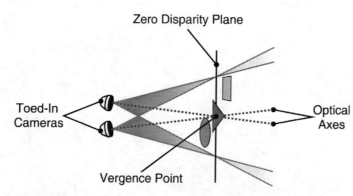

zero interaxial When the two images recorded by a 3D camera system exactly overlap — there is no interaxial distance separating them. The greater the separation between the images, the more pronounced the 3D effect. At zero interaxial, there is no 3D effect.

NOTE: This is often referred to as *zero interocular*, but technically interocular refers to the distance between the eyes, while interaxial refers to the distance between images or lenses in a 3D imaging system.
Compare **interocular distance.**

zero parallax; zero offset point When a point in the left-eye image is aligned with the conjugate point in the right-eye image in a stereogram. Conjugate points with zero parallax have no stereoscopic depth and appear to be at the same distance from the observer as the screen. *Compare* **negative parallax; positive parallax.** *See* diagram at **stereoscopic.**

zero parallax depth; ZPD *See* **zero disparity plane.**

zero parallax setting; ZPS Adjusting the relative horizontal offset of the left- and right-eye images in a stereogram so that the conjugate points that lie on the intended display plane have zero parallax.

zone of clear single binocular vision *See* **Panum's fusion area.**

zone of comfort; zone of comfortable viewing *See* **Percival's zone.**

zoom mismatch *See* **focal length mismatch.**

ZPD; zero parallax depth *See* **zero disparity plane.**

ZPS *See* **zero parallax setting.**

ZScreen An electro-optical liquid crystal modulator (polarization switch) used in RealD 3D projection systems. Essentially, an LCD panel without the last polarization layer. When the LCD panel is off, the projection light is polarized in the direction of the panel's linear polarizer. When the LCD panel is turned on, the polarized light is rotated 90° as it passes through the liquid crystals. *Compare* **dual-panel LCD 3D; RealD 3D.**

Selected Bibliography and Recommended Reading

Allen, Will, and Robert Ulichney, "Wobulation: Doubling the Addressed Resolution of Projection Displays," *SID Symposium Digest*, Vol. 36, May 2005.

Alliance for Telecommunications Industry Solutions, "ATIS Telecom Glossary 2007," www.atis.org/glossary, October 31, 2009.

Alter, Ethan, Carolyn Giardina, and Kevin Lally, "3-D Champions: Five advocates stating the format's case," *The Hollywood Reporter*, October 10, 2008.

American Press Services, "The HighDef Glossary of Terms," www.highdef.com/library/glossary.htm, November 27, 2007.

Beech, Michael, *Digital 3D Stereo Guide*, Arvada, CO: Michael Beech, 2008.

Berezin Stereo Photography Products, "Glossary," www.berezin.com/3d/glossary.htm, December 27, 2009.

Berman, Arthur, Matt Brrennesholtz, and Chris Chinnock, "3D in the Home: A Brief Look at the Current State of Affairs," *Insight Media*, September 19, 2007.

Brady, Terrance, "Film and Screenwriting Glossary," Third Millennium Entertainment, www.teak0170.com/glossary.html, October 10, 2003.

Cable Television Laboratories, Inc., "CableLabs Glossary," www.cablelabs.com/news/glossary, January 23, 2008.

Cooper, Rachel, "Basic 3D Viewing Terms," 1996–2010, www.vision3d.com/vocview.html, December 17, 2010.

Dubois, Eric, "Generation of anaglyph stereoscopic images," June 14, 2000, www.site.uottawa.ca/~edubois/anaglyph_000614.pdf, September 15, 2010.

Edwards, Mark, and Clifton Schor, "Stereo-Depth Aliasing," *Perception*, Vol. 28, August 22–26, 1999.

Evertz, "Glossary of Technical Film and Broadcasting Terms," www.evertz.com/glossary.php, November 27, 2007.

Fotokem, "Film Terms," www.fotokem.com/downloads/film_terms.pdf, September 14, 2008.

Fraser, Bryant, "In-Three on the Workflow Behind 3D Conversions," *StudioDaily*, April 7, 2010.

Futuresource Consulting, "The Strategic Impact of 3D," April 2009.

Gibson, James Jerome, *The Ecological Approach to Visual Perception*, Hillsdale, NJ: Lawrence Erlbaum Associates, 1986.

Goldman, Michael, "Rodriguez and 3D Post: Better Anaglyphs and Revised Workflow," *millimeter*, Vol. 33, No. 6, June 2005.

Haskell, Gary B., Atul Puri, and Arun N. Netravali, *Digital Video: An Introduction to MPEG-2*, Norwell, MA: Kluwer Academic, 1997.

Hautman, W.A., J.H. Roze, and W. Scheper, "Vertical Motor Fusion," *Documentia Ophthalmologica*, Vol. 44, No. 1, 1977.

Hayes, R.M., *3-D Movies*, Jefferson, NC: McFarland, 1989.

Hoffman, David M., et al., "Vergence-accommodation conflicts hinder visual performance and cause visual fatigue," *Journal of Vision*, Vol. 8, No. 3, August 2008.

Holben, Jay, "Conquering New Worlds," *American Cinematographer*, Vol. 91, No. 1, January 2010.

Holliman, Nick, www.binocularity.org, Creative Commons Attribution 2.0 UK: England & Wales License (creativecommons.org/licenses/by/2.0/uk), November 2, 2009.

Home Technology Specialists of America, "HTSA's 3D Technology Glossary," 2010, www.htsa.com/3D_glossary.aspx, December 14, 2010.

Insight Media, "Glossary of 3D Home Terminology," 3D@Home Consortium, May 2009.

Jones, Charlotte, "The Business Case for 3D," *Screen Digest*, December 1, 2008.

_____, "The Business Case for 3D: Part II," *Screen Digest*, September 16, 2009.

Kalloniatis, Michael, and Charles Luu, "Psychophysics of Vision," *Webvision: The Organization of the Retina and Visual System*, Salt Lake City, UT: John Moran Eye Center, 2009.

Kennel, Glenn, *Color and Mastering for Digital Cinema*, Boston: Focal Press, 2007.

Klooswyk, Abram, "Errors in Stereo History & The Chimenti Hoax," May 4, 2005, www.stereoscopy.com/faq/history-errors.html, October 4, 2009.

Konigsberg, Ira, *The Complete Film Dictionary* (2nd Edition), Harmondsworth, Middlesex: Penguin Books, 1997.

Krantz, John H., *Experiencing Sensation and Perception* (Draft), Hanover, IN: Hanover College, 2007.

Kroon, Richard W., *A/V A–Z*, Jefferson, NC: McFarland, 2009.

_____, *Technicolor's Guide to 3D for Film, TV, and Everything In-Between*, Hollywood, CA: Technicolor, 2011.

Lambooij, Marc, et al., "Visual Discomfort and Visual Fatigue of Stereoscopic Displays: A Review," *Journal of Imaging Science and Technology*, Vol. 53, No. 3, May-June, 2009.

Latta, Dr. John N. (Editor-in-Chief), "Video Compression Tutorial," *WAVE Report*, www.wave-report.com/tutorials/VC.htm, June 13, 2008.

Lerner, Sandy "The Dilettante's Dictionary," www.dilettantesdictionary.org, November 27, 2007.

Levoy, Mark, and Pat Hanrahan, "Light Field Rendering," *Proc. SIGGRAPH '96*, 1996.

Lipton, Lenny, "The Last Great Innovation: The Stereoscopic Cinema," *SMPTE Motion Imaging Journal*, Vol. 116, No. 11 & 12, 2007.

McIntosh, Heather, "Glossary," *Reality Film: Documentary Resources & Reviews*, State College, PA: Realityfilm.com, 2002–2003.

Mead, Bill, "Digital Update," *Film Journal International*, August 27, 2008.

_____, "The Return of 35mm 3D," *Film Journal International*, March 11, 2010.

Mehta, Neeraj, *Textbook of Engineering Physics*, New Delhi, India: Asoke K. Ghosh, 2008.

Mendiburu, Bernard, *3D Movie Making*, Oxford, England: Focal Press, 2009.

Merson, Gary, "3D Stereoscopic Glossary," December 5, 2009, www.hdguru3d.com/index.php?option=com_content&view=article&id=65&Itemid=60, November 17, 2010.

Morgan, Hal, and Dan Symmes, *Amazing 3-D*, Boston: Little, Brown, 1982.

Nave, Carl Rod, *HyperPhysics*, Georgia State University, 2005, hyperphysics.phy-astr.gsu.edu/Hbase/hph.html, February 21, 2010.

Poissant, Louise, and Lou Nelson, "New Media Dictionary," *Leonardo*, Vol. 34, No. 4, August 2001.

Rachlin, Harvey, *The TV & Movie Business*, New York City: Harmony Books, 1991.

Read, Paul, and Mark-Paul Meyer, *Restoration of Motion Picture Film*, Burlington, MA: Butterworth-Heinemann, 2000.

Schlemowitz, Joel, "A Glossary of Film Terms," *New School University Media Studies Department*, home page.newschool.edu/~schlemoj/film_courses/glossary_of_film_terms, July 31, 2003.

Siegel, Scott, and Barbara Siegel, *The Encyclopedia of Hollywood*, New York City: Avon Books, 1990.

Sklar, Robert, *Film: An International History of the Medium* (Second Edition), New York City: Harry N. Abrams, 1993, 2002.

_____, *Movie-Made America: A Cultural History of American Movies* (Revised and Updated), New York City: Vintage Books, 1975, 1994.

Slide, Anthony, *The New Historical Dictionary of the American Film Industry*, Lanham, MD: Scarecrow, 2001.

SMPTE, "Report of SMPTE Task Force on 3D to the Home," White Plains, NY: Society of Motion Picture and Television Engineers, 2009.

Staff, "Science: Three-Dimensional Movies?" *Time*, December 7, 1942, www.time.com/time/magazine/article/0,9171,774033-1,00.html, December 13, 2010.

_____, "Technical Glossary," *Widescreen Review*, 1995–2010, www.widescreenreview.com/eq_glossary.php, November 13, 2010.

Stereographer.com, "Glossary of 3D photography and stereography terms," stereographer.com/glossary.html, August 24, 2010.

Technicolor, "Technicolor Encyclopedia," www.technicolor.com/Cultures/En-Us/Support/Encyclopedia, June 13, 2008.

Thomson Grass Valley, "Dictionary of Technical Terms," www.thomsongrassvalley.com/docs/Miscellaneous/Dictionary, September 14, 2008.

Turing, Alan, "Computing Machinery and Intelligence," *Mind*, Vol. 59, No. 236, October 1950.

Video Clarity, "Glossary of Terms," www.videoclarity.com/glossary.html, June 16, 2008.

Warner, Jack, "3D cinema shows strength in depth," *Screen Daily*, June 18, 2009.

Weatherston, David, "Common Terms in Digital Photography & Photo Printing," www.troubleshootingphotos.com/definitions.php, December 11, 2010.

Wheatstone, Charles, "Contributions to the Physiology of Vision." *Philosophical Transactions of the Royal Society of London*, Vol. 128, 1838.

Wing, Paul, *Stereoscopes: The First One Hundred Years*, Nashua, NH: Transition, 1996.

Woods, Andrew, "3-D Displays in the Home," *Information Display*, Vol. 25, No 7, July 2009.

_____, Tom Docherty, and Rolf Kock, "Image Distortions in Stereoscopic Video Systems," *Stereoscopic Displays and Applications IV*, Proceedings of the SPIE, Vol. 1915, February 1993.

Yeh, Pochi, and Claire Gu, *Optics of Liquid Crystal Displays* (Second Edition), Hoboken, NJ: John Wiley, 2010.

Zone, Ray, "The 3-D Zone," www.ray3dzone.com, October 29, 2009.

_____, *Stereoscopic Cinema and the Origins of 3-D Film: 1838–1952*, Lexington: University Press of Kentucky, 2007.

Zou, William, "Defining 3D Home Master," *SMPTE Motion Imaging Journal*, Vol. 118, No. 5, July/August 2009.